Rethinking Racial Justice

Rethinking Racial Justice

ANDREW VALLS

OXFORD
UNIVERSITY PRESS

OXFORD
UNIVERSITY PRESS

Oxford University Press is a department of the University of Oxford. It furthers
the University's objective of excellence in research, scholarship, and education
by publishing worldwide. Oxford is a registered trade mark of Oxford University
Press in the UK and certain other countries.

Published in the United States of America by Oxford University Press
198 Madison Avenue, New York, NY 10016, United States of America.

© Oxford University Press 2018

All rights reserved. No part of this publication may be reproduced, stored in
a retrieval system, or transmitted, in any form or by any means, without the
prior permission in writing of Oxford University Press, or as expressly permitted
by law, by license, or under terms agreed with the appropriate reproduction
rights organization. Inquiries concerning reproduction outside the scope of the
above should be sent to the Rights Department, Oxford University Press, at the
address above.

You must not circulate this work in any other form
and you must impose this same condition on any acquirer.

Library of Congress Cataloging-in-Publication Data
Names: Valls, Andrew, 1966– author.
Title: Rethinking racial justice / Andrew Valls.
Description: New York, NY, United States of America : Oxford University Press, [2018] |
Includes bibliographical references and index.
Identifiers: LCCN 2018010835 (print) | LCCN 2018027738 (ebook) |
ISBN 9780190860578 (Updf) | ISBN 9780190860585 (Epub) |
ISBN 9780190860561 (pbk. : acid-free paper) |
ISBN 9780190860554 (hardcover : acid-free paper)
Subjects: LCSH: African Americans—Reparations. | Social justice—United States. |
United States—Social policy. | Affirmative action programs—Government policy—
United States. | African Americans—Social conditions—21st century. |
United States—Race relations—Political aspects.
Classification: LCC E185.89.R45 (ebook) | LCC E185.89.R45 V35 2018 (print) |
DDC 305.896/073—dc23
LC record available at https://lccn.loc.gov/2018010835

To Jessica

CONTENTS

ACKNOWLEDGMENTS

This book has its origins in the years I spent teaching political theory at Morehouse College. It was there, teaching "dead white guys" (as well as contemporary political theory) to my African American students, that I became interested in the issues explored here. My students challenged me to show them how some of the rather abstract theories on my syllabi applied to the "real world" and to the concerns of African Americans in particular. In trying to answer their questions I was pushed to think about familiar texts (to me) in new ways, and to think about issues that I had not thought much about before. I became interested in racial justice as a subject of research and philosophical argumentation, because of both its intrinsic intellectual interest and its pressing importance for people's lives. I am deeply grateful to my Morehouse students, and to my colleagues there. What I saw and learned at Morehouse is, I hope, reflected in these pages. I wish to thank especially Tobe Johnson, who was chair of the political science department at Morehouse while I was there. Professor Johnson (I still don't call him Tobe) was extremely kind and supportive, and I will be forever grateful.

I left Morehouse in 2003 for Oregon State University, and here too I have been fortunate to work with wonderful colleagues and supportive administrators. I wish to thank Bill Lunch, who was chair of the political science department when I arrived, and Denise Lach, who is Director of the School of Public Policy (of which the political science program is now a part) for all of their support. I also acknowledge and thank the Center for the Humanities at Oregon State for a fellowship that provided time to work on the book.

I have been working on this book and the issues with which it grapples, on and off, for nearly twenty years, and in that time I have accumulated many debts. I will not be able to record all of them here, but I want to try to acknowledge the help and support of some of those to whom I owe heartfelt thanks. I wish to thank the late Iris Young for her constant support—from serving on my dissertation committee, to providing feedback on an early précis of the book that I envisioned, and in other smaller ways until the time of her death. I also thank Margaret Walker and Steve Esquith for the interest that they took in me at a crucial time in my career. It meant a great deal to me, and I haven't forgotten.

Special thanks go to Andrew I. Cohen and the Jean Beer Blumenfeld Center for Ethics at Georgia State University, which hosted a two-day workshop on the manuscript in May 2015. It was both exhilarating and humbling for my work to receive such attention and searching criticism. I thank all of those who participated in the workshop. In addition to Andrew I. Cohen, they are William Edmundson, Timothy Kuhner, Charles Mills, Andrew Altman, Bill Lawson, Peter Lindsay, George Rainbolt, and Andrew J. Cohen.

I also thank Burke Hendrix for organizing a session on chapter 7 at the University of Oregon. Many thanks to Anita Chari, Bonnie Sheehey, Colin Koopman, and Joseph Lowndes for reading the draft and offering me their comments and suggestions. Thanks also to Alexander Livingston and Alex Zakaras for comments on chapter 7, to my colleagues in the School of Public Policy who offered their thoughts when I presented the chapter there, and especially to Brett Burkhardt, who offered guidance and support on the chapter when I needed it. The late Joel Olson provided very helpful comments on an early version of chapter 6. Chapter 6 was also presented at the workshop "Urban Justice" at the University of San Francisco in August 2016. I thank those who participated and offered comments on my paper there: Sharon Stanley, Justin Williams, Michael Iglesias, Shane Epting, and (especially) Ronald Sundstrom.

I have shared drafts of several chapters with the Portland-area Political Theory and Philosophy group. This group has become one of my primary intellectual communities, and I wish to thank its members, past and present, for all of the stimulation and critical engagement that our get-togethers provide: Tamara Metz, Bill Curtis, Chana Cox, Curtis Johnson, Nick Buccola, John Holzwarth, Jeannie Morefield, Paul Apostolidis, Peter Steinberger, Jeff Gauthier, Tom Balmer, the late Don Balmer, Alex Zakaras, Malcolm Campbell, Les Swanson, Julen Etxabe, Joseph Lampert, Evan Dudik, and Alex Sager.

Many thanks also to Alex Sager for reading the entire penultimate draft of the manuscript and offering many helpful comments. Thanks, too, to Daniel Andersen for reading large portions of the manuscript over the years—the last time as I furiously made final revisions.

Three students assisted with the book. I thank Misty Freeman and Sione Filimoehala for their help with research and in preparing the manuscript. And many thanks to Jake Fitzharris for proofreading the manuscript on a tight deadline.

A few portions of the book have been previously published, and I thank the venues in which they originally appeared for permission to reuse the material here. Much of chapter 4 was published in the *American Political Science Review* as "A Liberal Defense of Black Nationalism" (vol. 104, no. 3, 2010, pp. 467–81) and is reprinted with permission. I have borrowed two paragraphs in chapter 3 from "A Truth Commission for the United States?," which appeared in *Intertexts* (vol. 7, no. 2, 2003, pp. 157–69). And I have used three paragraphs in chapter 2 that originally appeared in the entry "Reparations" in the *International Encyclopedia of Ethics* (ed. Hugh LaFollette, Blackwell, 2013, pp. 4538–47).

At Oxford University Press, many thanks to Angela Chnapko for taking on this manuscript and expertly guiding it through the review and publication process. Thank you to Charles Mills, who not only attended the workshop at Georgia State but also served as a reviewer for OUP. I also thank an additional, anonymous reviewer for many helpful suggestions.

Finally, some personal notes. I want to thank my girls, Alma and Nora for bringing such joy into my life, and often providing a welcome break from my work. They have become nearly the sole purpose of my existence. My greatest debt is to my wife, Jessica Burness. She has given me unflagging support in too many ways to recount here. She also read the entire manuscript and provided comments that led to substantial rewriting of portions of the text. I thank Jessica for her generosity with her time and energy, and her generosity of spirit, which she always exhibits despite her own demanding and stressful career. This book is for you, Sweetheart. Long may we marvel at our good fortune.

Introduction

Race and Justice

The persistence of racial inequality in the United States raises profound issues of justice. The fact is that being "black" in the United States today places one at a substantial disadvantage in one's life prospects, and this runs afoul of any basic notion of equality of opportunity or equal life chances. Furthermore, the disadvantage of African Americans is a legacy of explicitly racist and discriminatory policies under slavery and Jim Crow. As a society, we have rejected these policies and the more informal practices that accompanied them, and have committed ourselves to equality under the law. Yet the inequality created in the past continues to be reproduced and to overwhelmingly influence life chances in the present. All of this takes place in a society that likes to see itself as democratic and liberal, in the sense that its citizens are to be treated as moral and civic equals, and all are to have a chance at a decent life. The persistence of racial inequality challenges this flattering self-perception and raises the question of what American society must do to address the legacies of its past.

In the political discourse on race in the United States today, two broad answers to this question are prominent. One view, associated with the political Right, holds that the very principles of equality and nondiscrimination that animated the civil rights movement now require public policy and political institutions to be race-blind—require, that is, that they do not take race into account in any way. To be race-conscious in policy, on this view, is to continue to treat race as relevant, whereas norms of equal treatment require it to be treated as irrelevant. While the government should enforce antidiscrimination laws, beyond that it should treat racial inequality with a kind of benign neglect. This view is perhaps best encapsulated by Chief Justice John Roberts's statement, in his decision in the *Parents Involved* (2007) case, that "the way to stop discrimination on the basis of race is to stop discriminating on the basis of race." Roberts's view is that any use of race in policy amounts to "discrimination" and that our political and constitutional principles forbid it.

The political Left has tended to be more supportive of actively pursuing racial equality. However, there are several tendencies in the Left's approach to race that are problematic from the point of view elaborated throughout this book. The first is that arguments for policies that take race into account are often defensive, even apologetic, and frame such policies as temporary. Advocates of race-conscious policies often hold that, while we must consider race in order to overcome the legacies of the past, as well as to address the problem of ongoing racial discrimination, the eventual goal should be to eliminate the need for such policies in the future. Second, efforts to overcome racial inequality often take the form of policies intended to achieve integration. This is certainly the case in education, but the tendency is also strong in other policy areas as well, such as housing. Third, policies that take account of race are often justified in the name of diversity and multiculturalism, which seek to encompass all minority groups—ethnic as well as racial, immigrants as well as native-born, gender- and sexual-identity groups, and so forth. "Valuing diversity" has become a catch-all phrase for including all kinds of groups in many institutional settings, and the claims of African Americans are often subsumed under, and understood through, this generalized multiculturalism.

This book takes issue with both of these sets of views. It argues (against the first position described above) that the principles to which American society is supposed to be committed, and those that animated the civil rights movement—the principles, broadly speaking, of a liberal society—require the pursuit of racial equality and permit (and in some cases require) race-consciousness in policy and institutions in that pursuit. In light of our history and current circumstances, neglect of racial inequality cannot be benign. Against the dominant tendencies in the Left's approach to race, the view defended here is agnostic about whether race-conscious policies will turn out to be temporary or permanent, and sees the insistence that they be temporary as causing harm to the cause of racial justice. It also argues against an emphasis on integration as the only route to racial equality, defending the value, in certain contexts, of predominantly black institutions and communities as a viable alternative. Finally, it argues against the tendency to subsume claims for racial justice, particularly as they regard African Americans, under more general arguments for diversity. Rather, the history and current predicament facing African Americans give rise to distinctive claims and distinctive arguments for those claims, and subsuming black claims under the heading of diversity underplays some of the strongest arguments in their favor.

JUSTICE AND LIBERAL THEORY

Every argument must start somewhere, and the arguments about racial justice that I make here draw on the premises of liberal political theory. The phrase "liberal political theory" (and its cognates, such as "liberalism" and "liberal theory") may be misleading to some readers because in American political discourse "liberalism" is associated with a leftist or progressive ideological orientation. Among political theorists and philosophers, however, liberalism has a different meaning. It refers to the tradition in political philosophy that traces its lineage to the seventeenth century, and emphasizes the importance of limited government, the rule of law, and individual rights. Canonical writers in the liberal tradition include John Locke, Adam Smith, John Stuart Mill, and John Rawls. Although issues of race and racial justice are discussed and debated in a number of registers today—legal, constitutional, ideological—I pursue them primarily as issues of normative political theory. In relying on liberal theory I draw on a tradition of political philosophy that influenced the authors of the

Declaration of Independence and framers of the US Constitution and that has always played a large role in American political discourse.

This is not to say that the United States actually *is* a liberal society, in the sense of embodying a set of plausibly liberal principles. Rather, it is better to think of the United States as "an aspirationally liberal political order" (Meister 1999, 135), one that is committed to liberal principles but has not lived up to them. Even this characterization will strike some readers as too optimistic. The liberal tradition is only one tradition of political discourse in the United States, and it has always coexisted with other traditions—some of which are compatible with liberalism, but some of which, such as explicitly racist views, are deeply incompatible (Smith 1997). When I say (borrowing the words of Robert Meister) that the United States is an aspirationally liberal society, then, I do not mean to suggest that everyone in the country espouses (some version of) liberal values. On the contrary, we know that this is not the case. What I mean is that liberal values inform some of the highest ideals reflected in American political discourse, ideals of liberty and equality to which one social movement after another has (often successfully) appealed—from the abolitionist movement of the nineteenth century to movements for legal and social equality in the twentieth and twenty-first centuries.

This book is not alone in exploring the implications of liberal values for justice toward a minority group. Many others have explored this terrain, and I engage and draw upon this work in the chapters that follow. As we will see, however, liberal multiculturalists tend to focus on minorities that are defined first and foremost by cultural differences, and they therefore neglect the case of African Americans. As one observer put it, "When liberal political theorists tackle matters of group difference, they often evade race in general and the case of African Americans in particular. On the subject of multicultural challenges to liberal neutrality, for instance, political theorists tend to focus on minority groups with a high level of cultural cohesion" (Fogg-Davis 2003, 557). Given this, much of the debate about liberalism and minority rights is of limited direct relevance to the case of African Americans. For although as a group African Americans arguably possess certain kinds of cultural distinctiveness, the primary sources of racial injustice are not cultural. Rather, they pertain to the history of slavery, racial discrimination under Jim Crow, and the ongoing sources of black disadvantage. Too few scholars have explored the implications of liberalism for racial justice (but see Appiah and Gutmann 1996; Cochran 1999; Lebron 2013; Shelby 2004; Shelby 2016; Spinner 1994, chap. 6).

The specific version of liberalism within which the arguments that follow are advanced is liberal egalitarianism, the school of thought associated with John Rawls. Liberal egalitarianism is committed to the moral equality of all people and sees each person as having interests and claims that are equally worthy of consideration. Liberal egalitarians generally defend a set of universal rights that protect individuals from having their most important interests sacrificed to the interests of others. Beyond these basic rights, liberal egalitarians require equality of opportunity, and they argue for constraints on the degree of economic inequality among members of a society.

One obstacle to pursuing a liberal-egalitarian view of racial justice is that liberal-egalitarian theories are often pursued on the plane of "ideal theory." That is, they ask, what principles of justice would be adopted if individuals choosing them knew nothing about their society or their position in it? This is a very different question from one that focuses on what we must do to remedy systemic injustice. This does not mean, however, that ideal theory is irrelevant to issues of racial injustice, for "Charges of injustice presuppose ideals of justice" (Shelby 2016, 12). Still, the principles generated by ideal theory provide limited guidance in responding to the specific forms of injustice that characterize a society. Addressing injustice places us in the realm of "nonideal" theory. A liberal-egalitarian approach to racial justice, then, must develop the implications of its principles—equal moral worth, civic equality, equal basic rights, fair equality of opportunity, and distributional equity—for the decidedly nonideal circumstances of deep and persistent racial inequality. Carrying this out requires engaging with not only theoretical arguments but also empirical and historical evidence, in an exercise in what Meira Levinson (2014) has called "grounded reflective equilibrium."

It should also be noted that despite the fact that I offer many arguments in the spirit of liberal egalitarianism, one need not be a liberal egalitarian to agree with my conclusions. Indeed, at certain points in the arguments below I appeal to other theoretical resources, such as (perhaps surprisingly) the libertarian theory of Robert Nozick. As Charles Mills (2017, 88) has noted, many of the violations of the rights of African Americans have been violations not just of liberal-egalitarian principles, but of the "negative" rights endorsed by libertarianism. Hence even libertarians should be deeply troubled by racial inequality, and they may be able to endorse some of the conclusions that I draw. At the same time, political theorists who identify with "critical" theory, and proponents of critical race theory, may be (pleasantly?) surprised to discover the far-reaching conclusions that I draw from liberal premises. Indeed, one point I attempt to make throughout the book is that liberal political theory is extremely demanding when it comes to the problem of racial inequality—it provides no comfort to the complacent.

To supplement liberal theory and to help us think through its implications for nonideal circumstances, I rely on the idea of "transitional justice." Transitional justice refers to the set of measures that societies undertake as they attempt to make a transition from a regime that systematically abuses human rights to a regime that is committed to upholding them. Such transitions have occurred over the last few decades in Latin America, Eastern Europe, and South Africa, among other places. These regime transitions have raised the issue of what must be done to address the abuses of the past and to establish a more just and legitimate successor regime. A rich literature now explores these and related topics. This literature is helpful in thinking about racial justice in the United States because many of the issues that it addresses have strong parallels in the United States. The central insight of recent reflections on transitional justice is that simply ending abuses and enforcing equal rights is not adequate for a just transition. A more thoroughgoing confrontation with the past is required, and public policy must deal with its legacies. Transitional justice is a valuable supplement to liberal theory because it introduces a temporal dimension to theorizing about justice, provides guidance for thinking about justice under nonideal conditions, directs our attention to relevant issues (such as reparations and the importance of collective memory), and furnishes concepts and principles that might apply in the circumstances that we face in the case of racial inequality in the United States.

The focus of the book, then, is on what justice requires, not what is politically viable or popular. I have no illusions about the prospects for adopting into policy the prescriptions defended here, particularly in the current political climate. The emphasis is on which public policies and institutional arrangements are compatible with, or required by, justice. In other words, the focus is mainly on what the state may, may not, or must do—as well as what other major institutions may, may not, or must do, if they are committed to liberal principles. While I agree with G. A. Cohen (2011) that we ought not conflate what justice requires and what the state should do, I believe that identifying what the state should do is an important part of developing a complete conception of justice.

RACE AND RACISM

The idea of racial justice obviously invokes the idea of race. Most scholars agree that "race" is a distinctively modern notion, a product of specific historical developments in the early modern period (see, for example, Hannaford 1996). Today, there is a strong consensus that race is a "social construction," that is, a culturally and historically specific idea that does not pick out any natural phenomena. Race is not a biological category but a social one. Still, philosophers and others continue to debate how we should understand the concept of race, whether we should continue to rely on it at all, and in what sense (if any) race can be considered "real" (see Boxill 2001; James 2016). The present work does not engage these debates on the "ontology" of race. It simply assumes that the overwhelming scholarly consensus is correct in concluding that there is no scientific basis for racial stereotypes regarding intelligence or behavioral tendencies. Rather, it assumes that race as a social category is deeply embedded in our history and culture. The idea of race shapes the way individuals see the world, and it has monumental consequences for those placed in certain racial categories. The consequences of race as a social phenomenon, then, are very real even if it is meaningless as a scientific or biological category. American society exhibits what Michael Omi and Howard Winant (1994) have called a "racial formation," or what Jennifer Hochschild and her colleagues (2012) have called a "racial order"—a fairly fixed racial hierarchy that deeply infuses the political, economic, cultural, and social life of the society. In the United States, as a matter of cultural norms and even (in the past) legal norms, to have any significant amount of "black blood" (or any at all, under the "single drop" rule) in one's background defines one as black (Davis 1991). I take as my focus the normative issues raised by the phenomenon of race as we find it in our society, while freely admitting that for other societies, with different histories and conceptions of race, different conceptions of racial justice may be appropriate. Still, to the extent that other countries have racialized minorities with a similar history, the arguments offered in this book may be of relevance elsewhere.

Philosophers and others have also devoted a great deal of attention to the nature of racism (see Harris 1999; Levine and Pataki 2004). Some argue that racism is best understood as a matter of individual-level psychology, while others argue for an understanding of racism as systemic or institutional. Among the former, some advocate a conception of racism (or racial bias) that is primarily cognitive (see Loury 2002), while others see racism as primarily a matter of affect or ill-will (see Garcia 1996). Elsewhere I have offered qualified support for the view of racism as primarily a matter of affect (see Valls 2005, 2009). Here, however, I do not focus on racism, in part because I do not see it as the primary driver of racial inequality. It is true that there is ample evidence of racial bias and its baleful effects, as we will see below. Most of us who are products of American society and culture carry around, at the very least, "implicit" bias. Furthermore, audit studies in the areas of housing and employment consistently demonstrate bias and discrimination against African Americans. While individual attitudes and biases no doubt contribute to the maintenance and reproduction of racial inequality, I see racial inequality primarily as deeply rooted in durable institutions and social arrangements. Racial injustice is a case of structural injustice (see Young 2011, chap. 2). In the words of Hayward and Swanstrom (2011), is a "thick injustice," reinforced by many overlapping and mutually supporting factors such as residential patterns, educational opportunities, and accumulated racial differences in wealth. While individuals' racial attitudes and biases—whether conscious and avowed, or unconscious and "implicit" (Banaji and Greenwald 2012)—certainly play a role, I think that it is a mistake to see racial inequality as primarily perpetuated by individual-level racial attitudes. Even if such attitudes were to change for the better, much structural racial inequality would remain.

The present work focuses on racial justice as it applies specifically to African Americans and the legacies of slavery and Jim Crow. While African Americans are not the only racial minority in American society, they constitute a very large and disadvantaged social group with a distinctive history and distinctive set of current conditions. This history and present-day reality, I argue, give rise to distinctive normative claims that cannot necessarily be made with equal force or plausibility by other groups. So despite the fact that there are other racialized groups, and other disadvantaged minorities, the issues related to African Americans deserve sustained attention in their own right.

Another way of putting this is to say that there is a trade-off between the detailed treatment of one group and a more general approach to group rights or multiculturalism. The latter may have the advantage of inclusiveness, but the cost is that the history, predicament, and issues that pertain primarily to one group may receive inadequate attention or emphasis. The result may be that some of the strongest grounds for certain claims that one or a few groups can make may be undermined in the search for grounds to which all groups can appeal. Thus the reliance on diversity, I suggest, has actually undermined arguments for some African American claims that could be advanced more persuasively on other grounds. If we wish to arrive at an overall theory of multiculturalism or minority rights, I suggest, it is best to do so inductively, by looking first at the claims that each group may have, and then looking for commonalities among them or searching for a way to accommodate all legitimate claims. It is a mistake only to discuss minority rights or multiculturalism in general, or only to advance arguments and claims that apply to all groups. Still, I hope that some of what I say will be of interest to, and relevant to, other disadvantaged groups. In arguing for measures that promote black empowerment and advancement, I appeal to general norms and principles that, in similar circumstances, will have similar implications.

A cogent conception of racial justice is badly needed because there is little reason to hope that racial inequality will diminish on its own. This has not happened in the fifty years since the civil rights movement and there is no reason to think that it will happen in the next fifty, at least in the absence of concerted effort. Such optimism would be unwarranted. I disagree with Jennifer Hochschild and her colleagues (2012), for example, when they suggest that the United States may be on the cusp of "creating a new racial order," one that is less fixed and in which African Americans are not stuck at the bottom. They argue that immigration, generational change, the rise of multiracial and multiethnic identities, and better understanding of genetics and the human genome are all undermining old racial categories and racial hierarchies. Yet there is little evidentiary basis for this optimism, and furthermore this perspective would seem to lend support to the very complacency on issues of race that has contributed to a lack of progress. We need a renewed sense of urgency about the problems of racial injustice, one that has not existed since the civil rights movement, and we also need a conception of racial justice to guide our thought and action.

In focusing on issues of justice that are raised by the conditions facing African Americans, I do not rely on the terminology of "recognition," nor do I see the arguments that follow as a case of "identity politics." Some political theorists have argued that one kind of injustice perpetrated against certain groups, distinct from injustices related to resources and opportunities, is the injustice of nonrecognition or misrecognition. These wrongs involve the failure to see members of a group as culturally (or otherwise) distinct, or failing to affirm and acknowledge them as differentiated from the dominant group (Taylor 1994). I do not see the main injustices related to African Americans as a case of misrecognition, but rather as relating to opportunities, resources, and the like. Now, some issues of racial justice do approach the terrain of recognition, especially ones related to collective memory and acknowledgment of the past, which are discussed in chapter 3. But even here, I find the language of recognition unhelpful because the main issues involve not recognition of distinctness, but the affirmation of African Americans as being of equal moral worth and as equal citizens. These are universalist, not particularist, claims.

Similarly, because the focus here is on structural and material inequality, we are not in the realm of identity politics. I agree with Iris Young when she writes that "the primary claims of justice [by African Americans] . . . refer to experiences of structural inequality more than cultural difference" (2000, 105). Arguments for addressing racial injustice also need not lead to the "balkanization" of society, nor must they undermine broad-based movements for progressive change—concerns that have variously been expressed by Arthur Schlesinger (1992) and Mark Lilla (2017), among others. Addressing the injustices facing African Americans must be part of any program for achieving a more just society. Justice overall cannot be achieved without addressing racial injustice.

Finally, the attentive reader will have noted that I used the terms "black" and "African American" more or less interchangeably (though I generally prefer the former as an adjective, the latter as a noun). This usage raises issues beyond mere terminology, for these categories are not necessarily coextensive. The term "African American" is conventionally used to refer to black Americans who can point to a long line of descent in American society—usually going back to slavery and Jim Crow. Yet some black Americans are recent immigrants (or their descendants) from the Caribbean, Africa, or elsewhere, and therefore do not have the same relation to the distinct history of African Americans in the United States. This is relevant to the normative arguments that follow because these often appeal to this history in grounding claims for justice. Yet even recently arrived black immigrants are subject to many of the same structural factors and forms of racial bias faced by African Americans (Portes and Rumbaut 2006, 258), so arguments about how the past structures present-day inequalities may apply even to those whose ancestors did not experience that past.

OVERVIEW OF THE ARGUMENT

The chapters that follow address an array of issues related to racial justice, and in each case I attempt to develop a distinctively liberal approach to the problem of racial inequality. In many cases, I argue that liberal principles have far-reaching implications for the requirements of racial justice. For example, I argue in the next chapter that a liberal conception of racial justice requires addressing the accumulated inequality along racial lines in American society. I argue, then, for black reparations, though I also argue that the usual philosophical approaches to this issue are in some ways less than helpful. I suggest using the conceptual resources of transitional justice as a way of formulating a compelling case for policies that directly address racial inequality. I also attempt to provide enough historical background to remind us of why the case for black reparations is so strong, particularly in light of the government's active role in creating present-day patterns of racial inequality and segregation.

The following chapter addresses another set of issues that often arises in regime transitions, namely issues of collective memory and acknowledgment of the past. I examine a number of specific issues that fall under this heading, and I assess the extent to which historical memory in the United States with respect to race should be seen as satisfying the demands of equal citizenship. I find some areas of hope and progress, such as the truth commissions and apologies that have addressed our racial past. These practices, along with the many memorials to the civil rights movement, are signs of progress in that they explicitly affirm the values of equal moral worth and civic equality. However, there are some troubling features of our symbolic racial politics as well, such as the persistence of Confederate war memorials and the continued use by state governments of the Confederate battle flag. These symbols, far from expressing a rejection of the racist aspects of our past, express a kind of nostalgia that is incompatible with the affirmation of the equal citizenship of African Americans.

If chapters 2 and 3 examine the material and symbolic dimensions of racial justice in our post-civil rights era, chapter 4 focuses on institutions and communities—especially the fate of black communities and institutions that played such an important role in the lives of African Americans before and during the civil rights movement. With its emphasis on integration, public policy has often played a role in undermining black institutions and communities, as Black Power advocates foresaw. I take up and defend some of the arguments of these black nationalists, as I attempt to show that integration as usually conceived imposes high costs on African Americans. Drawing upon recent debates over multiculturalism, I argue that a strong case can be made, on liberal grounds, that public policy should support black institutions and black communities rather than weakening them in the name of integration.

Affirmation of the value of black institutions and communities does not, however, imply the wholesale rejection of integration or of policies, such as affirmative action, designed to foster racial inclusion. I argue in chapter 5 that the history of affirmative action and the way it has come to be framed may help explain why its advocates seem perpetually on the defensive. Originally a policy aimed at African Americans and intended to compensate for past injustices, it came to include other groups, such as women and ethnic minorities. This required a shift in the justification to one that applies to all covered groups—hence the shift from compensation to diversity. Yet this shift has the effect of undercutting the case for affirmative action as applied to African Americans, since diversity turns out to be a weak basis for it, while the compensatory case (I argue) remains strong. I also attempt to rebut some of the main critiques of affirmative action, such as the idea that it actually harms its intended beneficiaries, and that it is incompatible with due consideration of merit.

One of the great causes of the persistence of racial inequality is residential segregation. African Americans remain highly segregated, and, particularly for poor blacks, this segregation is at the root of their diminished access to quality education, services, basic security, and economic opportunity. The integrationist approach to this set of problems is to disperse African Americans out of black neighborhoods, but as I argue in chapter 6, this approach is problematic because it does not take full account of the costs that it imposes on African Americans. Drawing on the arguments in chapter 4, I suggest that racial residential clustering is not itself the problem—rather, the injustice inheres in the terms on which that clustering takes place. A liberal-egalitarian approach to the issue must acknowledge the value that racial clustering may have for African Americans. Public policy should take account of that value even as it broadens the range of options available to African Americans regarding their choice of residence. The focus of public policy should be, not on dispersing African Americans, but on addressing directly the disadvantages that often are associated with black neighborhoods.

The geographic concentration of many African Americans has important effects on patterns of crime and policing. In chapter 7 I argue that race is deeply entwined with the problem of mass incarceration, since racial disparities in incarceration reflect both background racial inequality and disparate treatment within the criminal justice system itself. The latter is sometimes due to explicit policies of racial profiling, which I argue cannot be justified, as well as other kinds of racial bias in the criminal justice system. Sentences being served by prisoners in the United States are far too long, and African Americans are overrepresented among those serving long prisons terms. Perhaps the most important effect of the criminal justice system on racial inequality is the way that a criminal record affects one's prospects after release from prison. These "collateral consequences" impede the life prospects of ex-prisoners, their families, and communities. Hence justice requires far-reaching criminal justice reform, but also reform of policies outside of the criminal justice system that exacerbate racial inequality.

Another consequence of residential clustering is the existence of many schools in which African Americans constitute a majority of the student body. Such schools often have inferior facilities and are disadvantaged in other ways. As I argue in chapter 8, the problem of school segregation is too often framed as a failure of integration, which is assumed to be the ideal toward which policy ought to aim. As with residential segregation, the problem is often misidentified as racial clustering itself rather than as the terms on which it takes place. Integration, under some circumstances, may be a worthy goal, and recent Supreme Court cases restricting the use of race to achieve it are mistaken, I argue. Yet the pursuit of integration should be moderated by a recognition of the value of predominantly black schools. Public policy must to some extent take a pragmatic approach to enhancing educational opportunities for African Americans, but an over-emphasis on integration distracts attention from enhancing the quality of black schools.

Overall, then, the conception of racial justice that I advance indicates that American society has yet to live up to the demands that its liberal values place upon it. We have yet to fully address legacies of the past and to adequately confront ongoing sources of racial inequality. While integration and policies like affirmative action have their place in the pursuit of racial equality, these should not be seen as the sole requirements of racial justice. Rather, justice requires that pride of place be given to the freedom and equality of African Americans, and this in turn requires that public policy and institutional design provide not just routes to integration but also support for black communities and institutions.

I hope that the arguments in the following chapters will persuade some readers, but of course many will disagree—sometimes profoundly. Still, I hope that even for those who disagree, my arguments provide a service. I hope that by posing the issues as I do, I at least clarify some of what is at stake. Fundamentally, we need a conception of racial justice to guide our thought on the array of issues raised by racial inequality. I do not claim to have fully worked out this conception, or to have considered all of the issues a conception of racial justice should address. But I do hope that what follows constitutes a modest contribution to the (collective) endeavor of developing such a conception.

2

Racial Inequality and Black Reparations

Racial inequality in the United States is deeply rooted and persistent. The gap between African Americans and whites—as measured by any indicator of well-being such as wealth, income, employment, health, or education—is a profound injustice for two reasons: because of how it came about and because it continues to reproduce unfair disadvantage. The historical roots of racial inequality are important because they highlight the continuity between slavery and Jim Crow on the one hand and the current, post-civil rights era on the other. When one considers how little has changed with regard to racial inequality since the civil rights movement, it becomes clear that American society has not lived up to the ideals of that movement.

This is the situation to which some activists and scholars call attention by raising the issue of black reparations. The idea of black reparations is that the injustices of the past and their impact on the present provide powerful grounds for addressing racial inequality in public policy. The term "reparations" is sometimes taken to be synonymous with compensation, and it is true that material compensation is an important aspect of reparations. Yet the idea of reparations is broader, encompassing both material compensation and other efforts to engage in what Margaret Walker (2006a) calls "moral repair." Moral repair, or reparations in the broader sense, is required in the context of a society that has committed large-scale and systematic injustices that undermine social trust, political legitimacy, and civic equality. In chapter 3, I discuss a number of means by which the United States might explicitly acknowledge our racial past and engage in moral repair. This chapter focuses more narrowly on the material aspect of reparations.

Arguments for black reparations in the narrow sense of compensation entail some acknowledgment on their own, because policies of reparations (implicitly or explicitly) reflect a judgment that serious violations occurred and shaped present-day patterns of racial inequality. This may explain why advocates of reparations insist on framing the argument for racial justice, at least in part, in these terms—and also may explain why such arguments are resisted so strenuously by others. Arguments over material reparations are always also about the meaning of the past and its impact on the present, and therefore implicate people's sense of status and entitlement. They are about not only material resources but about the meaning of racial inequality in the United States. So while the focus in this chapter is on material compensation, issues of acknowledgment are never far from view. In what follows I argue that black reparations are demanded by justice, but that to appreciate the case for reparations requires putting it in its proper historical and theoretical context.

JIM CROW AND RACIAL INEQUALITY

The basic story about the origins of racial inequality is well known but it is worthwhile to remind ourselves of some of the salient facts, to lay the groundwork for the arguments that follow. The treatment here will necessarily be brief and highly selective, focusing not on slavery or the early decades of Jim Crow, but on developments roughly in the middle third of the twentieth century. I do this to show that the patterns of segregation and inequality that exist today, while in one sense having deep historical roots going back centuries, are also traceable to policy decisions that were made in the more recent past. During this period the federal government played an active role in promoting racial inequality, helping to make Jim Crow not just a southern, but a national phenomenon.

In the early days of Jim Crow, it was private individuals, and then state and local governments, that took the lead in enforcing racial subordination. As C. Vann Woodward (2001) shows in his classic work, the process of establishing Jim Crow segregation was slow and uneven. After the failure of Reconstruction and the withdrawal of federal forces from the states of the former Confederacy, southern whites began to reassert their dominance and re-establish many of the same institutions and practices that had existed under slavery. Sharecropping and debt peonage kept many African Americans living and working under conditions similar to those under slavery, and the criminal justice system came to be used to discipline and subordinate African Americans and subject them to "slavery by another name" (Blackmon 2008; Daniel 1973). All of this was abetted by the terrorist violence perpetrated by private citizens (usually with at least the acquiescence, if not the active support, of law enforcement) who engaged in intimidation, lynching, and "race riots" that destroyed whole black towns and neighborhoods.

Racial segregation became official policy in many southern states, which passed laws requiring separate accommodations for whites and blacks. This system of racial separation was given a stamp of approval by the federal government in the Supreme Court case of *Plessy v. Ferguson* (1896), which held that separate facilities were compatible with the Constitution's requirement of equal treatment under the law, as long as the facilities were equal. Of course, everyone knew that the two sets of facilities were not equal, but this was the fiction that permitted Jim Crow to develop and become entrenched. State and local governments, private businesses, institutions, and individuals worked together to ensure the social, economic, and political subordination of African Americans through explicit policy, social norms, and terrorist violence.

All of this is well known, but what is sometimes less well appreciated is how active the federal government became in promoting and enforcing racial inequality. As the power of the federal government grew over the course of the twentieth century, it often used its influence, not to limit the effects of racism perpetrated by states, localities, and private entities, but rather to exacerbate them. This is due in part to the role of southern politicians in the federal government, who often insisted that new federal policies and institutions accommodate the Jim Crow system. The effect was often to give federal support to extending and deepening racial inequality.

Consider employment. The federal government is itself a large employer, and through various policies it regulates and promotes employment. Beginning with the administration of Woodrow Wilson, the federal government segregated its employees based on race and engaged in systematic discrimination against African Americans, usually relegating them to more menial jobs and thereby reinforcing this norm for the entire country (King 2007, chaps. 2–3). During the New Deal, the federal government enacted a number of policies designed to boost employment, but these were often administered at the state and local level, where racial discrimination was practiced (King 2007, 182; Harris 1982, 102). Legislation regulating employment, which established minimum wages and working conditions, purposely failed to regulate sectors where most African Americans worked, such as agriculture and domestic service (Hill 1977, 97). The federal government also acquiesced in racial discrimination practiced by labor unions. In 1935 Congress explicitly rejected a provision of the Wagner Act that would have denied federal protection to unions that excluded African Americans (Harris 1982, 110; Jones 1998, 343; Moreno 2006, 172). As Philip Foner comments, federal law in this period "merely legalized for all American industry the pattern of racial discrimination that had long been the practice of Southern employers. . . . In acquiescing to the wage differential, the New Deal placed the government's stamp of approval on the principle of Negro inferiority" (1974, 200–201). And as another scholar concludes, the failure of the federal government to insist on equal treatment in federal employment programs "established a new degree of government complicity in economic racial discrimination. . . . [The New Deal provided] legal protections and benefits to white workers and [made] black workers more vulnerable to job discrimination. . . . [Under

New Deal legislation] informal discriminatory practices became structured and legally sanctioned" (Hill 1977, 98, 97, 100n).

The Jim Crow context decisively shaped other important areas of social policy as well. One of the most important achievements of the New Deal was the Social Security Act of 1935, which established three main programs: Old Age Insurance (what we now commonly call "social security"), Aid to Dependent Children, and Unemployment Insurance. As a number of scholars have pointed out (see Brown 1999; Lieberman 1998; Neubeck and Cazenave 2001; Poole 2006; Skocpol 1995), each of these programs discriminated against African Americans and denied them benefits extended to whites, but in different ways. Old Age Insurance was the only truly national program of the three, but it excluded the agricultural and domestic sectors. While this was changed in 1954, as Theda Skocpol points out, this delay meant that "such service and agricultural employees had already (compared to most other workers) lost many years of building eligibility for generous retirement pensions. . . . Thus African Americans have received less even from this relatively universal part of U.S. social provision than have whites" (1995, 143). Aid to Dependent Children was locally administered, permitting racial discrimination to take place. Indeed, a provision of the bill banning racial discrimination in ADC was removed (Neubeck and Cazenave 2001, 47). Unemployment Insurance, like Old Age Insurance, excluded agricultural and domestic workers (and this was not changed until 1976). Because Unemployment Insurance was structured as a benefit that was earned through previous employment, it disadvantaged African Americans, who were more likely to be unemployed for longer periods. It thus "ignore[d] the most serious problems of employment and unemployment for African-Americans" (Lieberman 1998, 178).

Finally, consider housing policy. As part of the New Deal, as well as in the GI Bill, the federal government got into the business of promoting homeownership. By insuring home mortgages and, later, by buying mortgages from banks, it fostered the housing boom that was essential to creating the post–World War II American middle class. The government also became deeply involved in the housing market by, for example, establishing national standards for home appraisals. The Federal Housing Administration's policies favored new construction and detached homes, so it was important to the development of suburban housing after World War II. By promoting suburbanization, however, it at the same time drained urban centers of middle-class residents by luring them to the suburbs with more favorable loan terms than they could receive on much of the older housing stock in the city. The appraisal standards introduced redlining, the practice of not insuring mortgages in certain residential areas—often those neighborhoods dominated by African Americans. As Kenneth Jackson states, "The lasting damage done by the national government was that it put its seal of approval on ethnic and racial discrimination and developed policies which had the result of the practical abandonment of large sections of older, industrial cities" (1985, 217). Massey and Denton reach similar conclusions. They write: "What was new about the postwar era was the extent to which the federal government became involved in perpetuating racial segregation. . . . It lent the power, prestige, and support of the federal government to the systematic practice of racial discrimination in housing" (1993, 51, 52).

None of the racial implications of these policies were accidental. They were fully foreseen, and in the case of many actors, fully intended. And they were understood by African Americans as well. As the NAACP noted about the New Deal, "From a Negro's point of view it look[ed] like a sieve with holes just big enough for the majority of Negroes to fall through" (quoted in Skocpol 1995, 142). From the advent of the New Deal onward, federal policy bore the marks of its Jim Crow context. African Americans were systematically denied benefits that were made available to others, particularly whites. As a result, they tended to have lower employment rates and lower wages, less income and less wealth, and fewer benefits under federal programs.

The patterns of segregation and racial inequality that were established in the middle decades of the twentieth century persist today. The restricted educational and occupational opportunities, combined with the more limited access to homeownership, have had a profound impact in the decades since the civil rights movement. While there have been some gains by

African Americans, relative to whites there has been little or no improvement for decades. Since the civil rights era, the ratios of white to black household income and wealth have been remarkably consistent. Median black household income has hovered at around 60 percent of median white household income. Black unemployment has been roughly double that of whites for decades. The black poverty rate has been two to three times that of whites over the same period (Protect Our Progress: State of Black America 2017).

The causes of this persistence of racial inequality are, of course, complex, but a number of scholars have pointed to the especially important role of wealth (see Conley 1999; Massey and Denton 1993; Oliver and Shapiro 2006). The employment, social, and housing policies discussed above meant that African Americans have had lower income and fewer opportunities to accumulate wealth, especially in the form of equity in owned homes. This in turn has meant that African Americans have had less money to save, less to invest in education, and less to pass on to their children. These patterns have persisted long after the policies that put them in place were repealed. Since the civil rights era, white median household wealth has continued to be about ten times that of median black household wealth, and at every income level, black households have much less wealth than their white counterparts. As Oliver and Shapiro show, "The growth and dispersion of wealth [today] continues a trend anchored in the economic prosperity of post–World War II America" (2006, 201). The benefits that were granted to whites but largely denied African Americans during the period of economic expansion in the middle decades of the twentieth century continue to reverberate, and this should not be surprising. In the absence of an effort to combat racial inequality commensurate with the problem, we should not expect these patterns to dissipate.

As we will see in other chapters, there have been some attempts to address the material legacies of Jim Crow: efforts to overcome discrimination in employment and higher education through affirmative action (chapter 5); to desegregate housing (chapter 6); and to integrate K-12 schools (chapter 8). However, as I will argue, all of these have been problematic in how they have been carried out, and limited in their scope.

None of them, singly or together, have been up to the task of overcoming the racial gap in income, wealth, and well-being. Racial inequality in the United States today continues to reflect the failure to engage in a concerted effort, with the necessary scope and resources, to fully address the accumulated effects of past injustice. So racial inequality in the United States is, among other things, a case of unrectified historic injustice. The question is, how can we best think about what justice requires today?

REPARATIONS AND LIBERAL THEORY

One way to think of the wrongs perpetrated against African Americans is to look at them as a large number of torts, and to think of black reparations as a way of aggregating all of the individual tort claims. Indeed, many accounts of reparations begin (if sometimes implicitly) with the model of compensation enshrined in tort law and attempt to extend this model to compensation "over time and between groups" (Hill 2002; see also Brooks 2004). The tort model posits two individuals, one of whom wrongly harms another, entitling the latter to compensation from the former. How that compensation is measured varies, but the most standard conceptions are that the wronged party should be restored to his status quo ante condition, or that he should be compensated to the point where he is as well off as he would have been had the violation not occurred. In the individual case, it is often relatively easy to identify the parties, the violation, and the appropriate remedy.

However, in extending the tort conception of compensation to large-scale cases of historic injustice such as that of African Americans, all of this becomes much less clear. What exactly is the wrong that provides the basis for present-day claims? Is it slavery or Jim Crow or both? If slavery, is it the unremunerated labor or the violation of rights? And who are the parties to present-day claims? Are all blacks entitled to compensation—even those who are well off? And who is liable to pay? Even if it seems plausible that some present-day African Americans are entitled to compensation, determining what form compensation should take, and how much should be paid, is a very difficult task. Much of the debate over black reparations and, more generally, compensation for historic injustice, has focused on these thorny questions: Who is entitled to what, and from whom?

One framework for thinking through these issues comes from a some-what surprising source, the libertarian theory of Robert Nozick (1974). Nozick argues that any distribution of goods is fair as long as it comes about through a series of consensual transactions that violate no one's rights. But what is to be done in cases where the present distribution did result in part from past violations? To handle this kind of case Nozick endorses (though he does not fully articulate) a principle of rectification. The principle holds that if the present-day distribution of goods has been shaped by past violations of rights, then justice requires bringing the distribution back to what it would have been in the absence of those violations (1974, 152–53). In some cases, this will be an impossible task because it requires detailed knowledge about long chains of actions and reactions involving large numbers of individuals across many generations—both those that actually occurred and those that would have occurred in the absence of past wrongs. At the individual level, the precise consequences of past wrongs cannot be known. Recognizing this, Nozick proposes the use of "rules of thumb"—that is, simplifying assumptions that allow for reasonable estimates about the impact of past wrongs on present-day individuals (1974, 230–31; see Litan 1977; Lyons 1981; Narveson 2009; Phillips 1979, chaps. 9 and 10; Valls 1999).

One need not be a libertarian to appreciate Nozick's reasoning here. Even if one does not agree that the process by which a distribution comes about is a *sufficient* condition for judging its justice, any plausible conception of justice includes fair processes and nonviolation of rights as a *necessary* condition of justice (Goodin 1991, 149–50). What the Nozickian approach to these issues provides is a way of thinking about justice within a temporal frame that may be useful quite apart from its libertarian commitments.

Yet critics have had little trouble finding difficulties with this kind of counterfactual argument for reparations. One objection focuses on the fact that we simply do not have, and cannot have, sufficient information about what would have happened in the absence of past violations. According to this objection, we cannot make even reasonable estimates about who is entitled to what. In the absence of reliable information, we cannot undertake a policy of redistribution using rules of thumb. Doing so risks perpetrating further injustice (see Kukathas 2006; Loury 2007; and Paul 1991).

Another objection is based on "the nonidentity problem," which is that in some cases the present-day individuals making reparations claims might not exist in the absence of the very injustices for which they claim compensation. If this is the case, it would seem to undermine the claim to reparations, since it may be more plausible to think of some present-day members of disadvantaged groups as having benefited from the past wrongs, rather than having been harmed by them (on the assumption that existence is better than, or preferred to, nonexistence). If present-day individuals have benefited from past injustices, it would seem they can hardly claim compensation for those very injustices (see Morris 1984; Schedler 1998, chap. 7; Sher 1979).

A third problem is that the events subsequent to the initial injustice may generate new legitimate claims to the very resources that are claimed by would-be recipients of reparations. This is the argument that Jeremy Waldron makes in his paper "Superseding Historic Injustice" (1992). Waldron argues that many reparations claims cannot overcome the objection that intervening developments can undermine reparations claims because changed circumstances change entitlements. Illegitimate possession can become legitimate over time, Waldron suggests, through subsequent developments (see also Sher 1981; Cowen 2006).

Now, I believe that all of these objections can be addressed from within the Nozickian framework (see Valls 1999), but there are other problems that the tort model of reparations faces. In the simple, small-scale tort model, there is a status quo ante that exists before the wrong is committed, and, after compensation is paid, there is some kind of closure. In large-scale cases involving long periods of time, there may be no way to think coherently about a status quo ante (Barkan 2000, 326; Walker 2006b). In the case of black reparations, there is no period of American history that

includes African Americans before their rights were violated; their initial incorporation into the polity involved the violation of their rights.
Similarly, there is little hope for quick closure in large-scale cases. While
a few commentators have argued for black reparations in the hope of
closing the subject of racial inequality (see Krauthammer 1990), such closure is neither possible nor desirable in the foreseeable future. Any plausible or morally adequate response to the injustices of the past will involve
an ongoing commitment to address is legacies.

Hence while the tort model and the Nozickian framework within which
it is often elaborated provide a way of thinking about justice in time, they
also entail problems that they may not be able to overcome. Furthermore,
the tort model is a private-law model; it suggests that the harms that call for
compensation were private harms, and it thus depoliticizes those harms
and the claims based on them. As we saw above, the wrongs suffered by
African Americans were not merely a series of torts but involved the active
participation of national and local governments in granting benefits to
some citizens while denying them to others. Finally, using a libertarian
framework suggests a lack of attention to forward-looking reasons to
address racial inequality; it implies that once reparations are paid, free
market principles would be appropriate, with all of the inequality that they
would permit.

An alternative approach for thinking about reparations is liberal egalitarianism, which does concern itself with ongoing inequality. Most
versions of liberal egalitarianism seek to protect basic rights and to limit
the degree of inequality in wealth and income in a society. The trouble,
according to some scholars, is that liberal egalitarianism has difficulty
dealing with the past. For example, Jeff Spinner-Halev argues that much
work on historic injustice demonstrates the limits of liberal justice. This is
because, according to Spinner-Halev, injustices such as those suffered by
African Americans are not historical, but "enduring," the difference being
that with enduring injustices the issue is not just what happened in the
past but the role of the past in causing present-day inequality. Enduring
injustices show the "*failure* of liberalism. . . . A better defense of individual
rights, and a modest or moderate redistribution of wealth, will often not

solve the enduring injustice" (2012, 64). This is especially the case, argues Spinner-Halev, when issues of memory, acknowledgment, and (dis)trust are intertwined with material inequalities related to past injustice.

Glenn Loury has made a similar, though distinct, argument (2002). For Loury the problem is that liberalism is committed to neutrality among individuals, in that it may not arbitrarily favor some over others. Loury argues that this means liberalism requires color-blindness and therefore makes liberalism incapable of explicitly addressing racial inequality. He argues that "liberal theory is inherently limited in its capacity to engage" the issue of "pronounced and durable racial inequalities." When it comes to "the historical fact of racial subordination and the continuing reality of racial inequality . . . liberal individualism gives no good answers" (2002, 115).

I think that Spinner-Halev and Loury are both right to an extent, but that they overstate their claims. While it is true that, under a certain interpretation of liberal theory, liberalism has difficulty addressing historic injustice, it is a mistake to argue that this is a necessary consequence of liberalism. Indeed, both Spinner-Halev and Loury go on to make arguments that are broadly compatible with what I will argue here, but they characterize their respective positions as going beyond liberalism, whereas I would characterize their efforts, and my own, as extending liberal theory and drawing out its implications for a case of historic (or, following Spinner-Halev, enduring) injustice. While they have identified certain tendencies within liberal theory as it has often been elaborated, I believe that it has greater resources for this kind of issue.

One way to explore both the potential and the limits of liberal-egalitarian theory for dealing with historic injustice in general and the question of black reparations in particular is to consider how these might fit within John Rawls's paradigmatic theory (1999, 2001, 2005). Rawls famously asks us to imagine ourselves in an "original position," behind a "veil of ignorance" that deprives us of knowledge about ourselves, our position in society, and the facts about our society and its history. We are then to decide upon principles of justice to regulate our society, and our ignorance about ourselves and our society guarantees that the principles both are fair and

do not depend on specific cultural or historical contingencies. The principles that would be agreed to under such conditions, Rawls argues, are ones
that would protect basic civil and political liberties, ensure fair equality
of opportunity, and limit the overall degree of inequality of wealth and
income (under what Rawls calls "the difference principle"). Rawls's argument is presented on the plane of what he calls "ideal theory," where the
point is to identify the most reasonable principles of justice in the abstract.
It is left to "nonideal theory" to determine how to pursue justice in a society that does not conform to these principles.

Scholars disagree about how useful Rawls's theory is for thinking about
racial justice. Some have argued that Rawls's inattention to nonideal
matters is a serious shortcoming of his theory. The most prominent advocate of this position has been Charles Mills, who argues that "the
abstractions of ideal theory are not innocent" but rather do much to di-
vert attention from the history of racism and racial injustice in American
society (2005, 181). More than this, Mills claims that the "ideal theory"
character of Rawls's work makes it largely irrelevant for thinking about
racial injustice, and perhaps even an obstacle to such thinking. Mills
asks how Rawls's theory can "serve to adjudicate the merits of competing
policies aimed at correcting for a long history of white supremacy," and he
answers, "Obviously, it cannot" (2009, 179–80). Ideal theory, by making
race invisible, is "likely to lend itself more readily to retrograde political
agendas" (2009, 180). Other scholars—such as Thomas McCarthy (2009,
39) and Elizabeth Anderson (2010, 3–7)—agree that Rawlsian theory is at
best unhelpful, and at worst an obstacle, for thinking about racial justice.

Others, most prominently Tommie Shelby (2004, 2005, 2013, 2016),
have defended a Rawlsian approach to racial justice. Two lines of thought
are prominent in this vein. First, some propose to modify the framework
of the original position to address historic injustice (see Boettcher 2009;
Carcieri 2010; Vaca 2013; Valls 2003). The way to do this would be to inform
the agents, at some point in their deliberations, of the past injustice and its
ongoing legacies in their society and ask them to formulate principles to
address this. The difficulty here is that it is unclear whether the choice situation in the original position allows for the backward-looking perspective

that reparations claims entail. As Simmons has noted, "Historical injustice goes unaddressed in Rawls's theory because the derived principles of justice are purely 'forward-looking,' because the choice problem given to Rawls's original contractors requires their choice of forward-looking principles" (2010, 33; see also Freeman 2002, 2007, 2008).

Another line of thought is to use Rawls's principle of fair equality of opportunity to pursue racial justice (see Kelly 2017; Matthew 2017; Shelby 2004). This principle requires that the institutions in society be arranged to ensure equal life chances, so that no one's prospects are harmed by the circumstances of one's birth. The difficulty is that it is a purely forward-looking principle. While fully satisfying the principle of fair equality of opportunity would reduce the racial gap in well-being, it would not be a reparations program. It cannot do the work of explicitly acknowledging the historical origins of present-day injustice. Charles Mills makes essentially this point in his critique of Tommie Shelby's attempt to use Rawls's principle of fair equality of opportunity to address racial injustice. Mills emphasizes that policies "must be carried out under the appropriate description" and that, even if Shelby is right about the effects of a fully realized regime of fair equality of opportunity in terms of its distributional effects, such an approach cannot do the reparative work that reparations are intended to do (2013, 13; see Shelby 2013).

The point here is not to condemn Rawlsian theory or the original position because it does not support reparations claims. Rather, the criticism that follows from these considerations is that the theory rules out backward-looking considerations of justice and therefore rules out reparations claims, by virtue of certain characteristics of the theory that require it to be forward looking. This does not mean, of course, that Rawlsian theory can be of no help whatsoever in thinking about racial justice. But the structure of the theory does seem to be an obstacle to applying it in any straightforward way to historic injustice in general or racial injustice in particular.

There is another way to think about reparations, one that avoids the problems of the Rawlsian and Nozickian approaches, and that has some virtues of its own.

REPARATIONS AND TRANSITIONAL JUSTICE

"Transitional justice" refers to an array of issues that are present in the aftermath of widespread, large-scale human rights abuses. Such abuses often take place during periods of war, including civil war, but they also occur under political regimes that systematically violate the rights of their citizens. The notion of transitional justice comes out of the experience of societies emerging from such conditions and confronting the issue of what justice requires in their wake. As a society attempts to make a transition from a regime that violates the basic rights of (some of) its members, what is to be done to address those wrongs and their legacies? A large body of empirical, legal, and normative scholarship now treats these issues, and if there is a consensus among scholars and activists, it is that doing nothing to explicitly confront the past is usually unjust, for at least two reasons. First, the abuses of the previous regime will often have important distributive consequences that, by virtue of their etiology, indicate that the resulting distribution of benefits and burdens in the society is unjust. Second, in addition to causing material injustice, the abuses often lead to nonmaterial harms, ones that involve psychological well-being, status, civic membership, and respect. The main argument for measures of transitional justice is that to leave the consequences of the past unaddressed is to (implicitly) condone the past, or at least to fail to repudiate it. Failure to confront the past is, in effect, to leave in place its unjust effects and hence suggests continuity rather than rupture, approval rather than disavowal, continuation rather than transition. Any attempt to create a more just society must involve an affirmation of the moral and civic equality of all members, a disavowal of the violations of the past, and an attempt to directly confront and ameliorate their effects (see Kritz 1995; Leebaw 2011; McAdams 1997; Minow 1998; Rotberg and Thompson 2000; Teitel 2000; Williams, Nagy, and Elster 2012).

While transitional justice is thus concerned with the past, it is forward looking as well. In the absence of explicit confrontation with and acknowledgment of the past, the legitimacy of the post-transitional political regime is called into question. If the prior, human rights-abusing regime was illegitimate, then the successor regime must, to the extent possible, distance itself from the prior one to achieve stability and political legitimacy. In addition to undermining political legitimacy, human rights-abusing regimes often undermine social trust, particularly when certain groups within society are affiliated with the regime and are beneficiaries of it, while other groups are its primary victims. Hence transitional justice not only concerns doing justice with regard to the past, but also addresses justice, legitimacy, and social trust in the future.

By now there is a fairly standard repertoire of transitional justice measures. First, in many transitions prosecution of the main perpetrators of the abuses has been essential to addressing citizens' sense of injustice and establishing the bona fides of the new regime as one that respects human rights and upholds the rule of law. Second, a just successor regime is often thought to require a change in personnel. Lustration, a method of ensuring that those complicit in the prior regime are excluded from positions of power in the new one, has been an important part of many transitions. Third, transitions usually involve institutional reform, including the writing of a new constitution, to help ensure that the abuses of the past will not be repeated and that citizens' rights will be respected. Fourth, a diverse set of practices have emerged as a way of establishing and acknowledging the record of abuses of the prior regime. The best known among these is truth commissions, but other measures under this heading include monuments and memorials, days of remembrance and national holidays, changes to national symbols, educational curricula, and official apologies. Finally, reparations have also been central to many cases of regime transition.

Each of these (sets of) transitional measures is complex within itself, and often there are necessarily trade-offs among them. The balance drawn among them is sometimes controversial, as when the South African Truth and Reconciliation Commission held out the possibility of amnesty for perpetrators of abuses under the apartheid regime in exchange for their testimony. This was seen as a trade-off between "truth" and (criminal) "justice" (Rotberg and Thompson 2000) and left many—particularly families of victims who wanted to see retributive justice done—deeply dissatisfied. Yet, regardless of the particular combination of transitional measures undertaken in a given case, there is broad agreement that some such measures are required for a just transition and a legitimate successor regime.

As Pablo de Greiff (2006b) emphasizes, the juridical conception of reparations (what I have called the tort model) does not capture how the term is understood in international law or in actual reparations programs that are enacted during political transitions. Rather, reparations in such circumstances must be understood as what de Greiff calls a "political project," with explicitly political goals. Reparations programs during political transitions are unlike compensation in a juridical context because the latter presumes that the harms that are to be compensated take place against the backdrop of generally norm-abiding behavior. If the abuses are systematic rather than an aberration, however, they exceed the capacity of any legal system to adjudicate. Reparations programs are policies and administrative procedures that, while they may not meet the standards of due process in a court trial, greatly reduce the "difficulties and costs associated with litigation" (2006b, 459). In addition, reparations programs during periods of transition have important forward-looking goals, which de Greiff characterizes as recognition of individuals as citizens, civic trust, and social solidarity. That is, among their other functions, reparations importantly contribute to the social and political preconditions of a stable and just democratic regime.

One other point that de Greiff makes is worth emphasizing. Reparations programs are usually deeply unsatisfying. The harms inflicted cannot be fully compensated even in principle, and their inadequacy is only exacerbated when the resources devoted to them are limited and involve serious trade-offs among legitimate goals. Victims are likely to feel that justice has not been done, even under the best of circumstances and even if all involved are well intentioned. The outcomes of reparations programs are not those that would likely be achieved through a series of successful individual lawsuits. Yet these shortcomings are not a reason to do without reparations entirely. It is a mistake, de Greiff argues, to make "the inference from premises regarding how difficult it is to establish fair and effective reparations programs to a conclusion claiming the impossibility of doing do" (2006b, 459). Despite the difficulties and inevitable shortcomings, the state nevertheless has a responsibility to attempt to design an adequate reparations program in cases of large-scale, systematic human rights abuses.

When one examines the discourse on reparations as it appears in the literature on transitional justice, then, one can see immediately how far removed it is from the debate on reparations that is framed by the tort model. Much of the philosophical literature on reparations is focused on intergenerational cases and preoccupied with issues of counterfactual reasoning and quandaries like the nonidentity problem. It also focuses on the issue of whether present-day individuals can legitimately claim reparations, and those skeptical of such claims often ground their arguments on standards of proof that would be appropriate for a civil lawsuit. These arguments entirely miss the large-scale nature of many human rights abuses and the political and administrative measures that are required to address cases of massive abuse.

To be sure, applying the transitional justice model of reparations to the case of African Americans involves extending the idea of reparations beyond the way that the notion is used in most transitional justice contexts. It asks the notion of reparations to do some of the work in arguing for policies that address deeply rooted, structural inequality. Some critics have worried that reparations talk is ill suited to do this work. They argue that those concerned about racial inequality should rely on straightforward (and forward-looking) egalitarian principles to pursue greater social and economic equality (Barkan 2007; de Greiff 2006a, 8; de Greiff 2006b, 470). Yet the reparations argument for pursuing racial equality should not be seen as a substitute for, but rather as a complement to, arguments for forward-looking egalitarian justice. I agree with those who argue that, where compensation and distributive justice conflict, there are strong grounds for preferring the latter (see Kutz 2004). But where the two perspectives converge—as in cases where victims of abuses are among the less well off—there is no conflict. In such cases, however, it remains important to keep the reparatory dimension in mind, since egalitarian arguments cannot perform the expressive function of reparations—that of acknowledging the specific harms that have been done and their relation to present-day disadvantage. In this kind of case, as Human Rights Watch (2001) has put it, given the availability of general norms of justice as grounds for a duty to address deep inequality, there is "a certain . . . redundancy" in making a reparations argument. But "there is something to be gained from speaking of this same duty as arising not only from [general principles] but also from the distinct obligation to remedy past racist practices. That is, we would provide another reason for doing the right thing."

In short, even if egalitarian and compensatory arguments converge to support the same set of policies to ameliorate racial inequality, it matters a great deal whether these policies are framed as an acknowledgment of the past. If they are, if reparative considerations are an important part of the justification and rationale for the policies, then they can be considered part of an overall reparations program. Here I make a point similar to the one that Robert Nozick (1974, 27) makes about what constitutes a redistributive policy. He suggests that, to count as redistributive, a policy not only should have redistributive effects, but should be undertaken to achieve redistribution. Hence what is crucial is the reason for the policy, not just its effect.

If transitional justice provides a way of thinking about "justice in time" (Meister 2011) that avoids the shortcomings of the Nozickian approach, it also provides a liberal basis for reparations that is largely missing in Rawlsian theory. The origins of the idea of transitional justice are precisely in places where the basic rights of citizens were systematically violated. The measures of transitional justice I have mentioned became the standard repertoire of means to affirm the dignity and humanity of all citizens, to disavow the wrongs of the past and the doctrines that rationalized them, and to attempt to establish a more liberal regime that abides by the rule of law. The origins of transitional justice in international human rights law point to its affinities with liberal theory. The norms of transitional justice provide a way of thinking about justice in the wake of massive and systematic abuses that has strong affinities with liberalism, and it can be seen as supplying some of the theoretical resources necessary for dealing with nonideal cases.

THE CIVIL RIGHTS ERA AS A REGIME TRANSITION

How can political transitions in places like South Africa serve as a model for racial justice in a consolidated democracy such as the United States? As I have argued elsewhere (Valls 2003), we should see the civil rights era as a political transition akin to more recent transitions from human rights-abusing regimes to regimes that aspire to respect citizens' rights. The civil rights era has many of the features that characterize such transitions. Before it, as a matter of both policy and social norms, basic rights and equal citizenship were denied to a large group, African Americans. During the civil rights movement, haltingly and imperfectly, state actors at all levels of government, as well as private individuals and institutions, became committed to ending this subordinate status and to respecting the rights of African Americans. The civil rights movement resulted in important court decisions, presidential orders, and acts of Congress—most prominently the Civil Rights Act of 1964 and the Voting Rights Act of 1965—as well as changes in the practices, policies, and norms of private individuals and institutions. The political regime, and much of the society as a whole, came to reject the racist policies of the past and affirmed the principle of equal citizenship.

This is the standard narrative about the civil rights era, and there is some truth in it. But there is another aspect of the civil rights movement that needs to be highlighted: the extent to which it was quite limited in what it accomplished, particularly when judged by the standards of transitional justice. Consider again the measures that I mentioned above that often accompany political transitions. On prosecution: few were prosecuted during the civil rights movement, even for the most brutal acts of resistance such as the murder of civil rights workers—let alone for the murders that took place routinely under Jim Crow. It is true that, in the decades that followed, some individuals were brought to justice for such acts committed during the civil rights movement, but these cases remained relatively rare.

With regard to lustration, what is remarkable about the civil rights movement is that there were few changes in personnel in positions of power. For example, officials in the education system, who enforced Jim Crow segregation in public schools, were usually left in place and relied on to carry out court orders to desegregate. This, of course, helps explain the slow and halting pace of desegregation.

There was also little institutional reform. The main reform was perhaps the creation of majority-minority legislative districts, which ensured black political representation. Yet, unlike the post–Civil War transition, which involved three amendments to the Constitution, no constitutional amendments resulted from the civil rights movement. Now it could be argued that none were necessary—all that was needed was that the post–Civil War amendments were given new life through changes in Supreme Court interpretation and new federal laws. And that may be so. But in hindsight it is striking that the range of debate on political and constitutional transformation was quite limited.

Finally, consider the other ways of confronting the past, namely the measures of acknowledgment (apologies, truth commissions, days of remembrance, memorials and museums, etc.) and material reparations. The former are the topic of the next chapter, so here I will be brief: few direct confrontations with the past occurred during the civil rights era, though many have been undertaken in subsequent decades. But with regard to material reparations, very little was done either during the civil rights era itself or since. Some policies begun during the civil rights era were indeed justified as compensatory measures, most prominently affirmative action and school desegregation. Yet school desegregation, at best, represents cessation of past practices of subordination; it does not compensate those who attended segregated schools in the past. And affirmative action (the subject of chapter 5) is far too limited, both in principle and as it has been practiced, to be sufficient compensation. It cannot bear the whole burden of rectifying the material inequalities accumulated along racial lines over centuries.

The civil rights era, then, closely matches the conditions that characterize a regime transition, yet by the standards of transitional justice the results of that era are inadequate. While the civil rights movement achieved the end of de jure segregation and subordination, it failed to achieve measures to directly confront the past and address its ongoing effects. Given the profundity of the inequality enforced by Jim Crow, the argument for reparations and other transitional measures would have been very strong during the civil rights era, but the failure to enact such measures has meant that American society continues to be shaped by its racial past.

So the "transitional" case for black reparations is straightforward: during a transition from a human rights-abusing regime to a human rights-respecting regime, there is a strong presumption in favor of compensating for the material and other harms done to victims of the former regime. The civil rights era was such a transition, so there was a strong presumption in favor of reparations to African Americans. Furthermore, as I have argued elsewhere (see Valls 2003), none of the considerations that might overcome that presumption are present in this case. There is little conflict between considerations of distributive justice and compensatory justice, since African Americans are overrepresented among the less well off. More generally, there was no obvious conflict between transitional measures such as reparations and more exclusively forward-looking concerns. There was also little tension between reparations and other transitional measures, such as acknowledgment or criminal prosecution, since these latter measures were not pursued at the time. Of course, the idea of black reparations was probably not politically viable, but this does not mean that they are not required by justice. Just as when dictators insist on immunity from prosecution in exchange for stepping down and allowing a transition to proceed, superior power or the ability to threaten violent resistance to transitional measures does not make the resulting political compromises just. As Rawls puts it, "To each according to his threat advantage is not a conception of justice" (1999, 116).

Looking at the civil rights era as a political transition to which norms of transitional justice apply suggests that the relevant wrongs that call for reparations are those of the Jim Crow era. By focusing on the Jim Crow era, I do not mean to suggest that slavery is irrelevant, or to imply that it should be forgotten. On the contrary, the way that slavery and events associated with it are remembered is critical to racial justice, as I will argue in the next chapter. However, I do agree with those who argue that, for purposes of material reparations, a far stronger case can be made if we focus on more recent history. Emphasizing Jim Crow places issues of racial inequality in a more helpful context: the wrongs that most clearly call for reparation today are ones that took place in living memory, in the middle decades of the twentieth century.

As Stephen Steinberg (1995, 109–13) points out, there was a lively debate during the civil rights era over the issue of compensating African Americans. The idea that the federal government should take positive measures to compensate African Americans for the material inequalities that resulted from past discrimination was defended by many, not the least of whom was President Lyndon Johnson himself. In his speech at Howard University in June 1965, Johnson famously said, "You do not take a person who, for years, has been hobbled by chains and liberate him, bring him up to a starting line of a race and then say, 'you are free to compete with all the others,' and still justly believe that you have been completely fair" (Johnson 1967, 126). Johnson's speech, and this passage in particular, has often been interpreted as an endorsement of affirmative action, but there is little warrant for this interpretation. Later in the speech Johnson briefly lays out a policy program grounded on his observation that African Americans continued to be disadvantaged in American society. The program included jobs (with no mention of preferential treatment in hiring; the emphasis is instead on creating jobs), housing, reformed welfare and social policies, and healthcare (1967, 130–31). Indeed, Johnson does not even state that any such policies would be explicitly race conscious; rather, the program he briefly describes is essentially his Great Society agenda, so one might fairly ask whether what Johnson endorses in the speech can reasonably be characterized as a program of black reparations at all.

I believe that it can, if we understand the notion of black reparations in a particular way. As I suggested above, a policy can be seen as part of a program of black reparations if at least part of its justification is to compensate African Americans for the disadvantages that they bear due to a history of discrimination. This can be so even if a policy is administered on a race-blind basis, and if some nonblacks benefit. Again, I take a position similar to that taken by Robert Nozick on the issue of what constitutes a policy of redistribution. Nozick states that "the term 'redistributive' applies to the types of *reasons* for an arrangement, rather than to an arrangement itself" (1974, 27). By the same token, a policy that has as one of its principal rationales compensating African Americans should count as (part of a program of) black reparations, even if it is also supported by other reasons and if nonblacks also benefit. I would also add the stipulation that to constitute reparations, a policy must actually achieve its intended effect, in order to rule out counting as reparations a policy that is enacted for the purpose of redressing the effects of past racial wrongs, but that fails to do so.

This may seem like an overly broad conception of reparations, precisely because it could include many policies that are race neutral and that benefit some whites. Yet I think that this conception of reparations resonates with the one implicit in much of the debate during the civil rights era. Many political actors, including Johnson, saw the need to go beyond the formal extension of rights to African Americans, to the provision of material resources that would compensate for previous discrimination. Yet for strategic political reasons, the compensatory intent, while acknowledged, had to be combined with other considerations, and the policies themselves, to be politically viable, had to be formally race neutral. On my conception of reparations, such policies may still be a part of a reparations program, as long as the compensatory element is one of the main justifications. After all, whether a policy benefits or harms a particular group is not necessarily related to whether it is explicitly group conscious. As Ira Katznelson details in his book *When Affirmative Action Was White* (2005), many formally race-blind policies under Jim Crow disadvantaged African Americans. It would be a mistake to think that policies intended to address the effects of such disadvantage must be explicitly race conscious, or must benefit only African Americans, to count as reparations.

[margin handwritten note: compensature for what's been taken unjustly]

The shift from focusing on explicitly race-conscious remedies to formally race-neutral ones that nevertheless retain their concern for racial inequality is exemplified in Martin Luther King Jr.'s book *Why We Can't Wait* (1963). In the final chapter of the book, King clearly endorses the idea of compensation to African Americans, invoking the Marshall Plan and the GI Bill as precedents. He calls for a "massive program [of] compensatory measures" (1963, 127). "Such measures would certainly be less expensive than any computation based on two centuries of unpaid wages and accumulated interest," King wrote, in an obvious reference to slavery (1963, 128). It is worth noting King's conception of compensation was very much in line with the understanding embodied in transitional justice discourse. He called for broad-based social policies to address racial inequality, not compensation to individuals on the tort model. Yet it is striking that King ends up calling for a "Bill of Rights for the Disadvantaged," which would include, he says, disadvantaged whites who have also been harmed by racial discrimination that lowered overall wages (1963, 128). This move was motivated, according to Taylor Branch, by King's desire that his proposal comport with Johnson's legislative program. "In the final book manuscript," Branch (1998, 211) tells us, "his 'Negro Bill of Rights' became a 'Bill of Rights for the Disadvantaged.' "

The idea of a program to attack accumulated racial inequality had broad support among both blacks and progressive whites during this period. The idea of a domestic Marshall Plan, aimed at black communities and modeled on the US policy to pour resources into the ravaged countries of Western Europe after World War II, was advanced by Whitney Young Jr., the executive director of the National Urban League—widely thought of as among the more conservative civil rights organizations (see Young 1963; Young 1965). This, in turn, was seconded by Tom Wicker of the *New York Times*, who, citing King's endorsement of the idea, and more specifically his plan to spend $10 billion a year for ten years on the effort, said that it was "Time to Pay the Piper" (Wicker 1966). Indeed, even the mainstream and decidedly moderate group of public figures who made up the Kerner Commission concluded in their report that a concerted national effort, including "unprecedented levels of funding," was needed to address the problems associated with black urban poverty. Although they did not use the language of reparations, they did make it clear that such policies were owed because, as they put it, "white society is deeply implicated in the ghetto. White institutions created it, white institutions maintain it, and white society condones it" (*Report of the National Advisory Commission* 1968, 2).

In the waning days of the civil rights movement, the issue of reparations was dramatically raised by James Forman when he interrupted the services at Riverside Baptist Church in New York on May 4, 1969, to demand $500 million from white churches and synagogues to support black institutions (see Forman 1969). Forman's "Black Manifesto" gave rise to a debate that turned out to be the last gasp for black reparations during the civil rights era (see America 1972; Bedau 1972; Bittker 1973; Boxill 1972; Browne 1972; Collins 1970; Main 1972; Marketti 1972). Since then, the issue has come to public attention only sporadically, such as when Randall Robinson published his book *The Debt* (2001) and, more recently, when Ta-Nehisi Coates (2014) published an article arguing for black reparations in *The Atlantic*. The point here is not merely historical. It is that the issue of reparations keeps coming up precisely because of the persistence of racial inequality. The deeply entrenched patterns that have their historical origins in slavery and Jim Crow are still with us. Justice requires measures to address the ongoing effects of past wrongs, and the very limited extent to which this has been done means that, even today, we are left with a profound case of unrectified historic injustice.

CONCLUSION

The upshot of this discussion is that justice requires a concerted effort to overcome racial inequality. The overrepresentation of African Americans among the less well off in American society reflects the persistence of an unjust past into the present. Public policy must therefore be directed at eliminating the racial gaps in wealth, income, educational attainment, employment, and other measures of well-being. In light of our history, these racial disparities will always serve as strong evidence of injustice. Some policies that address racial inequality can no doubt be color-blind, since policies that enhance opportunities for all, reduce overall inequality, and benefit the less well off will inevitably benefit many African Americans (as long as they are fairly administered). But other policies will have to take race into account, since it is unlikely that purely color-blind policies will be able to address, even indirectly, the specifically racialized character of inequality in the United States.

It is not my aim here to propose a specific set of policies to address racial inequality, but rather to establish the fundamental and prior point that some such set of policies are required by justice. I have argued that the issue of racial inequality is fruitfully viewed as a case of historic injustice calling for reparation, and more specifically reparation as understood in the discourse of transitional justice. As a political project, the point of reparations in a transitional context is to address both the material and the symbolic legacies of the wrongs of the past, and to do so through public policy rather than civil suits or individual cases. What matters most in the present context is that the prior regime created deep, structural inequality that continues to decisively shape individuals' life prospects.

While any reasonable theory of justice, from libertarian Right to liberal-egalitarian Left, converges on the conclusion that racial inequality in the United States today is a grave injustice that calls out for a remedy, the transitional case for addressing racial inequality captures the distinct meaning of racial inequality in the United States, and therefore the expressive and symbolic function that reparations perform. The language of reparations insists that racial inequality exists because of certain wrongs that have had lasting legacies, and not just because, say, some people lost out in a fair competition. It insists that while extreme poverty and lack of equality of opportunity violate purely forward-looking principles of liberal egalitarianism, in the case of African Americans they also result from the violation of even more basic principles that less egalitarian versions of liberalism endorse.

But if the United States has failed to enact a reparations program commensurate with the broad and deep character of racial inequality, it is nevertheless true that smaller acts of material compensation and other forms of moral repair are ongoing. As Lawrie Balfour (2008) has emphasized, we can think of reparations as being an accomplished "fact" or alternatively as an "act," a set of ongoing practices. Black reparations are clearly not an accomplished fact, but the act of engaging in moral repair related to our racial past is now a well-established feature of the political landscape. At the state and local level, and in civil society, there are many cases where particular aspects or episodes of the past are examined and acknowledged, and, in at least some cases, some form of material compensation results. Even where no material compensation comes out of these processes, they at least address part of the imperative of racial justice, acknowledging the past and conveying the appropriate symbolic expressions. It is to these efforts that I turn my attention in the following chapter.

3

Justice, Acknowledgment, and Collective Memory

In the previous chapter I argued that the material legacies of past injustices toward African Americans remain with us in the form of severe racial inequality that, as a matter of justice, must be addressed. Yet inequality of wealth, income, and opportunities are only one class of inequality, only one manifestation of the legacies of the past. These inequalities may be the most tangible and readily measured ones, but distributional issues do not exhaust the issues of justice raised by our racial past. As Iris Young (1990, chap. 1) has pointed out, too often liberal theories of justice have focused exclusively on distributional issues, or, when confronted with questions that do not fit the "distributive paradigm," they either attempt to redescribe nondistributional matters to fit the paradigm, or they define the issue as not being an issue of justice at all. I agree with Young that justice involves nondistributional questions, and in this chapter I focus on questions of collective memory, acknowledgment, and state speech as issues of justice. I argue that justice requires that the state acknowledge the harms of the past and reaffirm the equal status and equal moral worth of all citizens. It must reject the racist practices and norms and the symbolic and cultural expressions associated with them. It must attempt to create a collective memory that conveys the appropriate interpretations and evaluations. This applies to the federal government and state and local governments, as well as the major institutions of civil society that purport to uphold the fundamental values of a liberal society.

There is a diverse repertoire of practices that can convey rejection of the injustices of the past, contribute to appropriate memorialization, and affirm the equal citizenship of all. While these are matters of justice, it is not clear that justice requires a specific enactment or expression, or some particular combination of acts. Here I focus on some of the more obvious candidates: truth commissions, apologies, and the use of various kinds of memorials and symbols. All of these, I will argue, have been used to some extent with respect to the history of African Americans in the United States, and especially in connection with the Jim Crow era and the civil rights movement. As with reparations, while too little has been done at the federal level, there are a number of promising developments at the state and local level, and in civil society. There is now what we might call an established practice of acknowledgment, which often includes apology, other symbolic expressions, and memorialization. However, at the same time, there continues to be political conflict over the interpretation of the past, conflict that reflects a resistance to endorsing the civic equality of all, and indeed often reflects a nostalgia for the era of de jure racial hierarchy. Hence there are competing narratives, competing interpretations of the past and (therefore) of the present, and to some extent, this is as it should be. But to the extent that a significant portion of the population clings to the symbols of racial hierarchy, and certainly to the extent that the state seems to endorse their view, to that extent we still have far to go toward a racially just society.

LIBERALISM, ACKNOWLEDGMENT, AND MEMORY

While liberal theory has often had too little to say about the nonmaterial issues involved with acknowledgment and collective memory, it has had some things to say on these issues, and it has the resources to say quite a bit more. In claiming this, I contradict the view of some theorists who are generally pessimistic about liberal theory's capacity to encompass these matters. For example, as we saw in the previous chapter, Jeff Spinner-Halev thinks that liberal political theory is ill-equipped to deal with cases of historic or (to use his preferred term) enduring injustice. One reason for this, he argues, is that past injustice often creates mistrust on the part of a historically victimized group. Spinner-Halev states that "there is reason to be skeptical as to whether liberalism has the tools to fix these injustices" (2012, 79). He suggests, for example, that "acknowledgement and apology . . . lie outside of the usual liberal framework of justice, since they are not about rights or the redistribution of wealth" (2012, 87).

I have a more sanguine view of the resources of liberal theory to address the nonmaterial legacies of massive injustices. This is in part because I do not think that liberal theory is concerned only with the protection of rights and the distribution of wealth. I agree with Jacob Levy (2000, 230) when he writes that certain versions of liberalism have "some difficulty" with symbolic issues, but this has more to do with the traditional focus of liberal theory than liberalism's theoretical resources, as Levy's own discussion of symbolism and apologies makes clear.

In contemporary liberal theory, the importance of equal respect is exhibited in John Rawls's affirmation that "perhaps the most important primary good is that of self-respect" (Rawls 1999, 386). Although Rawls focuses on *self*-respect, he believes that the basic structure of society and the political regime have a great deal to do with whether individuals have self-respect and are accorded respect by others. While of course self-respect cannot be distributed (equally or otherwise) in a straightforward way, social and political institutions can publicly convey the equal status and worth of all citizens, and thereby provide what Rawls calls "the social basis of self-respect" (see generally Doppelt 2009; Eyal 2005; Thomas 1977–78).

Rawls, operating within ideal theory, focuses on the features of the basic structure of society, as regulated by his principles of justice, to provide the social basis of self-respect. Indeed, he thinks that his theory's capacity to underwrite this important good is a significant argument in its favor. But of course, in the context of a history of injustice, where that injustice was often justified by denying the equal status of members of a subordinated group, the generic equality of basic liberties is insufficient to provide the social basis of self- (and other-) respect. Justice requires that those whose equal status has been systematically denied should be reassured that the present political regime is committed to it. This is important not only for members of the oppressed group, but also for all members of society, especially those who harbor nostalgia for the prior order or who merely retain attitudes and beliefs associated with that order.

Tim Waligore (2016) has argued persuasively along these lines. Waligore suggests that, in the context of a history of denial of equal citizenship, particularized means of publicly conveying the equal status of all is required so that all citizens know, and are assured of, their equal status. It is not enough for the policies to change; what is needed is specific expressions of assurance by the state. In the absence of assurance, and, even worse, the presence of state symbolic expressions that send the opposite message, members of the historically oppressed group may reasonably believe that the political regime is not committed to their equal status.

Under nonideal conditions, then, affirming the equal status of all citizens requires affirmative expressions to counter the historically dominant narrative of unequal status and subordination. This, in turn, requires the past to be acknowledged and remembered, which points to the importance of collective memory. In recent years a number of philosophers and political theorists have explored the moral requirement to remember and the importance of memory in the wake of past injustice (see Blustein 2008; Booth 2006; Brendese 2014; Margalit 2002; Williams 1998). This theme is, not surprisingly, prominent in the transitional justice literature as well. Many arguments for acknowledging and incorporating into the collective memory of society the wrongs of the past focus on the loss of esteem or respect on the part of the victims, and the need to restore and reaffirm these. As Rejeev Bhargava puts it, "The demand that past injustices be forgotten does not address this loss of self-esteem. Indeed, it inflicts further damage. . . . Proper remembrance alone restores dignity and self-respect to the victim" (2000, 52–53). And of course this applies not only to individual victims, but also, in cases where individuals are victimized on the basis of their group membership, to members of the entire group—even those born after the end of the era of de jure subordination.

In a sense, the literature on transitional justice can be seen as working out the implications of liberal theory in the nonideal circumstances of past human rights abuses, and more recent work on liberal theory and past injustice is catching up to its insights. The two streams of thought converge on the conclusion that, in the context of a history of systematic injustice, symbolic expressions are often required to convey the message that all citizens are now to be treated as moral and civic equals. In the balance of this chapter, I examine a variety of ways in which this is being done, might be done, or is failing to be done in the case of African Americans in the United States. Each of the practices and expressions I examine below—truth commissions, apologies, memorials—can play a role in acknowledging the wrongs of the past and contributing to a public memory that rejects the norms of the prior era and thereby affirms the norms of moral and political equality. I argue that, while justice may not require a specific expression or action, some such expressions or actions are required by justice, and others prohibited. The specific cases taken up in this chapter represent some of the main options that are available in the US context for acknowledging the past and contributing to an appropriate collective memory—or, in some cases, actively resisting doing so by embracing symbols associated with historic injustice.

Much, though not all, of what I discuss in this chapter concerns "state speech," including expressions by the state via flags, monuments, memorials, and museums. As I have indicated, I will argue that justice requires certain kinds of state expression, and prohibits others, so it should be clear that I reject the notion that the state should be neutral on these matters, or should try to avoid endorsing certain values or norms. I agree with Corey Brettschneider (2012) that a liberal, democratic state may and should endorse the view that citizens are free and equal. It should promote this view, and should attempt to persuade all citizens to it, especially those who hold incompatible views. Some observers see a danger in the state performing this role. For example, Ruti Teitel (2000, chap. 3) worries that a state's attempt to establish an "official" truth about the past may have illiberal consequences. It may quash alternative interpretations or perspectives. Yet the state may, through memorialization, endorse a view of the past, and still leave plenty of room for differing interpretations. And even while it rejects views of that past that, say, glamorize those who defended racial hierarchy, it need not violate the rights of those who hold those views. The state can and should try to persuade citizens that such views are wrong without prohibiting them from being expressed.

TRUTH COMMISSIONS

One way to acknowledge the past and begin to construct appropriate collective memory is through a truth commission. Truth commissions, according to Priscilla Hayner (2002, 14), are officially sanctioned temporary institutions that focus on a pattern of abuses in the past and submit a report at the end of their investigation. Truth commissions usually are created as part of a regime transition to confront and expose the abuses of the prior regime. The main idea behind truth commissions, like other transitional measures, is that after a period of systematic abuses, merely ceasing the harms is not enough. Justice requires an explicit confrontation with the past, and truth commissions provide a process through which this can be done.

Advocates of truth commissions have identified many functions that they can serve (Minow 1998, 88; Crocker 1999), but some of the more important ones are to expose the truth about the abuses of the past; to officially acknowledge the harms done to the victims; to provide a forum in which victims can testify about their experiences; and to reconcile groups that were in an antagonistic relation with each other, as in a case where one is favored, the other disfavored, by the prior regime. They provide, in the words of Thomas Nagel, both knowledge and acknowledgment (Weschler 1990, 4). As reflected in the name of South Africa's well-known commission, they seek both truth and reconciliation.

While, according to Hayner's conception, truth commissions are creatures of regime transition and are officially sanctioned, there are other, similar institutions that can be thought of as quasi-truth commissions. For example, some commissions are unofficial but nevertheless seek to expose the crimes of the past, as in the cases of the commissions in Guatemala, Brazil, and Uruguay (Teitel 2000, 80; Hayner 2002, 21). Some commissions focus on the more distant past and are not a part of a regime transition, as in the case of Australia's investigation of its assimilationist practice of removing aboriginal children from their families and placing them with white families (Hayner 2002, 17–19). In the cases of these various truth commission-like institutions, the goals remain essentially the same: to expose and acknowledge the past; to promote reconciliation; and, as Michael Ignatieff puts it, "to reduce the number of lies that can be circulated unchallenged in public discourse" (quoted in Boraine 2000, 151).

The best-known truth commission, and the one that has received the most scholarly attention, is the South African Truth and Reconciliation Commission (TRC), which played an important role in that country's transition from the apartheid regime to a multiracial democracy. A number of features set the TRC apart from previous commissions. First, the TRC had a legislative mandate, giving it what Elizabeth Kiss has called "democratic legitimacy" (Kiss 2000, 84; see also du Toit 2000, 129; and Minow 2000, 252). While most previous commissions had been creations of the executive branch, the TRC was the result of a more democratic process, and therefore commanded greater moral authority. Second, the TRC process was very public. Its hearings were generally televised and broadcast on the radio, and a widely watched weekly television program showed highlights of its proceedings. This meant that the TRC process was an event experienced by the entire country, giving rise to many discussions about the issues it raised. It also meant that victims of apartheid who testified often reached a very wide audience; that victims who did not testify nevertheless saw their experiences reflected in those of others; that the perpetrators of human rights abuses who testified informed the entire nation about their actions; and that the horrors of apartheid were publicly exposed.

The arguments for truth commissions, and for the South African TRC in particular, are of two kinds. The first is pragmatic and consequentialist in character, resting on the effects that truth commissions are able to achieve, and the second is more principled, holding that truth commissions are required by justice (Allen 1999; Dyzenhaus 2000). The first kind of argument relies heavily on empirical observation about the effects of a commission, and in the case of the South African TRC, the evidence appears to be decidedly mixed. Many of the early assessments of its effects were positive, but as some commentators have pointed out these were often based upon anecdotal evidence and may have been influenced by wishful thinking (see Hamber 2001; Chapman and van der Merwe 2008, viii). Later, more systematic research emerged on the effects of testifying before the commission and on the broader societal impact of the TRC. Contrary to the hopes expressed by observers such as Martha Minow (1998, 2000) that giving and hearing testimony would be therapeutic, research has failed to find such positive effects (Kagee 2006; Stein et al. 2008). Yet studies also suggest that in society at large the TRC was successful in laying the foundations for future and ongoing reconciliation (Stein et al. 2008; Gibson 2004).

The justice-based argument for truth commissions is less vulnerable to the vicissitudes of empirical findings. It holds that truth commissions help to establish reasonable terms for reconciliation, which include acknowledgment of past wrongs and an assurance that the norms that permitted the wrongs to take place have been rejected. In this vein, Jonathan Allen writes: "Some of the claims concerning the tasks of truth commissions are better understood as moral claims than as empirical statements. . . . It is not that *no* reconciliation is possible without truth, but, rather, that morally justifiable reconciliation requires the disclosure of truth and some concern to see justice served" (Allen 1999, 317). Many scholars have emphasized the role of truth commissions in acknowledging the past (Kiss 2000; du Toit 2000) and have suggested that this acknowledgment is morally necessary in order to reaffirm the equality, dignity, and rights of the victims of the previous regime. If the abuses of the past are unacknowledged, then the new regime can reasonably be viewed as silently condoning them. As du Toit has argued, simply following a forward-looking approach, granting legal equality but ignoring the past and its present-day effects, would have been entirely inadequate from a moral point of view: "The TRC reflects a moral and political diagnosis that—at least in the case of victims and perpetrators of gross human rights violations—a general and formal restoration of citizenship alone would not be sufficient. Something more needed to be done: justice required a particularized procedure of public acknowledgement to restore human and civic dignity" (du Toit 2000, 134).

In the case of the United States, many observers have noted that public discourse on race suffers from a lack of the kind of knowledge and acknowledgment that truth commissions can help provide. Thomas McCarthy, for example, has argued that the United States has never had a public confrontation with its racist past, and this failure continues to distort public debate on racial issues. Even today, African Americans and whites have markedly different understandings of the past, with the former being well aware of its impact on the present, while the latter, by and large, have factually inaccurate beliefs about the past and present regarding issues of race. Building support for remedies to address the legacies of our racist past, McCarthy suggests, requires "a serious upgrading of public memory to provide the necessary background for public justification of a historical sort. From this perspective, then, there is a political need for historical enlightenment" (2002, 641).

Kevin Bruyneel (2013) has called into question this diagnosis. He characterizes accounts like McCarthy's as "liberal rationalism," which presumes that the main obstacle to policies that address racial inequality is a cognitive one—that people simply do not have sufficient knowledge of the relevant facts, and that if they did, all would be well. This ignores, Bruyneel contends, the investment that white Americans have in their identity, and the way that this identity is tied to a particular historical narrative that requires the downplaying of past racism and its present-day effects. Bruyneel is no doubt correct that the problem is not only cognitive but also affective. But it remains the case that having a factually correct understanding of the past and its links to the present is a necessary, if not sufficient, condition for pursuing racial justice.

In addition to the need for more information and knowledge, however, there is the need for a public mechanism of acknowledgment. That is, public consciousness must be informed not merely by knowledge about the past and present, but by an acceptance of the responsibilities that this knowledge should create. Acknowledgment is required to affirm the dignity of victims of injustice, and to create the preconditions for effective policies to overcome those injustices. Since there has been too little public acknowledgment of the past, and only halfhearted (at best) commitment to undo its legacies, African Americans can reasonably conclude that the conditions for a just reconciliation have not been created. At the same time, whites may wrongly feel entitled to their privileged position.

A truth commission could help address these problems. Ideally, like the South African TRC, it would have a legislative mandate and would educate the public about the brutality of our racial past—and the way in which that past continues to shape our society. It would thereby, one would hope, "reduce the number of lies that can be circulated unchallenged in public discourse," or, to put it less tendentiously, it would provide some historical context for discussions that so badly need it.

Some commission-like institutions have already contributed to the needed examination of the past, and the creation of such institutions is now a well-established practice. Sanford Levinson (2000) has suggested that the hearings of the Civil Rights Commission and of administrative agencies and congressional committees may be thought of as playing roles akin to truth commissions. The Kerner Commission report, issued in 1968 in response to the urban riots of the previous years, can be seen as a quasi-truth commission, though the process that produced it was not as public as a truth commission would normally be, and it had only executive, not legislative, mandate.

The clearest case of an attempt to focus on race at the national level in the post-civil rights era is President Clinton's Initiative on Race. This involved fourteen hundred conversations across the country, in which about eighteen thousand people participated. However, the initiative's impact was limited by a number of factors. First, it was not really an independent commission, but rather an advisory board; real control of the initiative remained with the White House staff. Second, the initiative was a creature of the executive branch rather than the legislature, limiting its claim to moral authority. Third, the initiative framed its discussion in terms of multiculturalism and the claims of not only African Americans but also Hispanics, Asians, and other immigrant groups; it therefore failed to focus on the legacies of slavery and Jim Crow. Fourth, media attention was limited and often focused on the issue of whether the advisory board included a member who opposed affirmative action. Finally, the release of the board's report was overshadowed by the scandal involving President Clinton's affair with Monica Lewinsky. On the whole, then, the initiative has been viewed as either empty symbolism or a missed opportunity, but in any case it clearly failed to perform the important functions of a truth commission (see *One America in the 21st Century* 1998; Loury 1997; Goering 2001; Kim 2000, 2002).

Yet as Kiss (2000, 92–93) has suggested, the greatest prospects for truth commission-like efforts to acknowledge the racial wrongs of the past may be at the local, rather than the national, level. One such case is Oklahoma's investigation of the Tulsa Race Riot of 1921. The riot, which has been well explored by historians (see Ellsworth 1992; Madigan 2001; Hirsch 2002; Brophy 2002), involved an attack by whites on Greenwood, a thriving black neighborhood. The attack resulted in the destruction of a thirty-five-block area, leaving over a thousand residences destroyed and over ten thousand African Americans homeless. It also left a number (the exact figure is disputed) of African Americans dead and hundreds injured. Local police failed to protect the black population from the onslaught and were complicit in other ways. In 1997 the state legislature established a commission to investigate the riot, and in 2001 the commission issued a report that, among other things, recommended reparations to survivors and their descendants. The state legislature rejected these recommendations and instead established a corporation to provide scholarships to descendants. In one sense, then, Oklahoma's actions are an important acknowledgment of state complicity in a particularly ugly chapter of racial violence. But despite this, the absence of an explicit apology or appropriate reparations makes this a case of only partial acknowledgment and partial acceptance of the responsibilities that should flow from a full reckoning with the past.

A more successful case of acknowledging the past is Florida's confrontation with a similar riot, the Rosewood Massacre of 1923. Rosewood was a town of nearly two hundred black residents that was destroyed in a week of violence perpetrated by a white mob that grew as the days passed. Many African Americans were killed and the rest were driven out of town, never to return. Every black residence was burned, and local whites appropriated the property. Local law enforcement did little to protect the victims, and, as in Tulsa, no one was ever prosecuted. After the massacre was brought to light by journalists and began to receive media attention, the Speaker of the Florida House created a committee of historians to investigate in 1993. In response to the committee's report, the Florida legislature passed the Rosewood Claims Bill. The act provided for compensation to the few remaining survivors of the massacre, and additional funds to compensate the families of victims for the loss of their property. It also created a scholarship fund for descendants and for "minorities in general." Florida's actions constituted an important form of acknowledgment. "Because of the passage of this bill," said one descendent of a victim of the massacre, "when I hear something like 'America the Beautiful' or 'God Bless America,' it has a different meaning. . . . It has a real meaning now" (quoted in Finan 1995, 30; see generally Barkan 2000, 296–99; Bassett 1994; Dye 1996, 1997; D'Orso 1996; Rosewood Forum 1994).

Unofficial truth commissions can play a similar role, even without any governmental sanction. Consider the commission that examined the Greensboro Massacre of 1979. This case involved the attack by members of the Nazi Party and the Ku Klux Klan on a racially mixed group of demonstrators, killing five and wounding ten others. As in the other cases just discussed, lack of police protection played an important role in the massacre, and indeed there is evidence of actual coordination between the police and the attackers. Two criminal trials resulted, one state, one federal, but in both cases all-white juries acquitted the accused. A civil trial in 1985, however, found the City of Greensboro, the Klan, and the Nazi defendants jointly liable, and the city paid $400,000 in settlement. In 2000 two civic organizations approached the International Center for Transitional Justice, which advises transitional regimes around the world, and asked for assistance in a truth and reconciliation project. The ensuing process took place without any governmental involvement—indeed, the city council voted along racial lines to oppose the commission. Still, a commission committee was selected, and hearings were held that gave survivors, as well as a few police officers and Klansmen, an opportunity to testify. The resulting report documents the events and the city's complicity in them. One survivor of the attack who testified at the hearings concludes her reflections on the process by stating that the report "made a significant impact on Greensboro" and that the process undertaken there "can serve as a model for other similar projects in the country" (Bermanzohn 2007, 109; see generally McIvor 2016; Magarrell and Wesley 2008).

However imperfect each of these undertakings may have been, they suggest that there is now an established practice of examining and acknowledging the race-related wrongs of the past. While there has not been anything like a comprehensive truth commission at the federal level, these local efforts may play an important role in bringing to light, and raising public awareness of, our racial past. Similar initiatives have also been undertaken by institutions in civil society. For example, a number of universities have undertaken a public process of examining their ties to slavery and have considered what action is appropriate in light of what they find (Schuessler 2017). Still, one should not be too sanguine. These local and institutional efforts are relatively few and far between. Furthermore, when they focus on individual events, they may convey the false impression that the incidents they examine are aberrations or isolated occurrences. And it remains that case that, overall, there is too little official acknowledgment of the past, and that public discourse on race-related issues continues to suffer as a result.

APOLOGIES

Apologies are another way in which wrongs of the past can be acknowledged and their legacies addressed. In the context of interpersonal relations, an apology serves several functions: it acknowledges that certain events took place; the apologizer accepts responsibility for his or her actions and expresses regret about them (Kort 1975; Gill 2000; Davis

2002; Smith 2008). In the process, the apologizer affirms the validity of the norm that was violated, acknowledges the dignity and respect due the victim, and makes a commitment not to repeat the wrong in the future (Govier and Verwoerd 2002). In cases of a serious wrong, the very continuation of the relationship may depend on the acknowledgment performed though an apology. That is, in the absence of an apology following a serious wrong, it might be unreasonable for the person who committed it to expect the other party to continue in the relationship. In this case, the wronged party has no assurance that the perpetrator rejects the act in question and affirms the norm it violated. In that absence, the victim has no assurance that such acts will not be repeated in the future.

This familiar practice in interpersonal contexts has become a prominent feature of public life. Many official apologies have been offered by governments, heads of state, corporations, religious bodies, and civic organizations for wrongs that the organizations have committed in the past—sometimes the distant past. To mention just a few examples: Germany and Japan have apologized for many of their actions during World War II, such as the Holocaust, the attack on Pearl Harbor, and the treatment of Korean "comfort women"; the Catholic Church has apologized for many of its past misdeeds, such as the Crusades and the Counter-Reformation; and Canada, New Zealand, and Australia have apologized for their treatment of indigenous peoples. In the American context, the US government has apologized for its internment of Japanese Americans during World War II and to Native Hawaiians for the takeover of Hawaii in 1893. President Clinton apologized for inaction during the Rwandan genocide (Nobles 2008). The proliferation of public and official apologies has led observers to declare that we live in "The Age of Apology" (see Brooks 1999; Gibney et al. 2008).

Yet some have questioned whether extending the practice of apologizing from the interpersonal context to larger-scale collective, institutional, or state apologies makes any sense at all (see, for example, Smith 2008). Janna Thompson has suggested that such apologies are problematic because the individuals who do the apologizing may owe their very existence to the wrongs for which they would apologize. Can they sincerely regret events and actions in the absence of which they would not exist (Thompson 2000; see also Levy 2002)? Another objection is that such apologies involve certain individuals apologizing for the actions of others. There seems to be something odd about this. In the interpersonal context, one can express regret about the actions of others or events in which one has played no role, but one cannot really apologize for them. An apology is appropriate only when one apologizes for actions one has actually performed (or failed to perform). How can one apologize for the actions of prior generations? It was on these grounds that Prime Minister Howard of Australia (in)famously refused to apologize to aboriginals for their treatment at the hands of previous Australian governments (Zutlevics 2002).

Following others, I would argue that both of these objections rest on an overly individualist interpretation of what is going on in state and institutional apologies (see Cohen 2017; Harvey 1995; Cunningham 1999; Joyce 1999; Weyeneth 2001; Winter 2015). In such cases individuals apologize, not qua individuals, but as representatives of the corporate bodies or institutions that they represent. There are many other ways in which such corporate or collective bodies are thought of as persisting through time, even after all of the individuals who comprise them at one point have been replaced with others. Hence legal contracts between corporations survive changes in personnel; international treaties remain binding after a change in government; and indeed constitutional and legal provisions remain in force in the absence of positive action to change them (Zutlevics 2002). "If states make treaties and accept obligations of reparation, then they should also be able to make genuine apologies" (Thompson 2008, 38). It is true that, in moving from the interpersonal to the collective context, certain features of apologies either drop out or are significantly altered. For example, the feelings, beliefs, and attitudes of the apologizer are of great importance in the interpersonal context. These, however, are less important in institutional apologies; here, the subjective states of the apologizer matter much less, if at all, because they are not apologizing as individuals but as representatives of organizations and institutions.

Spinner-Halev (2012, chap. 4) sees a number of problems with official apologies, but his main argument is that apologies are supposed to be transformative, to create a new reality, yet they often fail to perform the work that their most ardent defenders claim for them. Spinner-Halev suggests that greater emphasis should be placed on acknowledgment than apology. Apology takes place at a moment in time, he suggests, whereas acknowledgment requires an ongoing process. Yet while it is true that an apology alone will often be insufficient as an acknowledgment of the past, an apology is one important way to acknowledge and, in combination with other measures, apologies can contribute significantly to moral repair.

One goal of apologies is to make people feel better, and thereby facilitate reconciliation between the offender and the offended parties. But do institutional apologies achieve this goal, or are they merely "'political correctness' at its silliest" (Weyeneth 2001, 29)? Some evidence suggests that apologies do in fact make a positive difference and contribute to reconciliation. The fact that victim groups often demand an apology reflects its importance to them (Harvey 1995). Sometimes victims see compensation alone as an insufficient response to past wrongs when they are not accompanied by an apology (Weyeneth 2001, 31–32). Perhaps the strongest evidence that we have on this issue comes from James Gibson's study of the South African Truth and Reconciliation Commission. Gibson found that South Africans were much more likely to perceive amnesty for apartheid officials to be fair if the perpetrator apologized for his actions (2004, 277). While the available evidence remains incomplete, there is certainly some support for the notion that apologies can make a positive difference (Blatz, Schumann, and Ross 2009).

Yet the argument for apologies does not depend entirely on empirical evidence. Like other transitional measures, apologies can be justified in terms of their role in creating reasonable terms of reconciliation. And indeed apologies have been prominent in regime transitions and other cases where serious human rights violations have occurred (Cunningham 1999; Nobles 2008, appendix). These apologies can perform many of the same functions in large-scale contexts that they perform at the interpersonal level: where serious and widespread human rights violations have occurred, the humanity, dignity, and equality of the victims and victim-groups may be in need of reaffirmation (Gibney and Roxstrom 2001). At the same time, human rights norms and the victims' membership in the community are also reaffirmed (De Greiff 2008). Such a reaffirmation may be necessary for victims and victim-groups to reasonably believe that a transition has taken place, and that the new regime rejects the practices of the prior one. Hence an apology, as with other transitional mechanisms of acknowledgment, both helps to constitute the regime transition and provides evidence of it. This argument for apologies does not rest on their immediate consequences but on their intrinsic features. As an expressive act, apologies help to create the conditions under which reconciliation is reasonable, and in their absence members of oppressed groups may doubt the commitment of the political regime to their equal status, which in turn may undermine its political legitimacy.

What does all of this imply for racial justice in the United States? It certainly suggests that apologies are one way for the society to acknowledge the history of slavery and racial oppression. And indeed there have been some such apologies. In particular, President Clinton has apologized for the Tuskegee syphilis experiments conducted by the US government, in which black men, infected with syphilis, were permitted to go untreated (Harter, Stephens, and Japp 2000). The US Senate has apologized for its failure to pass antilynching legislation during Jim Crow (Poe 2007). And the House of Representatives has apologized for slavery (Fears 2008). While significant, both individually and cumulatively, none of these actions satisfy the "gold standard" of an apology, which would involve both houses of Congress passing, and the president signing, an official apology acknowledging the history of racial injustice in the country.

The model to which proponents of an apology to African Americans often point is the Civil Liberties Act of 1988. This act followed the creation of a commission by Congress to review the facts surrounding the internment of Japanese Americans on the West Coast of the United States during World War II, and to recommend remedies. The act offered an apology to the internees and provided compensation of twenty thousand dollars to the victims who were still alive at the time of the passage of the act (Brooks 1999, part 4). This act has a number of virtues, but the most relevant one in the present context is that it included an apology in a law that was passed by both houses of Congress and signed by the president. Hence it is not merely an utterance by a head of state or another official, but carries "the full weight" of a government apology that results from a deliberative process (Nobles 2008, 5). Since 1989 Congressman John Conyers has proposed the establishment of a commission, modeled on the one that led to the 1988 act, to look into the history of injustices toward African Americans. It would propose appropriate remedies, potentially including both an apology and reparations. It has never made it out of committee.

While many advocates of an apology (and reparations) for slavery and Jim Crow have been disappointed by the failure of the Conyers bill to pass, it is a mistake to focus exclusively on an apology by the US government as a measure of progress on this issue. Rather, as with truth commissions, many important developments have been taking place below the level of the federal government, in state and local governments and in civil society (Glynn 1997, 35). At least six state legislatures have apologized for their support of slavery (Cave and Sexton 2008). Florida (Fortin 2017) and Georgia (Blinder and Fausset 2017) have apologized for specific race-related miscarriages of justice that took place decades ago, and the president of an association of police chiefs has apologized, more generally, for the mistreatment of minorities at the hands of police that has fueled mistrust between the two (Williams 2016). Beyond the governmental realm, many organizations have issued apologies for their past support of, or complicity in, slavery and Jim Crow. Some of these organizations have been religious, such as the Southern Baptist Convention (Glynn 1997). Others have been professional organizations; for example, the American Medical Association has apologized for its long support for discrimination against black physicians and patients (Washington 2008). Many businesses, such as banks and insurance companies, have also apologized.

So what we have is a well-established and ongoing practice of looking to the past and apologizing for racial wrongs. As many commentators have noted, while apologies are backward looking in that they address events in the past, they are also forward looking in that they attempt to establish a more legitimate and just future (Joyce 1999, 171; Gibney and Roxstrom

2001, 916; Nobles 2008, 2). As Danielle Celermajer puts it, "The apology is, in its first movement, an acknowledgement of a collective failure to live up to an ideal ethical principle and, in its second, a public, performative declaration of a new commitment, a new covenant for *now* and into the future" (2009, 247). The practice of apologizing on behalf of governments and other institutions for their complicity in racial injustice can play an important role in creating a more racially just society. Ideally, the federal government would undertake something like what Congressman Conyers has proposed, a truth commission-like process that would result in policy prescriptions to address racial inequality and an official federal apology. But in the absence of that, the proliferation of these practices at the state and local level, and in civil society, is a promising reflection of a society attempting to grapple with its racial past.

CIVIL RIGHTS MEMORIALS AND MUSEUMS

Truth commissions and apologies are limited in time. Truth commissions are, by definition, temporary institutions, and apologies, while often the result of a lengthy process, are issued at one point in time. I have argued that both, either separately or together, can do a great deal to reject the practices of the past, reaffirm the dignity and equality of victims and victim groups, and contribute to collective memory, but their temporary nature entails certain built-in limitations in their ability to do so. Societies have other, ongoing, ways to acknowledge the past, including monuments, memorials, and museums. These have long been means by which collective memory is created and with it (sometimes) a shared national identity (Johnson 1995).

In a regime transition, or in a postconflict context, memorials and museums can play an important role in publicly establishing a historical record. They can also provide a means by which to honor victims and create heroes. At the same time, memorials and museums implicitly (and sometimes explicitly) endorse some values and norms and condemn others. In honoring the victims of the past they condemn the victimizers, the political regime that permitted the abuses to occur, and the ideas that justified them. Hence memorials and museums can play a particularly important and public role in symbolically rejecting the wrongs of the past and affirming the equal dignity of all (Barsalou and Baxter 2007; Megret 2010).

In this context one of the noteworthy developments of the latter part of the twentieth century and early decades of the twenty-first is the growth of civil rights memorials and museums. The emergence of monuments, memorials, and museums dedicated to the civil rights movement marks "a watershed event in the representation of American history in public space" (Dwyer 2002, 32). In the past, according to Dwyer and Alderman (2008, 46), African Americans were largely ignored in most American memorials, and "when they were present, they were included in order to testify to the superiority of whites. Civil rights memorials dismantle this legacy, at once calling shame upon it and contradicting its claims. In a sense, these memorials are an extension of the Movement itself." In the way that these memorials and museums portray the civil rights movement, and the practices of Jim Crow that it protested, an unmistakable message is sent: civil rights activists are valorized as heroes, fighting a righteous cause, and the defenders of segregation are cast as villains. While this is not entirely unproblematic, as I note below, at a basic level the message affirms the equal citizenship and dignity of all. To that extent, the memorials play an important role in officially and publicly repudiating the racism of the past and endorsing the values of a liberal democratic society.

Civil rights memorials and museums vary a great deal in form, content, and focus. The Civil Rights Memorial in Montgomery, Alabama, designed by Maya Lin (who also designed the Vietnam War Memorial in Washington, DC) presents a cone-shaped black marble table, inscribed with some of the important names and dates of the civil rights movement, including the killing of many activists. The Martin Luther King, Jr. National Historic Site consists of some thirty-five acres along Auburn Avenue in Atlanta, Georgia, including King's birth home, the King Center, and a visitor's center that includes a museum depicting the civil rights movement and King's role in it. Kelly Ingram Park in Birmingham, Alabama, was the site of the famous confrontations between "Bull" Conner and young civil rights protesters in 1963. The park now features a number of statues, including ones portraying German Shepherd dogs with their teeth bared, reflecting the use of such police dogs against the protesters. The National Civil Rights Museum in Memphis, Tennessee, was created out of the Lorraine Hotel, where Martin Luther King Jr. was assassinated. The Martin Luther King, Jr. Memorial is located on the National Mall in Washington, DC, and includes a thirty-foot high statue of King. These are just a few of the more prominent examples of the memorialization of the civil rights movement. Others are less well known and include hundreds of streets, schools, and buildings named after Martin Luther King Jr. and other leaders of the movement.

Many of these sites have been subjected to a great deal of scrutiny both by scholars from diverse disciplinary backgrounds and by the popular press. While generally seen as a positive development in constructing a collective memory that acknowledges and records important events of the movement, a number of lines of criticism are also prominent. First, the narrative of the movement presented by them is often quite selective and limited. Most memorials focus on the period between the Supreme Court's *Brown v. Board of Education* decision in 1954 and the assassination of King in 1968 (Raiford and Romano 2006, xiv). Remarking on this aspect of Maya Lin's memorial, one observer charges that this "lifts this period out of the long-term context of African American struggle" (Upton 1999, 25). Second, the focus is often on the best-known, mainstream leaders of the movement, and particularly on King himself, to the neglect of grassroots activists, women, and more radical elements of the civil rights movement such as black nationalists. In the process, the memorials often portray the movement as being more unified than it was, as if all activists shared a single goal or set of goals. Third, the movement is usually portrayed as victorious, its limited goals met, and inevitably so (Dwyer and Alderman 2008, chap 1; Wilson 2001). The narrative, then, is a triumphalist one: Jim Crow defeated, racial equality achieved.

There is, of course, some truth in this narrative, but its limits are also obvious and its implications potentially troubling. One implication concerns our understanding of the past. The past that is presented, critics charge, is a sanitized one (Wilson 2001). The goals of the movement are presented as quite limited, and as such they "jettison the more encompassing visions" of the movement and "endorse the definition of the civil rights movement as a simple campaign for legal rights" (Upton 1999, 32). Some of the more radical views held by Martin Luther King Jr., such as in his shift to economic justice in his last years, are usually downplayed or ignored entirely (Bruyneel 2014; Inwood 2009; Raiford and Romano 2006, xviii; Upton 1999).

The other main implication of this dominant narrative concerns our understanding of the present. If the problem was de jure segregation and deprivation of basic legal rights, then the Supreme Court cases, executive orders, and acts of Congress that marked some of the movement's most important achievements solved the problem. Any discussion of contemporary racial problems is usually "conspicuously absent" (Dwyer 2006, 16–17). The movement is a "won cause" (Dwyer and Alderman 2008; Eskew 2001). No further activism is necessary, since racial justice has been achieved. These are the implications that can be drawn from some civil rights memorials, at least according to their critics.

There are also sometimes troubling aspects to the siting of the memorials. They tend to be away from the center of the city, away from "the traditional places of civic memory—City Hall, the courthouse lawn, and Main Street" (Dwyer and Alderman 2008, 80; Dwyer 2002). Instead, civil rights memorials are often situated in or adjacent to predominantly African American neighborhoods or business districts. In some cases, like the "Sweet Auburn" area of Atlanta and the area around the National Civil Rights Museum in Memphis, these were thriving black neighborhoods during the Jim Crow era, and their diminished state vividly demonstrates some of the costs of integration and the objectives that the civil rights movement did not achieve (Upton 1999). The siting of civil rights memorials, then, often undercuts their triumphalist narrative both due to their displacement away from the center of public space and their setting in depressed African American areas of the city.

Some of the features of civil rights memorials are explicable in terms of the political and financial support on which they depend. Many of them are supported by civic leaders who wish to burnish the reputation of their cities in order to combat the negative images that came to be associated with them during the civil rights movement. Often the memorials depend on corporate sponsorship (Shaw 2009). Civil rights memorials are also part of a large and growing industry of "multicultural heritage tourism" (Dwyer 2004, 419). They must therefore be concerned about attracting tourists, and an uplifting message is helpful in this (Dwyer 2006).

Other forms of memorialization partake of many of the same features as the memorials discussed so far. Martin Luther King Jr. Day, a federal holiday since 1986, is an important recognition of the importance of all that King has come to represent, and the holiday is sometimes used as an occasion to reflect on ongoing racial issues, especially in educational institutions. But the version of King that is celebrated is too often the sanitized, safe version portrayed by other memorials. And in focusing on King himself, the holiday always runs the risk of distracting attention from other participants in the movement and the divergent visions and goals that they had.

Perhaps the most common form of memorialization is place names, and here again the most common name that has come to be attached to schools and streets is that of King. Street names have the advantage of being a part of the landscape that is experienced by many people who are not seeking out memorials. They are encountered by thousands each day. Yet many of the streets named after King in cities and towns across the country are in predominantly black areas. Naming a street after King often faces stiff opposition from whites, who see King as "belonging" to African Americans rather than to all Americans, and who fear depressed property values and diminished business from an address bearing his name. Yet to many African Americans, having a street named after King remains of great symbolic importance. "Black activists envision being able to engage in commemoration as part of the democratization of society. . . . [Naming a street after King] is conceptualized by some blacks as an antiracist practice, a way of inscribing a new vision of race relations into the American landscape" (Alderman 2006b, 218, 222; see also Alderman 2006a, 2008).

Despite their limitations, ironies, and ambiguities, civil rights memorials both reflect and help to constitute the important changes in the American racial regime over the last half century. They affirm the dignity and equality of African Americans, and they repudiate and disavow the practices of the past. They are necessarily partial, but they nevertheless encourage further reflection and dialogue on issues of race in American society. And the activism that has brought the memorials into being can be seen as part of an ongoing effort to direct attention to issues of race. In this way, "The struggles over the memory of the civil rights movement are not a diversion from the real political work of fighting for racial equality and equal rights in the United States; they are key sites of that struggle" (Raiford and Romano 2006, xxi).

CONFEDERATE MONUMENTS AND STATUES

Civil rights memorials coexist and compete with another, generally older and more ubiquitous set of memorials, especially in the South. Immediately after the Civil War, both the North and the South quickly began erecting memorials to their soldiers. In the South the earliest memorials tended to be simple obelisks, usually erected in cemeteries. After the end of Reconstruction, however, more monuments began to be erected in town centers and often featured a "common soldier" standing high atop a pedestal. The early part of the Jim Crow era was the most active period of monument construction in the South, when hundreds of memorials were erected to honor Confederate soldiers. Many of these retain their prominent position in towns large and small across the South today. In addition, there are statues of particular individuals, such as those of Confederate generals on Monument Avenue in Richmond, Virginia (see generally Piehler 1995, chap. 2; Foster 1987; Savage 1997; Widener 1982; Mills and Simpson 2003; Levinson 1998).

Interpreting the meaning and message of these monuments is fraught; they present, as Levinson puts it, "wrenching semiotic issues" (1995, 1107). At one level, many of them are simply memorials to fallen soldiers and therefore arguably unobjectionable (see Schedler 2001). Savage suggests that one of the points of the monuments was to "smash" the equation of the South with slavery, so that the monument could be focused not on the issues underlying the Civil War, but on military valor (1997, 129–30). Yet Savage also emphasizes that "the common soldier is . . . always white and Anglo-Saxon in physiognomy [which] suggests that the memorials offer up not a neutral individual body but a collective body conceived with certain [racial] boundaries and allegiances" (1994, 131; see also Savage 1997, 186–88). In the case of the statue of Robert E. Lee on Monument Avenue in Richmond, which portrays Lee sitting high on his horse, Savage argues that the stature rests on a "disguised racism" that makes claims "for the prerogatives of Southern white manhood [that are] not lost on many people" (1994, 133–34). This kind of statue can easily be interpreted as "celebrat[ing] not just the veteran but also his cause. It signifie[s] the South's conviction that it had acted rightly" (Foster 1987, 131). Poole argues that the monuments are "provocative statements of Confederate nationalism . . . [that are] an image of defiance" (2005, 127). They reflect the idea that "the struggle for the South's peculiar institution would carry on, albeit in a largely symbolic warfare" (Poole 2005, 129). Furthermore, it is a mistake to attempt to glean the significance of Confederate memorials individually, for as Savage emphasizes, their effect is cumulative (1997, 209). The fact is that the southern landscape is filled with monuments to those who defended the old order of slavery and white supremacy. The Southern Poverty Law Center (2016) finds that there are over fifteen hundred of them on the American landscape, mostly (though not exclusively) in the South.

While memorials to Confederate soldiers are problematic, simply removing them is not necessarily the solution. In this respect, there are parallels to the cases of Soviet-era statues, many of which were torn down with the fall of the communist regimes in the Soviet Union and its satellites (Levinson 1995, 1998). As Levinson shows, even some dissidents under the prior regime were ambivalent about tearing down its monuments. He quotes one such dissident as lamenting that "Bolsheviks topple czar monuments, Stalin erases old Bolsheviks, Khrushchev tears down Stalin,

Brezhnev tears down Khrushchev, and now this" (1998, 14). This quotation reflects a discomfort with what might be considered "victor's justice," where supporters of a new regime can "erase" the prior one without regard to the historical value, ambiguity, or complexity of such symbols.

What, then, ought to be done with Confederate monuments? Some have been moved to less prominent positions or removed entirely. In other cases, the explanatory materials on plaques or on the base of the monument has been changed to place the monument in context and to resist valorizing the southern cause in the Civil War. In still other cases, the approach has been to add additional monuments to the site. One example of this is the addition of a statue of Arthur Ashe, the African American tennis player, to Monument Avenue in Richmond, the city of his birth—thus undermining the exclusively Confederate (and white) character of that site (Leib 2006). Levinson (1995, 1998) surveys the various options, but comes to no firm or general conclusion, and I agree that no single approach is necessarily the correct one. Each case raises questions of interpretation and meaning, but also questions of process—who should decide, and how? The disposition of these monuments can give rise to fruitful dialogue, and the outcome of this dialogue ought not be prejudged or forced into a one-size-fits-all approach. Most of the monuments should probably be removed, but not necessarily every last one. In some cases, augmentation or contextualization rather than removal may be defensible.

Instead of dialogue, though, some Confederate statues and monuments have become sites of protest and even violence. In August 2017, in Charlottesville, Virginia, a group of neo-Nazis and other white nationalist groups staged a protest over the city's decision to remove a statue of Robert E. Lee. This drew counterprotesters, one of whom was killed when a neo-Nazi sympathizer drove his car into a crowd. The events in Charlottesville seem to have accelerated the trend of cities removing their Confederate monuments, sometimes in the dead of night so as to avoid protests (*New York Times* 2017). This has also become an explicit election issue, with the Republican candidate for governor in Virginia in 2017 "running ads extolling his support for Confederate statues" (Martin and Peters 2017).

It would be a mistake to think that the only issue here is whether to remove monuments and place names associated with the Confederacy that have been part of the landscape for many decades. As Dwyer (2004, 427) has noted, "Neo-Confederate memorial activists have been very busy" in recent years, trying to add new memorials. The best-known case of this is probably that of a bust of Confederate general Nathan Bedford Forrest, who before the Civil War was a slave trader and afterward become the first grand wizard of the Ku Klux Klan. During the war he oversaw the massacre of black Union troops who had surrendered. In 2000, a group calling itself "Friends of Forrest" installed the bust on the grounds of a city-owned antebellum house that is used as a museum, in a predominantly black area of Selma. In response to public protests and pressure from the business community, the city moved the bust to a cemetery that already had a Confederate memorial (Dwyer 2004; Dwyer and Alderman 2008, 89–93). In 2012, after years of vandalism to the bust, it disappeared, but it was replaced with a new one in 2015 (Edgemon 2015).

The conflict over memorialization, then, is ongoing, with those who seek to honor the civil rights movement, its leaders, and its goals vying with those who wish to retain or add to memorials of those who fought to defend the Confederacy and slavery. This conflict is played out on the landscape itself, with civil rights memorials and Confederate memorials coexisting in an uneasy standoff. Sometimes this reaches absurd heights: in Selma there is an intersection where Rosa Parks Avenue crosses Jefferson Davis Avenue (Dwyer and Alderman 2008, 95).

Universities campuses have also become sites where this conflict plays out. Many universities, often prompted by student protests, are considering renaming buildings named after individuals associated with slavery or the Confederacy. I disagree with David Cole (2016) when he writes that such efforts are "misguided" and "a sideshow [that] substitutes cheap symbolism for the concrete measures needed to achieve real progress." The debates about monument removal and name changes should instead be seen as an important part of the ongoing reckoning with the past. As I have tried to argue, "real progress" must be made not only on material issues but at the discursive and symbolic level as well. The state and major institutions in civil society (such as universities) must not continue to honor those strongly associated with white supremacy. Changing the messages conveyed by monuments, memorials, and place names is part of the work of transitional justice. Although some memorials and place names may be ambiguous in terms of what they convey, many are sufficiently problematic to require removal, or at least clarification and contextualization so as to disavow any support or nostalgia for white supremacy.

CONFEDERATE FLAGS

More troubling, and less ambiguous, are the interpretive and normative issues raised by official displays of Confederate flags. During the Civil War, the Confederate States of America adopted a flag, commonly referred to as the "Stars and Bars," composed of two red and one white horizontal stripe, with a blue field containing one star for each state of the Confederacy. However, this flag was deemed by some to be too similar to the American flag, and so the Confederate Battle Flag, with its blue St. Andrew's Cross containing the stars representing states, all on a red field, was informally adopted as the symbol of the southern cause (Coski 2000; Bonner 2002). It "came to represent the Confederacy itself for most white southerners" (Poole 2005, 125). Many Confederate states also adopted new flags during the Civil War or afterward, and in the decades after Reconstruction many southern states adopted official flags that either incorporated or strongly resembled the Confederate Battle Flag or the Stars and Bars. Though Coski states that "legislative records offer no clue whether the new flags were intended as references to the Confederate Battle Flag," it can hardly be a coincidence that, as he later adds, the "flag changes . . . coincided with the passage of formal Jim Crow segregation laws throughout the South" (2005, 79–80). Far from symbolizing a decisive transition from the white supremacy of the Old South, these flags reflected southern resistance to the equality of African Americans, and were to that extent appropriate symbols of Jim Crow. The Confederate Battle Flag went on to be widely used by white supremacist groups such as the Ku Klux Klan.

In 1948 the Confederate Battle Flag was revived, after decades of disuse, to become the symbol of Strom Thurmond's "Dixiecrat" run for the US presidency on a segregationist platform. In the following years of the civil rights movement the Confederate Battle Flag become a potent symbol of southern segregationist resistance. It was in the 1950s that Georgia changed the design of its state flag to prominently incorporate the Confederate Battle Flag, and South Carolina began flying the Confederate Battle Flag over its state capitol. Today, several states of the former Confederacy have official flags that evoke, to varying degrees, the Stars and Bars, the Confederate Battle Flag, or, in the case of Arkansas, a single star intended to refer to the Confederacy. In some states residents may obtain a license plate for their car bearing the insignia of the Sons of Confederate Veterans, which features the Confederate Battle Flag (see generally Coski 2005; Liptak 2015; Martinez, Richardson, and McNinch-Su 2001; Prince 2004; Woliver, Ledford, and Dolan 2001).

The politics of the Confederate Battle Flag was given new life in the aftermath of the murder of nine African Americans in a church in Charleston, South Carolina, in June 2015. Pictures of the killer with the Confederate Battle Flag were found online, and the incident exposed the close connection between racism and this symbol. Soon political pressure built for states and other institutions to stop displaying the flag. South Carolina, which had continued to display the flag on its capitol grounds, finally removed it. Yet the momentum to cease official displays of the flag was short-lived, and led to a backlash (see Blinder 2016; Inwood and Alderman 2016; Webster and Leib 2016). This backlash coincided with the rise of Donald Trump, as the Confederate Battle Flag often appeared at his rallies (Adams 2016; Fausset 2016).

Some have argued that symbols of the Confederacy are not necessarily racist and, properly understood, should give no offense (see Schedler 1998, 2000). Yet as critics have pointed out, it is difficult to maintain this position in light of the relevant history (Alter 2000a, 2000b). The display of these symbols of the Confederacy has, as we have seen, been revived at moments of southern resistance to civil rights. It is difficult to escape the conclusion that they are symbols of such resistance, and of opposition, therefore, to racial equality. The southern "traditionalist" position that the flags merely symbolize southern heritage or culture, divorced from slavery and Jim Crow, strains credulity. To the extent that the meaning of these symbols is shaped by the contexts in which they were created and then resurrected, that meaning is inextricably linked to resistance to racial equality.

Furthermore, the notion that southerners' support for the Confederate Battle Flag has nothing to do with racism is simply not borne out by the empirical evidence. There are now several empirical tests of the "southern heritage defense" of Confederate symbols, which use multivariate analysis to discover whether racial attitudes or southern pride explains support for the Confederate Battle Flag. These studies generally conclude that such support is closely related to negative racial attitudes (Clark 1997; Reingold and Wike 1998; Orey 2004; Cooper and Knotts 2006; but see Wright and Esses 2017). According to the best evidence that we have, then, it is simply not true that support for these symbols of the Confederacy has nothing to do with racism.

Quite apart from this empirical evidence, it is the meaning of the Confederate Battle Flag that is offensive. State displays of the symbols of the old racial order violate the requirement of justice that the equal citizenship of all is to be affirmed. In the realm of state speech, such displays should be deeply troubling, and they are reasonably interpreted by African Americans and others as calling into question the extent to which the current political regime affirms their equal status and is committed to racial equality.

A constitutional argument along these lines has been made by James Forman Jr. (1991). Forman argues that the display of the Confederate Battle Flag by southern state governments violates the US Constitution by inhibiting speech by an oppressed group (violating the First Amendment's protection of freedom of speech) and by denying citizens equal protection of the laws (violating the Fourteenth Amendment). Whatever the merits of Forman's constitutional arguments may be, the more important question for our purposes is what liberal democratic norms require—or, as Sanford Levinson puts it, what decency requires (1995, 1110; 1998, 111). The Confederate Battle Flag is "a metonym for the white South" and "a powerful symbol [of] . . . white supremacy" (Poole 2005, 125, 136), and as such it privileges white citizens over black citizens by expressing nostalgia for the period of official black subordination. It represents a refusal to disavow historical injustices and undermines the civic equality to which the post-civil rights movement United States is supposed to be committed.

It is important to keep in mind that the issue here is official, public displays of the symbols of the Confederacy (putting aside displays for educational purposes, such as in museums). State displays of the Confederate Battle Flag are wholly incompatible with a commitment to moral and civic equality. Hence California's decision to ban the sale and display of the flag by the state should be welcomed. This ban, it should be noted, does not prohibit private individuals from exhibiting the flag, even on state property, and so does not threaten freedom of speech (*Los Angeles Times* 2017). And the Supreme Court correctly decided the case *Walker v. Texas Division, Sons of Confederate Veterans* (2015), in which a group sued to have its emblem, which includes the Confederate Battle Flag, available on state license plates. The Court held that license plates are state speech, not private speech, and that Texas was within its rights to deny the request. But establishing that the state has no obligation to display a symbol of white supremacy is a small victory. What I have tried to suggest is that justice prohibits the state from doing so.

CONCLUSION

I have generally avoided drawing hard-and-fast conclusions about the requirements of justice in this chapter. Instead, my concern has been to insist that justice requires some confrontation with the past and some acknowledgment of it, in order to create an appropriate collective memory that affirms the civic and moral equality of all. At the same time, satisfying this requirement entails particular disavowals and affirmations through a variety of means and expressions, and in a variety of sites. While it is difficult to say that justice requires a specific expression (say, a particular monument, situated just so in a particular site, bearing specific words on its plaque), justice does impose some constraints on what are appropriate messages to send with respect to racial equality. In particular, it prohibits state use of symbols that implicitly endorse racial hierarchy.

Most cases of regime transition involve several means of acknowledgment, complementing and mutually supporting each other. We have seen, for example, that truth commissions often lead to apologies. The various means of providing knowledge and acknowledgment discussed here should be seen as working together to collectively convey the commitments of the political regime, including racial justice and the full equality of citizens. Moreover, these symbolic expressions should accompany an effort to achieve justice with respect to wealth, income, and opportunity. As others have noted, symbolic measures in the absence of policies to achieve material justice can easily become empty and meaningless. Justice requires, I have argued in the last chapter and this one, policies that pursue both material justice and appropriate means of knowledge and acknowledgment that affirm the equal moral and civic standing of all citizens.

final paper

4

Supporting Black Institutions and Communities

In addition to material inequality and the denial of moral and civic equality, the history of racial injustice in the United States has produced patterns of segregation. This segregation can be observed in where people live, where they go to school, where they work, where they go to church, and the social networks to which they belong. Racial segregation, in short, is manifest both geographically and in many institutions. These forms of segregation have profound implications for racial justice. Living in a predominantly black neighborhood often means living with higher rates of concentrated poverty, inferior educational resources, fewer employment opportunities, and higher rates of crime—all of which add up to much poorer life prospects.

Because segregation is such an important linchpin in the perpetuation of racial inequality, many of those concerned with racial justice have argued for policies that attempt to break up black communities and institutions and integrate African Americans into predominantly white ones. This focus on integration has been an important strand of thinking about racial equality since the civil rights era. Indeed, integration is sometimes thought of as a straightforward policy implication of liberal values and principles.

There is another strand of thinking about racial justice that has long challenged the more dominant integrationist view. This alternative, associated with black nationalism, argues that integration is not the only, or even the best, route to racial equality, and indeed that attempts at integration often entail serious costs for African Americans that are unacknowledged. It argues that certain forms of black separatism have important benefits for African Americans that ought to be preserved. Black nationalism has come in various forms, from advocating a separate nation-state for African Americans to more modest demands for community and institutional autonomy. These claims for more modest forms of autonomy are often known as "community black nationalism," and were prominent in the Black Power movement of the 1960s and 1970s.

Simplifying greatly, then, there are two main approaches to addressing racial segregation, one integrationist (and often assimilationist), and one advocating separation and autonomy for black communities and institutions. One place to look for guidance on these matters is the large literature on liberal theory and minority rights—particularly minority rights that include rights to (various degrees of) autonomy and self-determination. In recent years political theorists and philosophers have devoted a great deal of attention to these issues, and in the process they have challenged the notion that liberal values and principles require the integration and assimilation of minorities (see Tamir 1993; Taylor 1994; Kymlicka 1995; Levy 2000; Laden and Owen 2007; Patten 2014; Phillips 2007). Yet this view of minority rights is rarely extended to African Americans.

In this chapter I draw upon liberal theories of minority rights to argue that many defenses of minority autonomy and self-determination, suitably modified, also apply to African Americans. I argue that the exception that is made for African Americans, who are often excluded from making the sort of claims seen as appropriate to other minorities, is unwarranted. I argue for a version of black nationalism that is compatible with liberal commitments, and I thereby challenge the view that black nationalism and liberalism are necessarily opposed (see Dawson 2001, 13).

KYMLICKA, NATIONAL MINORITIES, AND
AFRICAN AMERICANS

Will Kymlicka's arguments for liberal multiculturalism are well known among political theorists and philosophers and constitute an important achievement in giving minority rights firm grounding in liberal values and principles. For both of these reasons, Kymlicka provides a helpful starting point for the present discussion. However, Kymlicka also exhibits a general tendency on the part of liberal multiculturalists, which is to neglect and distort the case of African Americans. While Kymlicka discusses African Americans in a number of places, he puts them in a residual category and withholds support for claims made on behalf of African Americans that are similar to the ones he defends for other minorities. He does so on the grounds that African Americans lack a distinct culture and language, but I attempt to show that, despite this, much of Kymlicka's framework for minority rights, suitably modified, can support some black nationalist claims.

Kymlicka argues that liberal theory can underwrite minority rights by focusing on national minorities. A national minority is "an intergenerational community, more or less institutionally complete, occupying a given territory or homeland, sharing a distinct language and history" (1995, 18). Such minorities have what Kymlicka calls a "societal culture," by which he means "not just shared memories or values, but also common institutions and practices." Societal cultures are "institutionally embodied—in schools, media, economy, government, etc." (1995, 76). Because minority nations are "institutionally complete," and provide for the whole range of needs of their members across their lifetimes, they have a strong claim to self-government.

Kymlicka's argument for self-determination of national minorities focuses on the conditions necessary for the realization of two liberal values, liberty and equality. He observes that one such condition is that people need a stable cultural and institutional context that make certain choices available and meaningful (1995, chap. 5). Individual liberty requires a stable context in which to formulate and carry out a life plan.

Kymlicka then argues that, in light of this, liberal equality requires that members of minority nations receive certain provisions such as a degree of self-government, in order to protect them from the vulnerability that is created by their minority status. Members of the cultural majority that dominates the central state can take for granted the survival of their language and culture, and the institutions that embody these, but members of the minority cannot take this for granted. Without some protections, members of a national minority often have two options: to assimilate to the majority culture, or to attempt to maintain their minority culture and institutions without the support of the state. Both of these options impose costs that are unjust because they are a product of individuals' unchosen cultural membership. There is also a cost to the self-respect of minority group members: the vulnerability of a minority culture would mean that its members would be uncertain that they can carry out their life plans, creating what Rawls called "social conditions that undermine self-respect" (1999, 386). Kymlicka argues that liberal egalitarianism must make a distinction between choices and circumstances and compensate for differences in circumstances that place individuals at a disadvantage in pursuing their conception of the good life. Membership in a minority nation is such a disadvantage.

Kymlicka contrasts national minorities with ethnic groups, which usually lack a societal culture, geographic concentration, and so on. Furthermore, national minorities are often incorporated into a state involuntarily, while ethnic groups arise through voluntary immigration, Kymlicka argues. The latter have legitimate claims of inclusion in the larger society through reasonable accommodation of some cultural differences, but have no claim to autonomy or self-determination.

What are the implications of Kymlicka's theory for African Americans? The first thing to note is that African Americans fit neatly into neither of Kymlicka's main categories. African Americans are unlike national minorities in that they are not concentrated in a single geographic region where they constitute a majority of the population. Yet their original incorporation into the polity was not voluntary. Furthermore, when Kymlicka focuses on culture and language as a basis for minority institutional autonomy, his argument seems not to apply directly to African Americans. Though we may speak loosely of a "black culture," this culture has great overlap with, and influence on, "mainstream" American culture. For African Americans, the main sources of vulnerability and inequality have little to do with a distinct language or set of cultural practices.

Kymlicka is of course aware of all of this and says that "we should not expect policies which are appropriate for either voluntary immigrants or national minorities to be appropriate for African-Americans" (1995, 25). Still, Kymlicka believes that most minorities are either national minorities or ethnic minorities, and that the case of African Americans is "anomalous" (1989, 257). He suggests that "the situation of African-Americans is quite distinct," "very unusual," and even "virtually unique in the world" (1995, 24, 60). Elsewhere, Kymlicka provides a typology of minorities, which includes the following categories: national minorities, immigrants, isolationist ethnoreligious groups, metics (that is, noncitizen guest workers), and African Americans (2002, 348–65). It is striking that only the last specifies a particular group, rather than a type.

Kymlicka notes that integration on the immigrant model has failed in the case of African Americans and suggests that "it is increasingly accepted that some new model of integration will have to be worked out" (1995, 25). Elsewhere he briefly sketches what such a model might look like (2001, chap. 9; see also 2002, 360–62). He notes that, under Jim Crow, African Americans developed a somewhat separate society with a parallel set of institutions, and states that, in this respect, they constitute something "closer to the 'national minority' pattern than to the immigrant pattern" (2001, 181). But he emphasizes that African Americans did not have "an already existing culture," distinct from white American culture, which they sought to preserve through these institutions. "In terms of their uprootedness, therefore, African-Americans are much closer to immigrants and refugees than to national minorities" (2001, 181). Kymlicka also notes that the effect of integration during and after the civil rights movement was to undermine black institutions while at the same time blacks continued to feel excluded from white institutions, leading many "to look with some nostalgia at the era of separate institutions" (2001, 182).

Kymlicka concludes that "we have no clear theory or model for under-standing or meeting the needs of African-Americans," but suggests that such a model might include measures appropriate to both immigrant communities and national minorities: policies promoting inclusion in the larger society plus some policies to support black institutions (2001, 184). Still, he emphasizes that the support for such black institutions would constitute "short-term separateness and colour-consciousness [that] is needed to achieve the long-term goal of an integrated and colour-blind society" (2001, 184).

Kymlicka's position is problematic and may reflect a tendency to see African Americans as being (more) like immigrant groups, which may lead him to presume that, like immigrants, African Americans ought eventu-ally to be assimilated into "mainstream" American culture and institutions. Kymlicka may be supposing that this is what African Americans want, or what they should want, but in any case the normative implication is that any vision of racial justice that does not embrace a color-blind society as its long-term goal is beyond the pale. Despite the qualifications and nuances he has added to his reflections on African Americans over time, Kymlicka's analysis is still driven by the nation / ethnic group dichotomy, with African Americans being shoehorned into the latter category.

This problem may originate in the specific arguments that Kymlicka offers for minority autonomy. Kymlicka's defense of minority institutions is based on their role in preserving culture and language, so when it comes to African Americans, he sees no grounds for protecting black institutions indefinitely. Yet minority institutions can serve other important functions and may be justified on other grounds. Kymlicka points to language and culture as the source of unchosen costs to members of a minority, but other kinds of costs may justify similar claims. In this light, some of what Kymlicka says about the value of minority institutions may be relevant to African Americans, but it must be decoupled from the rationale of protecting language and culture and grounded instead on the particular history and current predicament of African Americans.

Many reactions to Kymlicka's work attempt to undermine the privi-leged position of national minorities in his theory and displace culture and language as the grounds for minority autonomy. Margaret Moore (2003), Anne Phillips (2007), and Iris Young (1997) all argue that it is a mistake to place too great an emphasis on culture, language, and nationhood in arguing for minority rights. All argue instead for an account that focuses on more historical and contextual factors, and for one that avoids the sharp distinctions and the reification of culture and language that Kymlicka's approach arguably entails. Other theorists, such as Jacob Levy (2004) and Yael Tamir (1993), concur that one cannot delineate in advance the features that characterize a nation, and then proceed on this basis to a normative argument for a right to self-determination. These critiques of Kymlicka suggest that his reliance on culture and language, and on a conception of nation that is sharply distinguished from other kinds of groups, is problematic. Greater reliance on historic injustice and on context may more successfully ground an argument for some minority claims.

JUSTICE AND COMMUNITY BLACK NATIONALISM

We are now in a better position to assess the claims of community black nationalism, the view that supports "black control of political and economic institutions in the black community, and the building of autonomous black organizations" (Dawson 2001, 101). This was a dominant form of black nationalism during the Black Power movement of the 1960s and 1970s, though it was not the only variant. As historians have shown, the Black Power movement consisted of an array of organizations that had differing, and often conflicting, goals (see Ogbar 2004; Joseph 2006; Ahmad 2007; Goldberg and Griffey 2010; Bloom and Martin 2016). Yet community nationalism, emphasizing the value to African Americans of predominantly black institutions, often couched in terms of "community control," was certainly prominent during this period (Van Deburg 1992, 113–29; D. Robinson 2001, chap. 5).

Some observers might doubt whether community black nationalism is properly labeled as a form of nationalism, since it is not a program for an independent state. After all, minority nationalist claims usually have a territorial basis, which community black nationalism would seem to lack. At the time of the Black Power movement, some activists did declare a Republic of New Africa, comprising several states of the South, but under the prevailing circumstances sustaining this claim would have required a reversal of at least some of the migration of previous decades—not a likely prospect (Draper 1970, chap. 5; Hall 1978, 129–38). Community nationalists had to find a way of revising traditional nationalist ideas to suit the conditions that they faced—especially the concentration of much of the black population in urban centers. Thus, they came to see black neighborhoods in urban areas as the territorial basis of their claims (Dawson 2001, 97–100). Since this territory is noncontiguous, being disbursed among a number of cities, and since African Americans did not have the long-standing tie to these "territories" that national minorities often have to "their" land, community black nationalist claims to autonomy are not precisely analogous to other minority nationalisms.

But I am not so much concerned with whether community black nationalism is a genuine case of nationalism. I am interested in retrieving some insights from what is commonly called "black nationalism" for issues of racial justice today. My use of the terms "black nationalism" and "community black nationalism" is meant only to refer to a set of claims that remain worthy of consideration. If black nationalism does not qualify as true nationalism, this does not bear on the merits of the claims. That is, if black nationalism is nationalism only in an attenuated, or even metaphorical sense, then so be it. This does not affect the substance of the argument.

In any case, for community black nationalists, the important thing was not so much land itself as control of certain institutions. Malcolm X reflects this shift from land to institutions when he states that the struggle is "to gain control of the land and the *institutions that flow from that land*" (quoted in Dawson 2001, 99, emphasis added). Roy Innis similarly shifted from territory to institutions: "Large, densely populated black areas, especially in urban centers, must have a change in status. They must become political sub-divisions of the state, instead of sub-colonial appendages of cities. Blacks must manage and control the institutions that service their areas" (1997, 177).

Which institutions, exactly, did community black nationalists seek to control? As a group, they were often vague and inconsistent on this question. Sometimes the institutions are "churches, professional societies, schools and social groups" (Ogbar 2004, 124); sometimes "credit unions, co-ops, political parties" (Student Nonviolent Coordinating Committee 1997, 122); sometimes schools, housing authorities, and businesses (Ture and Hamilton 1992, 167–73); sometimes governmental bureaucracies and programs that serve black communities (Ture and Hamilton 1992, 183); and sometimes "schools, hospitals, and government agencies" (Van Deburg 1992, 115). These lists include institutions in civil society, such as churches and professional associations, so that the "demand" to "control" them would seem odd; as voluntary associations, all that is required is that African Americans have the freedom of association to form and participate in the institutions. Similarly, supporting black businesses is presumably a matter of individual choice. Other cases, however, might require state action to support black control—particularly schools, government programs, and housing (at least with regard to public housing). And even in the case of economic institutions and those in civil society, public policy can play a role in determining the conditions under which they operate, and thus in determining their chances of success. In any case, there is no definitive list of the institutions community black nationalists had in mind, though generally their emphasis was on the institutions that, as Malcolm X put it, "flow from" the areas where African Americans predominate, and that exercised direct authority in those areas (Innis 1997, 177; Baraka 1997, 153; Foner 1995, 178–79).

While black nationalists demanded control of the institutions most directly related to black communities, they realized that, given the limited nature of the territory dominated by African Americans in any given city, complete autonomy would not be practicable. So they usually called for the extent of autonomy appropriate to these circumstances, and for fair representation in decision-making where it took place at a jurisdictional level where African Americans did not predominate. "This is what they seek: control. When the black people lack a majority, Black Power means proper representation and sharing of control. . . . [They seek] the inclusion of black people at all levels of decision-making. We do not seek to be mere recipients from the decision-making process, but participants in it" (Ture and Hamilton 1992, 46, 183). Community black nationalists "demanded inclusion while advocating autonomy and self-determination" (Ogbar 2004, 2). Hence, while this program contains separatist elements, it is a mistake to characterize it simply as separatism or to place it in opposition to integration itself. Black Power advocates were well aware—how could they not be?—that African Americans were a minority in the United States, and that (barring secession) total separation from whites was not possible. What they objected to was not integration but "integration-as-assimilation" (D. Robinson 2001, 71). Hence Ture and Hamilton, in their book, *Black Power*, are careful to reject, not integration itself, but "integration as it is currently practiced," which they characterize as "a one-way street" (1992, 55). Black Power "embodied . . . the desire of a minority to be included, *but on its own terms*, within a society that it could never dominate" (Fredrickson 1995, 315). One can say that their position is "both anti-integrationist and anti-separatist" (Draper 1970, 119) in that it is opposed both to the mainstream vision of integration and the total separation of classical black nationalism. We might call this vision, following Bush (1999), "pluralist integration," or, following Brooks (1996), "partial separation."

But what was the *argument* for "community control"? I suggest that community black nationalists made two arguments, one based on justice and addressed to the broader, white-dominated society, and the other addressed to their fellow African Americans to support black institutions. I treat the former in the remainder of this section, and the latter in the next.

Community black nationalists argued that justice demands the support of black institutions and communities by the broader society. This argument focuses on the costs to African Americans of integration as it was usually understood—costs that were unfair to impose on them. These costs are similar to those to which Kymlicka draws attention in his argument for autonomy for minority nations, and the circumstances and vulnerabilities underlying the costs are also similar. Kymlicka emphasized that stable communal and institutional contexts are necessary for individual freedom. Without these, individuals cannot make and carry out coherent life plans. In the context of the civil rights movement and its aftermath, the implications of this insight for the case of African Americans are clear. Under Jim Crow, African Americans possessed something very close to a societal culture. Though they operated under very adverse conditions, black institutions—schools, businesses, professional organizations, media, hospitals, churches, and so forth—provided for a substantial degree of black autonomy. Though born of oppression, these institutions took on a life of their own and came to be deeply valued by many African Americans. While the conditions that gave rise to black institutions were unjust, undermining or destroying these institutions in the name of integration was a further injustice. At the very least, the fate of these institutions should have been an explicit topic of discussion during the civil rights movement and its aftermath. Yet this issue was largely ignored (Peller 1995).

After the civil rights movement, under the banner of integration, African Americans were essentially told that racial discrimination and de jure segregation would no longer be tolerated as a matter of policy, but that further progress toward racial equality would be achieved through integration. This, in turn, would be carried out through, as Norman Podhoretz put it, "the gradual absorption of deserving Negroes one by one into white society" (quoted in Steinberg 1995, 110). This way of conceiving the route to racial equality imposes enormous costs on African Americans and represents a great disruption to the context in which they had formed their life plans. It undermines the associative and communal ties that many deeply valued. It is also, many black nationalists argued, incompatible with the self-respect of African Americans to place themselves in the position of supplicants, hoping to be found "deserving" by whites. Black nationalists often focused on the "price" of integration (Ture and Hamilton 1992, 54; Browne 1968, 51)—a price that they argued was unfair to impose as a condition of racial equality, and a price that many whites, taking white culture and institutions as normative, usually failed to see at all. Furthermore, the disruption to African American communities and individuals' lives had little analogue in white communities: African Americans were being asked to bear costs that white Americans were not. Black individuals, institutions, and communities were to be transformed while little was asked of their white counterparts beyond "tolerating" the presence of a few African Americans. Hence, considerations of both liberty and equality support black nationalist claims in resisting the costs that integration imposed on African Americans, and support their alternative vision of maintaining stable black communities and institutions.

Some might argue that the costs associated with integration—the disruption to African American individual life plans and communities—were necessary and inevitable, but this is not so, at least not to the extent threatened by the dominant conception of integration. These costs are a result of a set of policies that place little or no value on the continued health and prosperity of black institutions and communities. An alternative set of policies might offer African Americans a different array of choices: between participating in well-funded, thriving predominantly white institutions, on the one hand, or participating in well-funded, thriving predominantly black institutions on the other. But this is not the set of choices African Americans were offered. Instead, the set of choices that African Americans faced came to be, essentially, between well-funded white institutions on the one hand and black institutions that had been underfunded and disadvantaged under Jim Crow and continued to be so during and after the civil rights movement. They faced an intrinsically coercive set of choices that heavily favored integration into white institutions. This is precisely the kind of assimilation pressure that national minorities have rightly resisted.

Community black nationalists did not call for a return to segregation. They affirmed that African Americans ought to be included in predominantly white institutions, and ought to be able to pursue the opportunities offered by the wider society without facing racial discrimination. What they contested was the terms on which African Americans must make their choices about where to live, where to work, with whom to associate, and so on. As we will see in the following section, black nationalists did argue that their fellow African Americans should choose to associate with their racial kin, but the justice-based argument is distinct: it is a matter of principle and of policy, addressing the institutional constraints that African Americans should and should not face in pursuing their life plans.

Of course, black nationalists realized that institutional autonomy was not enough; resources were needed as well. As one observer put it, "In reality, of course, control can operate to our advantage only if we have something to control, if we have the necessary resources" (Tucker 1971, 116). So an essential part of the black nationalist program was the call for redistribution from white institutions to black institutions, on both compensatory grounds and more forward-looking, equity grounds. James Forman's "Black Manifesto" (1969) is an example of this. It called on white churches and synagogues to pay $500 million as part of a program of reparations to which other institutions, including the federal government, would contribute. The money would be spent on supporting institutions that serve African Americans, including banks, publishing houses, television networks, and job-training programs. The Black Panther Party also combined demands for black control with demands for resources as compensation for Jim Crow (Foner 1995, 2–4). So it is not accurate to say that black nationalists who advocated community control failed to realize that the sources of many of the problems in the black community lay outside of it (see D. Robinson 2001, 102–3). They did realize this, and the call for black reparations was one attempt to address this problem.

Black nationalists often compared their program to what immigrant groups had achieved for themselves, and sometimes couched their demands as in line with the ethnic pluralism that already existed in the United States (see Hough 1968; McCartney 1992; Van Deburg 1992). Yet to compare their own case with that of immigrants was a mistake, because it substantially understates the grounds for their claims. Given the nonvoluntary and highly unjust conditions under which black institutions and communities were formed, African Americans have a much stronger case for autonomy than many immigrant groups.

A LIBERAL "NATION-BUILDING" PROJECT?

Achieving the goals of community black nationalism requires not only establishing just conditions vis-à-vis the society at large, but also gaining the support of African Americans themselves. So the other argument that black nationalists made was addressed to their fellow African Americans, whom they urged to reject integration on the terms on which it was offered, and instead to rally around the communities and institutions of which they were a part. Black nationalists urged African Americans to see black institutions, not as necessarily inferior to white ones, but as an aspect of and vehicle for community self-determination. I call this a "nation-building" project to emphasize the similarities between the community black nationalists' efforts and those undertaken by some national minorities. But the scare quotes are meant to indicate that it is not actual nation-building that the black nationalists were engaged in, except in a loose sense. (Following Eamonn Callan [2005, 498], one might also call it "quasi-nation building.")

What reasons did community black nationalists offer in their call to African Americans to support black institutions and communities? There were several. First, black nationalists appealed to African Americans' interests, arguing that they would be better served in thriving black institutions than as a minority in predominantly white ones. Given the continued salience of race, they argued, African Americans would be better off controlling "their own" institutions rather than being a minority within institutions dominated by whites (Ogbar 2004, 3; Innis 1997, 176). Second, some argued that African Americans had a moral duty—to themselves or to their racial kin—to support black institutions. That is, even if some African Americans could do well for themselves in predominantly white contexts, they nevertheless had special obligations to other members of the black community to support institutions on which others depended (Boxill 1992, 176). Third, black nationalists argued that African Americans should see integration (in its dominant, assimilationist guise) as an affront to their self-respect, since they interpreted it as carrying the message that white norms and institutions are superior to their black counterparts (Boxill 1992, 176–85; McGary 1999, 49). Fourth, some argued that American society remained racist and that the promise of integration was essentially a sham or a ploy—that integration, even on whites' terms, would not take place in the foreseeable future (Dawson 2001, 87; Ture and Hamilton 1992, 44).

I find these arguments to be plausible, but the argument I wish to make need not endorse them or establish their plausibility. Rather, the important thing from the perspective of a liberal conception of racial justice is that black nationalists should be able to make these arguments under conditions in which African Americans are not coerced into rejecting them by the nature of the choices available to them. That is, the argument from justice discussed above requires that black nationalists making their appeals to support black institutions should be able to do so under conditions that are fair and that give black "nation-building" a fighting chance.

That is not all a liberal conception of racial justice has to say about the community black nationalist project, since it must concern itself not only with threats to liberty and equality that arise from conditions under which the project is pursued, but also with the way it is pursued. The call by black nationalists for African Americans to get behind their program worried some liberals, and there would seem to be reason to be concerned. After all, black nationalism has often been charged with being patriarchal and even misogynist (Shelby 2005, 8). More generally, it has sometimes been identified with what Michael Dawson describes as "nonliberal elements" in black politics. "Perhaps the most obvious example of a nonliberal (some would say antiliberal) political tradition within Black politics has been the consistent demand that *individual* African Americans take political stands that are perceived by the *community* as not harming the Black community" (Dawson 1995, 206). These concerns raise important questions about the internal dynamics of black institutions and the appropriate liberal stance toward community black nationalism.

These questions are not unique to black nationalism, but have strong parallels in debates over liberal multiculturalism. As with black nationalism,

other minority nationalisms make claims to a degree of institutional autonomy that then raise the question of the treatment of individuals within
those institutions, that is, of the position of "internal minorities" (Green
1995; Weinstock 2007). These concerns have been pressed particularly
by feminists worried that empowering minorities merely empowers the
dominant forces within them and deprives internal minorities of the
protections offered by the dominant liberal legal and institutional framework. Ever since Susan Moller Okin asked, "Is Multiculturalism Bad for
Women?" (1999), this has been a prominent theme in work on liberal multiculturalism (see, for example, Eisenberg and Spinner-Halev 2005).

Simplifying greatly, the ensuing debate has fallen roughly along the
following lines (Deveaux 2006, chap. 2). On one side there is a group of
theorists who argue that liberal multiculturalism, while extending certain
kinds of autonomy and accommodation to minorities, must uphold the
rights of individuals within the minorities. These include the right to equal
consideration and to participation in democratic decision-making. For
these theorists, minority autonomy must not become an excuse to oppress
"minorities within minorities" (Deveaux 2006; Song 2007; Phillips 2007).
On the other side is a group of scholars who argue that toleration requires
that a liberal state take a more "hands-off" approach to certain minorities,
even those that are patriarchal or that deprive their own members of certain rights. This is permissible, it is argued, as long as minority group
members have a right of exit (Kukathas 2003; Spinner-Halev 2005). If they
do, then their association with their cultural kin is voluntary, and the liberal state has no right to interfere with their choice to go on associating
with the group—even if, in the minds of some observers, this makes
members of internal minorities complicit in their own oppression.

I cannot fully engage this debate in the present context, but I want to endorse the position of the former camp, that the proper liberal approach to
the problem of internal minorities is to ensure that they are not oppressed
by "internal majorities," or by the dominant powers within their group.
The most telling argument against the hands-off approach is that it does
not take adequate account of the costs of exit, and therefore there is little
warrant to infer that, if internal minorities choose not to exit, then their

association must be voluntary. Once we reckon with the costs of exit, it is not plausible simply to say that the failure to exit implies consent. "If circumstances are sufficiently extreme in terms of coercion or probable consequences of exit . . . we would not want to say that the right of exit is genuinely enjoyed by all" (Deveaux 2006, 52).

This is the position taken by Kymlicka, who distinguishes between external protections accorded minorities (which he defends) and internal restrictions that minorities impose on their own members (which he rejects) (1995, 35–44). Kymlicka also emphasizes that the competition, so to speak, between the majority nation's nation-building (which may attempt to persuade some minority group members that they should see themselves as members of the cultural majority) and the (would-be) minority nation's nation-building efforts should take place on fair terms. They may use the same methods of persuasion, but both must also respect the same constraints, particularly respecting individual rights. Fairness requires, he suggests, that "national minorities should have the same tools of nation-building available to them as the majority nation, subject to the same liberal limitations. What we need, in other words, is a consistent theory of permissible forms of nation-building within liberal democracies" (2001, 29).

The implications of this position for the community black nationalist project are clear. Black nationalists may engage in attempts to rally their fellow African Americans to see themselves as members of "a nation within a nation," to affirm their black identity, perhaps to embrace a particular vision of black culture, and to support and participate in black institutions. At the same time, predominantly white institutions may attempt to attract black members by propounding a vision of an integrated multiracial society, affirming the value of diversity, engaging in affirmative action, and the like. Liberal theory should concern itself with the fairness of the terms on which each of these projects pursues its goals. Black nationalists may make their case on fair terms, though they have no guarantee of success.

The present argument resonates with Anne Phillips's notion of "multiculturalism without culture," a vision, she says, that "put[s] human agency more at its centre" (2007, 9). For in the argument presented here, as with some other recent treatments of liberal multiculturalism, culture and its preservation do not play a dominant role. The point is not, for example, to protect a set of cultural practices from contamination or from other influences that might induce change. Rather, the emphasis is on protecting individual members of minority groups both from undue pressure to integrate into the majority and from undue pressure from the minority to toe the line. A consistent liberal approach to these issues is equally concerned with both kinds of threats to individual freedom.

Now, it may be that the black nationalist project is doomed to fail, as many commentators have suggested, but it can fail for different reasons, and we must distinguish between failure due to unfair conditions, on the one hand, and failure because it just cannot attract adherents, even under fair conditions, on the other. That is, it is one thing if the project fails because of the unfair circumstances in which black nationalists make their case, where black communities and institutions are so disadvantaged that anyone with the option to exit them will choose to do so. It is quite another if, in the context of a fair competition between predominantly black and white institutions, African Americans choose the latter. We simply do not know whether this would occur, however, because such fair conditions have not yet been created.

Some commentators have suggested that black nationalists are doomed to fail because they have only bad arguments. Their arguments are said to presume identity of interests among African Americans, whereas in fact African Americans have diverse and divergent interests depending on their gender, sexual orientation, or (especially) their class position. Or their arguments are said to presume a black culture that is common to all African Americans, or to presume that blacks have a moral duty to sacrifice their own interests for that of the group (see Glaude 2002; Reed 2002). On the interpretation offered here, however, black nationalism need not presume these things—rather, the project is best understood as attempting to create what its critics say it presupposes. That is, it is an attempt, among other things, to convince African Americans that they ought to see their interests as closely connected to that of other African Americans; that they ought to embrace a certain version of racial or cultural identity; or that they ought to affirm special duties toward other African Americans. There is nothing incoherent or obviously absurd about this project. After all, interests, identities, and one's sense of special obligations to others are not objective facts, but mediated by one's self-understanding. The black nationalist project is an attempt to advance one such self-understanding among African Americans.

Once fair conditions of individual choice for African Americans are created, it would not be surprising if the black nationalist project proved successful given what we know about black attitudes toward community nationalism, which tend to be very positive—even under current conditions. Michael Dawson tells us that blacks' sense of a "linked fate varies very slightly with socioeconomic variables" (1994, 79). That is, better-off African Americans are about as likely as less well-off ones to see themselves as sharing a common interest with other African Americans. Dawson (2001, chap. 3) also finds little support for the classical nationalist goal of a separate nation-state but finds substantial support for more modest kinds of black autonomy and self-determination. According to Dawson, "There is broad support for a moderate position in favor of controlling, building, and supporting institutions in the black community. . . . Black nationalism . . . remains, particularly in its 'community nationalism' variant, a strong force in black politics and public opinion" (2001, 123, 133). Many scholars have found strong support for community black nationalism among African Americans, and this support is often even greater among middle-class blacks than among the poor (Brown and Shaw 2002; Davis and Brown 2002). Black solidarity, then, is alive and well, with many African Americans expressing a willingness to support black institutions. In fact, it is remarkable that community nationalism enjoys the support that it does in light of the often-disadvantaged conditions that predominate in black institutions. If there were a more equitable distribution of resources, then the disincentives of supporting black institutions would only diminish.

Finally, the focus on threats to the liberty and equality to African Americans posed by the conditions under which they choose whether to support black institutions marks a significant divergence between the position defended here and that of Tommie Shelby. Shelby's book *We Who Are Dark* (2005) is a sophisticated theoretical engagement with black nationalism, and in many respects Shelby's conclusions are similar to those defended here: Shelby argues that (a version of) black nationalism is compatible with liberal principles and that black nationalism need not rest on a conception of black essentialism or on a belief in a distinct black culture or identity. Yet Shelby argues that any liberal approach to black nationalism places such severe constraints on the black nationalist project as to make it unviable as a strategy for institution- and community-building. He argues that the interests of individual African Americans are now so widely divergent that the idea of building black institutions as the path to advancement is not realistic. Shelby is rightly concerned about the potential threat posed by the black nationalist project to individual liberty—the threat that advocates of the project will pressure or coerce others to "get with the program" to advance a vision of collective black interests at the expense of their own interests. In particular, Shelby argues that the class interests of better-off African Americans are so different from the less well off that the former cannot reasonably be expected to be interested in the black nationalist project.

Shelby's diagnosis of the prospects for community black nationalism may be accurate under present conditions, but it focuses on only one of the two sources of threat to the freedom of African Americans: those internal to the black community. His argument, focused on the choices likely to be made by better-off African Americans, takes as given the current conditions under which those choices would be made. That is, Shelby assumes that the options among which better-off blacks would choose are, on the one hand, deprived black neighborhoods and institutions, and, on the other, more comfortable but more racially mixed neighborhoods and institutions. Yet, as I suggested above, these are the very conditions of choice that black nationalism challenges on grounds of justice. The choice ought not to be between deprived black settings and well-resourced settings where African Americans are a minority. For the conditions not to be highly coercive, and for them not to entail unfair costs, these disparities must be addressed. Yet Shelby accepts as given these disparities, which community black nationalism challenges, and then relies on them as the basis of an objection to community black nationalism.

This reflects an interesting asymmetry in Shelby's view. His argument reflects an acute awareness of the danger of coercive pressure within the black community, and he staunchly defends the right of better-off African Americans not to sacrifice their own interests and autonomy for the sake of some conception of the common interests of black Americans. He is right to do so, since a liberal black nationalism must respect this autonomy. Yet Shelby is arguably too willing to accept the coercive pressures that are created by the unjust circumstances of choice that better-off—and indeed all—African Americans face. In confronting the possible danger of coercion internal to the black community, he inadequately scrutinizes the very real presence of external coercion created by the circumstances of choice. Justice requires, I have argued, that African Americans not be faced with the set of choices that Shelby accepts. Only if African Americans have a choice between equally well-resourced predominantly black settings and settings where African Americans are a minority can their choices be considered uncoerced.

ANDERSON'S DEFENSE OF INTEGRATION

While Shelby's treatment of black nationalism implicitly accepts the integrationist pressure of current conditions, Elizabeth Anderson's argument explicitly endorses integration and seeks to increase the integrationist pressure on African Americans. Indeed, Anderson's book *The Imperative of Integration* (2010) is the most robust recent defense of the integrationist perspective to which black nationalism is opposed. If Anderson is right that integration is an imperative of justice, then the position I have defended here is mistaken. We must, therefore, confront Anderson's arguments for integration as the only route to racial equality.

Anderson conceives of segregation as having "two basic modes: *spatial segregation*—processes that assign groups to different social spaces and institutions—and *role segregation*—processes that assign groups to different social roles" (2010, 9). The view that I defend here agrees with Anderson that roles should be integrated—that is, that positions of power and authority in American society should not exclude African Americans, and that positive steps should be taken to ensure their inclusion. As we will see in the next chapter, I join Anderson in endorsing affirmative action policies. The issue, then, is spatial integration: does justice require racial integration in residence and in institutional settings such as schools?

Anderson claims that it does, and she has two main arguments for her position: that integration is essential for equal citizenship and democracy; and that it is essential for equal opportunity and distributive justice. Consider the former argument first. Anderson argues that racial segregation is bad for, indeed, incompatible with, genuine democracy. Anderson endorses a very thick conception of democracy, one that includes not just majoritarian political processes but also a deep commitment to equality that is embraced by all citizens. "The democratic ideal holds that justice requires equality in social relations" (2010, 102). Democracy also requires deliberation among citizens, that they come together as equals and bring together their various experiences and perspectives. I find nothing to disagree with as far as this goes, but when Anderson writes, "Negotiation and deliberation, in turn, requires integration" (2010, 99), I must ask, which aspect of integration does she have in mind here? The sentence that immediately follows seems to answer the question: "If insular elites are allowed to work out 'solutions' for themselves, without having to consult excluded groups, their answers will neglect the interests of those excluded" (2010, 99). Anderson seems to have in mind role, not spatial, segregation. It is easy to agree that democracy requires an integrated elite, in the sense of an elite (say, political leaders and officeholders) that includes all racial groups. But does democracy require spatial integration, that is, residential and institutional integration? ᴺᴼ, ᴺᴼᵗ ᶠᵒʳᶜᵉᵈ ⁱⁿᵗᵉᵍʳᵃᵗⁱᵒⁿ

Anderson seems to think that it does, but she never states this explicitly. Anderson argues that common citizenship requires the creation of "an integrated 'us'" (2010, 188). To the extent that racial identity conflicts with national identity, racial identity must be subordinated. She further seems to think (but again does not explicitly argue) that such common citizenship is incompatible with spatial segregation or clustering. Yet this is a difficult position to defend. Many democratic societies are composed of a number of racial, ethnic, and cultural groups, and these groups, even when characterized by spatial clustering, are not necessarily antithetical to a sense of common citizenship or the well-functioning of democracy. If Anderson wants to maintain that spatial integration of all racial and ethnic groups is a necessary condition for democracy, she would have to confront the vast amount of evidence that contradicts this claim.

Furthermore, as some of Anderson's critics, such as Sharon Stanley (2014, 2017) and Tommie Shelby (2014; 2016, chap. 2) point out, it is implausible to argue that African Americans have a duty to integrate, regardless of what they see as serving their own interests. Stanley argues that "it would be difficult to begrudge black citizens for resenting a nation that demanded such a sacrifice of them in exchange for a still-abstract, still-deferred future unity" (2014, 15). This appears to be yet another case where African Americans are asked to give something up in exchange for promised benefits that may never materialize.

Anderson's second argument, that a socially just society requires racial integration, relies heavily on empirical evidence. Anderson cites an impressive array of studies that show that integration in residence, schools, and other contexts often produces benefits for African Americans (see esp. 2010, chap. 5). She relies on this evidence to conclude that integration is an imperative of justice. Yet several things are noteworthy about this argument. First, Anderson sometimes states her claim about the relation between integration and justice as an analytic one, rather than as a synthetic and contingent one. "If racial segregation is the problem, it stands to reason that racial integration is the remedy. Since the problem is an injustice, the remedy is an imperative of justice" (2010, 112). If matters were that simple, then Anderson would not need the copious amounts of empirical data to support her case. But of course the claim that integration is, on principle, an imperative of justice cannot withstand scrutiny. It does not follow from the fact that de jure segregation is an injustice that justice requires integration. So that leaves us with the empirical case for integration.

The empirical evidence is much more mixed and ambiguous than Anderson sometimes suggests. I will make this argument in more detail in chapters 6 and 8, on residential segregation and education, respectively. But for now several general features of Anderson's argument can be highlighted. First, from the premise that some African Americans have benefited from integration, it does not follow that integration is a necessary condition of black advancement. Anderson's claims on behalf of integration are actually comparative, though she rarely makes this explicit. The question is what the appropriate comparison should be. Anderson's comparisons are often with cases where integration has not been pursued, where African Americans live, work, and go to school under severely disadvantaged conditions. In this light, it is not surprising that those in more integrated settings generally do better. But I would argue that the appropriate comparison is not to such deprived conditions, but to other alternatives, where resources are devoted to improving black neighborhoods, schools, and other institutions. Anderson makes no attempt at this comparison, and so is silent on the issue of whether integration really does produce better outcomes for African Americans than alternative policies. She often leaps from evidence that African Americans benefit from integration to the conclusion that *only* through integration can African Americans' lot be improved. Despite her claims to the contrary, Anderson simply has not presented evidence for the claims that integration is "the only feasible" (2010, 179) or "an indispensable" (2010, 180) means to achieving racial equality.

Furthermore, though Anderson early on rejects the assimilationist vision of integration, she later comes very close to endorsing it. "Blacks need to change," she writes, and though she immediately adds, "Whites need to change, and we all need to change" (2010, 186), she leaves no doubt about who must change the most. Anderson suggests that "considerations of inertia and cost call for more change on the part of minority groups, in the direction of assimilation" (2010, 115). Since Anderson's vision of integration mostly involves integrating blacks into predominantly white settings, it is clear that African Americans will have to change much more, whites less. Sure, Anderson admits, there are "costs" to African

Americans—but these costs are a necessary price for the benefits of integration. How different is this from the assimilationist vision of integration that black nationalists, rightly, have always found so objectionable?

Finally, there is the issue of the fate of black neighborhoods and institutions under Anderson's conception of integration. Anderson is very clear and explicit, emphatic in fact, that racial equality requires spatial integration. She acknowledges the costs of integration to African Americans, including "the loss or alteration of cherished racially homogeneous institutions" (2010, 180). And yet Anderson considers the view that integration threatens black neighborhoods and institutions "confused" (2010, 113). She never explains how spatial integration is compatible with the very kind of clustering that she has portrayed as a major obstacle of racial equality, nor even acknowledges the tension. There may be ways to resolve the tension, to reconcile the importance of thriving black communities and considerations in favor of integration (see Stanley 2014, 2017). But such a reconciliation must give full weight to the liberty and equality of African Americans and to the legitimate reasons that they may have to resist integration.

Despite its virtues, Anderson's book reflects the dominant view of racial justice in the United States since the civil rights movement. Anderson's view is essentially indistinguishable from the common attitude that the route to racial equality involves African Americans moving into predominantly white settings. This view, I have argued, takes inadequate account of the costs to African Americans of integration and ignores the reasons that they may have to participate in and support black institutions and communities.

CONCLUSION

In the final analysis, black nationalists argued for changes both in policy and in attitude toward racial concentration. The attitudinal change they urged combated the dominant view among whites (but also shared by some African Americans) that any geographic or institutional clustering of African Americans should be viewed negatively, as a reflection of American society's failure to achieve an integrated society. To the contrary, they argued that such racial clustering is often valued by African Americans, and quite reasonably so. The problem of racial justice in the United States is the terms on which that clustering takes place, and the maldistribution of resources associated with it. The policy change that follows from this perspective is that public policy should support black institutions and communities rather than undermine them in the service of integration. Across a broad range of policy issues, black nationalism challenges the terms on which integration has taken place (to the extent that it has) in the post-civil rights era, and more generally challenges the terms of mainstream discourse on race that has led to a set of policies that have failed to benefit many African Americans.

One of the perennial issues in African American political thought is whether African Americans are better served through integration or through some version of separation—whether emigration, secession, or the more limited separation of community black nationalism (see Cruse 1967, 564; Brooks 1996; 2009, chap. 4; Boxill 1992, chap. 8; McGary 1999, chap. 3). The position outlined here supports the community black nationalist position, but in a provisional way. It supports community black nationalism to the extent that black institutions are necessary for the liberty and equality of African Americans. If, however, individual African Americans, under fair conditions of choice, ultimately abandon black institutions and communities, then the liberal conception of racial justice that I have sketched will have no argument against this. The concern here is with the fair conditions of choice that promote individual freedom, not the ultimate success of the "nation-building" project. So the position outlined here cuts across the integration/separation debate by focusing on the terms on which the debate should be decided.

5

Affirmative Action

I argued in the previous chapter that predominantly black institutions and predominantly white ones can each vie for the participation of African Americans, and that justice does not require one particular outcome of this competition but does require it to take place under fair conditions. Affirmative action is one means by which predominantly white institutions vie for black participation. It is one way in which an array of institutions, such as schools and employers, attempt to attract African Americans. Traditionally, African Americans have been either excluded or sorely underrepresented in these institutions, and affirmative action seeks to overcome the present-day legacies of this history. In this way, affirmative action is fundamentally an integrative policy: it seeks to integrate African Americans into predominantly white institutions. In light of what I argued in the previous chapter, affirmative action cannot be a complete approach to racial justice, and it cannot bear the full weight of remedying our racial ills. Indeed, it may well be that too much attention has been given to affirmative action in public and academic discourse on race. Still, as part of an overall approach to racial justice, affirmative action has an important role to play. But placing affirmative action in the context of the conception of racial justice articulated throughout this work casts many of the issues that it raises in a distinctive light.

SOME HISTORICAL CONTEXT

Although there is some debate among historians about when the story of affirmative action begins, in its contemporary usage the phrase "affirmative action" is usually traced to an executive order by President John F. Kennedy in 1961. The order created the President's Committee on Equal Employment Opportunity, and it directed the federal government and companies contracting with it to end racial discrimination and to take "affirmative action" to hire "without regard to . . . race, creed, color, or national origin" (T. Anderson 2004, 60). The phrase "affirmative action" was meant to convey the idea that merely ceasing discrimination would not be enough. Employers had not only a "negative" duty not to discriminate but also an affirmative duty to ensure equal opportunity.

As some observers have pointed out, there is a certain "irony" in affirmative action (Skrentny 1996), since in both Kennedy's order and the subsequent Civil Rights Act of 1964, the emphasis in the text is on hiring "without regard" to race, yet affirmative action calls for just the opposite—it involves the use of race as one consideration in hiring and contracting (and later in admission to institutions of higher education). How did this shift come about? It is important to see that it arose immediately and necessarily from the original goal. Affirmative action from the outset conveyed that something more than the mere absence of discrimination would be required. It required positive efforts. And how could it be known whether these efforts were being undertaken effectively? How would the government ensure that employers, who for decades had practiced systematic racial exclusion, had begun to make efforts to include African Americans? Clearly, in light of their history, these employers were not in a position to say, "Trust us." The only way to know whether effectual steps were being taken was to look at the results.

And this is exactly what the Kennedy, Johnson, and Nixon administrations did: they insisted on concrete evidence that African Americans were being hired, as evidence of the fact that they were not continuing to suffer from discrimination. It is important to remember in this context that until this time, not only employers, including the federal government, but also unions engaged in widespread and systematic exclusion of African Americans. Where this was the case, and where unions had a monopoly or near-monopoly on certain trades, African Americans were excluded. Hence, the Philadelphia Plan, which was started under Johnson and continued under Nixon, required unions to admit and employers to hire African Americans. In 1970 the Philadelphia Plan was extended to apply to all businesses, making affirmative action the general policy of the federal government (T. Anderson 2004, 124–25).

Though the main impetus behind these policies came from the executive branch, Congress did little to impede or thwart them. These early affirmative action policies survived constitutional challenges and judicial scrutiny as well. For example, in *United Steelworkers of America v. Weber* (1979) the Supreme Court upheld an affirmative action program under both the Constitution and the Civil Rights Act of 1964. The following year, in *Fullilove v. Klutznick* (1980) the Court upheld an affirmative action program for federal contractors. As Terry Anderson (2004, 157) puts it, "Between 1969 and 1980 all three branches of government lined up and supported [affirmative action]." While there certainly were dissenters, it was widely agreed that, in the context of a history of systematic exclusion, merely stopping discrimination was not enough: positive steps were needed to begin to overcome that history.

Along the way, however, some subtle changes were taking place in how policymakers and the public thought about affirmative action. At its inception, two things were clear about affirmative action: it was intended to benefit primarily African Americans, and it was intended to compensate for the diminished opportunities that they had faced up until that time. These two features are, of course, closely linked. At the height of the civil rights movement, the focus was on racial equality and on overcoming Jim Crow segregation. This placed the attention squarely on African Americans, and affirmative action was intended to meet the urgent need to ensure that the previous limitations on their educational and employment opportunities would not be a bar to their employment opportunities in the present and future. To merely cease discrimination would leave in place many of the consequences of past discrimination. Hence affirmative action was needed to compensate African Americans for the injustices of the past and their ongoing legacies.

But the focus on African Americans and on compensation would not last. Already in Kennedy's 1961 order, we saw that the language focused on individuals being hired "without regard to . . . race, creed, color, or national origin." Though African Americans were the primary intended beneficiaries, the language suggests that all groups that had traditionally faced barriers to equal opportunity might benefit. The same would apply to women once they were protected by the Civil Rights Act of 1964. As the beneficiaries of affirmative action came to include Hispanics, Asians, and women, a more inclusive justification was required—one that didn't depend so much on a history of blatant discrimination. At the same time, even as it was upholding affirmative action in employment, the Supreme Court ruled in *Regents of University of California v. Bakke* (1978) that a general history of societal discrimination could not justify affirmative action in higher education. The only justification the Court would accept from colleges and universities that wished to engage in affirmative action (in the absence of a history of discrimination practiced by the institution in question) was that the policy was necessary to create a diverse student body, which, in turn, was necessary to provide a rich educational experience for their students.

The *Bakke* case has had an enormous impact on the public discourse on affirmative action. First, much of this discourse is focused on higher education, and this drives many of the presumptions about the policy—particularly in criticisms of it. It must be remembered, however, that affirmative action, both originally and even today, applies to trades and occupations where many people meet the qualifications to be hired or admitted, and above that threshold it is difficult to distinguish the more from the less qualified. Second, since the only constitutionally permissible rationale for affirmative action in higher education, according to the Supreme Court, is diversity, there has been a tremendous effort in institutions across the country to foster diversity and emphasize the need for it. Now, of course, the *Bakke* decision alone is not responsible for this, and there may be some positive consequences of this development. But an unfortunate effect has been to take the focus away from African Americans and to eclipse the compensatory rationale for affirmative action. In the effort to be inclusive and "diverse," one of the main justificatory rationales for affirmative action has been largely forgotten. I will have more to say on this point below.

The essential ruling of *Bakke* remains the law of the land. In *Grutter v. Bollinger* (2003) the Supreme Court upheld the ruling, allowing the University of Michigan's Law School to take race into account as part of a holistic evaluation of each applicant. Then, in 2013 and again in 2016, in *Fisher v. University of Texas*, the Court upheld affirmative action but also held that the use of race must be justified on the grounds that no race-neutral means exists to achieve the goal of creating a diverse student body. So at the time of writing, affirmative action remains permissible, but only based on its indispensable role in fostering diversity.

WHAT, THEN, IS AFFIRMATIVE ACTION?

As I suggested above, there was an ambiguity built into the idea of affirmative action from the outset. It conveyed aggressive efforts at nondiscrimination, but it also entailed taking race into account when examining evidence of whether previously excluded groups, especially African Americans, were in fact being included. The phrase "affirmative action" quickly came to be equated with race- (and other group-) conscious hiring, contracting, and admission to higher education. At a very basic level, all informed observers probably agree on a core definition of affirmative action, yet advocates on both sides of the issue seem to disagree on how best to conceive of affirmative action. As we will see, some conceptions of affirmative action have unfortunate implications, and some depart markedly from usage in ordinary language. Any plausible definition of affirmative action, I suggest, should both capture the shared understanding of it and at the same time convey why the policy is so controversial—while not prejudging the normative issues that it raises.

Robert Taylor (2009), drawing on an argument by Thomas Nagel (1973), presents a fivefold typology of affirmative action policies, ranging from formal equality of opportunity, to what he calls aggressive formal equality of opportunity (which can include efforts such as outreach), to "compensating support" such as special training programs, to "soft quotas," and finally "hard quotas." Each of these categories is reasonably clear and the typology may very well capture a range of policy options. But Taylor insists that each of these five categories is a type of affirmative action (2009, 478–79). It is difficult to see how formal equality of opportunity (whether aggressive or not) can be thought of as affirmative action. If affirmative action can amount simply to formal nondiscrimination, then what is the opposite of affirmative action? What contrast does the phrase draw? Clearly, this conception goes beyond what most observers would consider affirmative action.

Some scholars argue that the key distinguishing feature of affirmative action is the justification or rationale for the policy. For example, Daniel Lipson (2008) has argued that the affirmative action debate has become detached from its civil rights roots and that the justice-based argument for affirmative action has been largely forgotten. I agree. But Lipson goes further to argue that a policy justified by its effects in promoting diversity is not affirmative action at all. "Racial inclusion policies are not affirmative action policies unless they are implicitly or explicitly rooted in a civil rights rationale of seeking to achieve equality by actively including members of historically excluded groups" (2008, 694). Applying the label "affirmative action" to policies not based on this rationale is an "abuse[]" of language" (2008, 693). I entirely agree with Lipson that the description of, and rationale for, a policy can make a crucial difference for its meaning (as I argued in the case of reparations), but I am not sure that it is helpful or clarifying to say that affirmative action policies justified in the name of promoting diversity are not affirmative action at all. This is simply at odds with too much firmly established ordinary usage.

Some attempt to define affirmative action in terms of its goal. For example, James Sterba (2009, chap. 3) has suggested that affirmative action policies are those that are justified by the immediate goals of outreach, remedying past and ongoing discrimination, and promoting diversity, and that have the ultimate goal of achieving a color-blind society. This has the implication that any policy that does what affirmative action policies generally do, but that does not aim at the ultimate goal of a color-blind society is not an affirmative action policy. Sterba does add that by color-blind he means racially just, but here too he is prejudging a number of important normative issues rather than offering a neutral definition that will allow the normative argument to proceed.

Some scholars have interpreted affirmative action primarily in terms of its relation to integration (see Anderson 2010; Warnke 1998). It is true, as I noted at the outset, that affirmative action necessarily has integrative effects, but is it unhelpful, I believe, to define affirmative action as a policy of integration. Take, for example, Elizabeth Anderson's (2010, 135) formulation: "By 'affirmative action,' I refer to any policy that aims to increase the participation of a disadvantaged social group in mainstream institutions, either through 'outreach' . . . or 'preference.'" This definition is too broad, because it includes many policies that would not generally be considered affirmative action. Consider two policies that aim to increase the participation of disadvantaged groups in "mainstream" institutions: integration of public schools and gerrymandering of legislative districts to promote the representation of disadvantaged groups through the creation of "majority-minority" districts. Both of these would seem to fit Anderson's conception of affirmative action. But is it helpful to lump these policies under the same heading as the much more controversial policies that form the core of our understanding of affirmative action?

If a plausible definition of affirmative action should capture its core meaning, it must also mark out those features that make affirmative action particularly controversial. What makes affirmative action so much more controversial than other policies that pursue integration is that it operates in contexts where important goods and opportunities are being distributed on a competitive basis. It therefore is seen by some as pitting considerations of race against those of merit, and this is the feature to which its opponents take such strong exception. The assignment of students to public schools and of individuals to different legislative districts, on the other hand, is not done on a competitive basis; one school, or district, is supposed to be as good as another. Now, of course, particularly in the case of schools, we know that this often is not so. Nevertheless, the distinction I am drawing is an important one: in principle, students are usually assigned to schools by place of residence along with other considerations, but (except with magnet schools and similar cases) students do not *compete* for positions in public, K-12 schools. Job applicants, prospective contractors, and applicants to colleges, universities, and professional schools do compete. And when race and other similar factors are taken into account in awarding the associated benefits, this is what is distinctive about affirmative action and what gives rise to the fierce political (and philosophical) battles over it.

If this is right, then it is perhaps best to think of affirmative action as *a policy that aims at ensuring that members of historically disadvantaged groups are among those selected for competitively awarded benefits*, such as contracts, employment, and admission to institutions of higher education. The distinction that this conception allows us to draw between affirmative action and other integrative strategies reflects the way courts have treated the issues. There is a clear divergence, for example, between *Brown v. Board of Education* (1954) and its progeny down to *Parents Involved* (2007) on the one hand and *Bakke, Grutter*, and *Fisher* on the other. To be sure, the two are not unrelated, and there are important points of contact—and tension. For example, when the Supreme Court struck down the use of race to integrate the public schools in Seattle and Louisville, it had to strain to explain why diversity is a compelling interest in higher education but not in K-12. (I will have more to say about this in chapter 8.) Nevertheless, the two lines of cases have proceeded largely independently of one another, and this is possible precisely because affirmative action raises issues that the integration of public schools does not.

It must also be said that affirmative action looks very different in different contexts. The bulk of the public and scholarly attention has been devoted to affirmative action in higher education, and why this is so should be clear from what I said above: to its critics, affirmative action pits "irrelevant" characteristics such as race against "merit," and this tension is most clear in the context of admissions to institutions of higher education—particularly highly selective ones. In the case of contractors or prospective employees for many jobs and in many trades, on the other hand, while merit still plays a role in selection, it is more difficult to suggest (as it is often suggested in higher education) that one can rank all applicants according to objective criteria of merit, and that affirmative action overrides these criteria in favor of other considerations. While tradesmen (and tradeswomen) and contractors no doubt have important skills, it is more difficult to maintain in this context that, among competent and qualified applicants (or bidders), some are clearly more meritorious than others.

In light of the differences in affirmative action in different contexts, perhaps it would be best if different terminology were used in these divergent contexts. But this suggestion proposes to dramatically revise ordinary usage and is therefore not practicable. Besides, as I argue below, the case of affirmative action in higher education is actually much more like the analogous policies in employment and government contracting than is usually recognized. So it is appropriate to use the same label for the policies in these different contexts.

One advantage of the conception of affirmative action proposed here is that it leaves open the important normative issues that it raises: can the use of race and similar characteristics in the distribution of competitively awarded goods be justified?

THE MISMATCH THESIS

Since the consequences of affirmative action are complex and varied, it is impossible to construct a compelling, overall utilitarian argument for (or against) it, and therefore consequentialist arguments have tended to focus on the policy's consequences for a particular institution or a particular group. One group that is harmed by affirmative action, according to some of its critics, is the policy's intended beneficiaries, especially African Americans. If this were true, it would be powerful critique of the policy.

The argument that students are harmed when admitted to institutions of higher education under affirmative action programs is often called "the mismatch thesis." The argument asserts that African Americans in particular are often harmed because affirmative action places them in educational institutions for which they are poorly prepared and in which they are likely to be among the most poorly performing students. Minority students admitted into a highly competitive college or university under an affirmative action policy, the argument runs, would be better off attending a less selective and less demanding institution.

Two of the most prominent advocates of the mismatch thesis are Stephen and Abigail Thernstrom (1997). The Thernstroms rely heavily on SAT scores, and more precisely on *average* SAT scores in their argument against affirmative action in higher education (1997, chap. 14). They assume that the black-white gap in the average SAT scores of admitted students at an institution reflects the degree of preference given to black students in the application process. The corresponding assumption is that if there were no preference given to black applicants, the average SAT scores of admitted black and white students would be the same, or nearly so. The "typical" black student would not differ very much in academic preparedness from the "typical" white student at any given selective institution, and the black and white test score distributions would be roughly the same.

William Bowen and Derek Bok, in their book *The Shape of the River* (1998), have shown these assumptions to be false. It is well known that, nationally, the distribution of SAT scores among African Americans is lower than among whites. This means that if a race-neutral standard were used, there would still be a gap in the average SAT scores of admitted black and white students. "For example, if a school admitted every applicant with SAT scores over 1100 and none with lower scores," the white average among admitted students would be higher than the black average because there would be more African Americans concentrated closer to the 1100-point cutoff (Bowen and Bok 1998, 16). So the SAT score gap among admitted students is not a measure of the preference given to African American applicants but is partially a result of the national distribution of the scores. Indeed, as Bowen and Bok remark, "The only way to create a class in which black and white students had the same average SAT score would be to discriminate against black candidates" (Bowen and Bok 1998, 16).

There is a further problem with the Thernstroms' reliance on averages and on the notion of "the typical white student" (1997, 416). The fact is that many white students fall below the "typical" white student in academic preparedness, so it is unclear why it is problem if some black students do as well. If we assume a fairly normal distribution, and take "typical" to mean "median," then many white students will be below the typical white student. To expect most black students to approximate the typical white student is to place an additional burden on them that is not placed on white students. Assuming some dispersion in the distribution, many admitted students will fall below the typical white student. That is the nature of a distribution.

There is another obvious point that the Thernstroms miss but that is brought out by Bowen and Bok (1998, 37–38). A black applicant who is admitted under affirmative action does not displace a white applicant who is "typical" of the white students admitted to the institution. The comparison of average SAT scores of admitted black and white students implicitly assumes that, were it not for affirmative action, more "typical" white students would have been admitted. But most likely, in the absence of affirmative action, more white students below the median would have been admitted. Bowen and Bok also show that while affirmative action makes an enormous difference in the number of black applicants admitted, eliminating it would neither substantially increase the average level of preparation among black college students at selective institutions, nor would it significantly increase the odds of admission for white students (1998, 42).

Perhaps the most conclusive rebuttal of the mismatch thesis comes out of Bowen and Bok's analysis that combines school selectivity, SAT scores, and graduation rates among African American students (Bowen and Bok 1998, 61, figure 3.3). The authors divide the schools in their data set into three categories of selectivity. They then divide black students by SAT interval and determine the graduation rate for black students within each interval at schools with different levels of selectivity. If the hypothesis advanced by the Thernstroms were true, we would expect to find that black graduation rates are highest at the less selective schools. In fact, the opposite turns out to be the case. Black students graduated from the most competitive schools at the highest rates, no matter what their SAT score. In fact, school selectivity is a much better predictor of whether a student will graduate than the student's own SAT score (Bowen and Bok 1998, 65).

So the mismatch hypothesis turns out to be unsupported by these data. If it were true, graduation rates for black students within a given SAT interval would go down as one moves from less selective schools to more selective ones, but instead the rates go up. To be fair, it must be noted that the Thernstroms did not have the benefit of these data when they were conducting their analysis. But as was noted above, even in light of the data they used, there was good reason to be suspicious of the mismatch hypothesis. That suspicion turns out to be well founded.

Indeed, years after graduation, students who attended more selective schools earned higher incomes and expressed greater satisfaction with their college experience (Bowen and Bok 1998, 114, 142–44, 207). Hence, both subjective measures and objective measures fail to reveal any cost to black students associated with the supposed lack of fit between themselves and the institutions they attended. They were, Bowen and Bok conclude, "well advised to go to the most selective schools to which they were admitted" (Bowen and Bok 1998, 144).

Two other prominent advocates of the mismatch thesis are Richard Sander and Stuart Taylor (Sander 2004; Sander and Taylor 2012). Sander (2004) argues that many black law school applicants are mismatched with the schools that they attend because of affirmative action. Using data that include LSAT score and undergraduate GPA, he finds that students who are better matched with their law school earn higher grades and pass the bar exam at higher rates. Affirmative action, Sander argues, has the

effect of actually lowering the number of African Americans who become lawyers. He concludes that black law school applicants are better off
attending schools where their credentials place them closer to the middle
of the entering class, rather than following Bowen and Bok's advice that
they attend the most selective institution that admits them.

Sander's article almost immediately inspired a number of critiques (see
Ayres and Brooks 2005; Chambers et al. 2005; Wilkins 2005; and the reply
by Sander [2005]). These critics show, using Sander's own data, that in fact
African Americans who attend more selective law schools graduate and
pass the bar at higher rates (Ayres and Brooks 2005) and that eliminating
affirmative action would substantially reduce, not increase, the number of
black lawyers (Ayres and Brooks 2005; Chambers et al. 2005). In addition,
as these and other critics have pointed out, Sander makes the same error
committed by the Thernstroms: he assumes that affirmative action is the
source of most of the difference in average black and white levels of academic preparation among the students admitted, and that eliminating it
will therefore eliminate that gap (Ayres and Brooks 2005, 1808; Kidder
2013, 93). In fact, given the difference in the distributions of black and
white entering credentials, even a race-blind admissions process would
result in differences between the black and white mean test scores, as
Bowen and Bok pointed out.

The most recent round of debate over the mismatch thesis surrounded
the book by Sander and Taylor (2012), which presents Sander's argument
about affirmative action in law schools (substantially unaltered in light
of any of the criticisms to which that earlier analysis was subjected) but
adds a new argument based on data before and after the 1996 passage of
California's Proposition 209, which banned the use of race-based affirmative action in higher education. The publication of the book coincided
with the oral arguments in the *Fisher* case. Sander and Taylor submitted an
amicus brief to the Court, ostensibly in support of neither party, but generally arguing against affirmative action based on the analysis presented
in the book.

Sander and Taylor rely on the "natural experiment" provided by the
passage of Proposition 209 to analyze the effects of eliminating affirmative

action in higher education. They argue that, while Proposition 209 caused a decrease in African American enrollment at the flagship University of California campuses in Berkeley and Los Angeles, it led to an increased rate of black attendance at UC campuses overall, as well as in California state universities and community colleges, and an overall increase in both the number of black graduates and the graduation rate among black students.

But critics point out flaws in Sander and Taylor's analysis. Kidder, for example, shows that in the years after the passage of Proposition 209, applications to the UC system rose, and the number of slots available did not keep pace. "Consequently, the UC system became more selective," which would tend to close the racial and ethnic gaps in graduation, independent of the elimination of affirmative action (Kidder 2013, 104–5). Other analyses that rely on the same natural experiment come to conclusions quite different from those of Sander and Taylor (see Kurlaender and Grodsky 2013).

The balance of the empirical evidence, then, weighs strongly against the mismatch thesis. But it is important to emphasize that, even if confirmed, the mismatch thesis does not require any particular normative conclusion. It would not follow from its truth that affirmative action policies are wrong, or ill advised, or that black applicants to higher education are better off going to less selective schools. Even if statistically the mismatch thesis were born out, there would still be many individual black students who would do well and even thrive in the challenging and competitive atmosphere in the most selective schools. And each individual applicant is in the best position to make this judgment; as some observers have pointed out, there is something paternalistic and patronizing in counseling that black students should aim lower for their own good (Kurlaender and Grodsky 2013).

There is another kind of mismatch that does seem to be a serious problem, however. It is not a problem of students attending schools for which they are underqualified, but rather of students failing to attend selective schools for which they *are* qualified. William Bowen and two coauthors call this problem "undermatch": the phenomenon of well-qualified high school students who either go on to a less selective college or university than they would be competitive for, or who fail to go to college at all (Bowen, Chingos, and McPherson 2009). This is the kind of mismatch we should be concerned about.

THE TROUBLE WITH DIVERSITY

If the mismatch thesis is often used as the main consequentialist argument against affirmative action, the main consequentialist argument in its favor is based on the benefits of diversity. The attractions of grounding affirmative action on diversity are undeniable. It is intuitively plausible that bringing together students from different walks of life would enrich the college experience, both in and out of the classroom. It detaches affirmative action from the particular case of African Americans and places the justification for it on more general grounds that potentially apply to many groups. It therefore might undercut the perception that affirmative action amounts to treating African Americans as "special" or that arguments in its favor amount to special pleading on their behalf. The appeal to diversity may also be seen as a brilliant move on the part of affirmative action's defenders, an attempt to seize the rhetorical high ground. After all, who could be against diversity?

But there are serious limitations associated with relying on diversity as a justification for affirmative action, and (intentionally or not) when the Supreme Court upheld affirmative action on these grounds alone, it seriously undercut the case for affirmative action, particularly as it applies to African Americans. The focus on diversity has distorted the legal, and therefore the broader public, debate over affirmative action over the last several decades.

For example, as others have noted, the focus on diversity undermines the connection between affirmative action and concerns about injustice and inequality. Daniel Lipson (2008) has traced the transition of affirmative action from being a means to greater equality to a policy of maintaining diversity, and has further argued (as I discussed above) that policies aimed merely at achieving or maintaining diversity do not deserve the label "affirmative action." More polemically, Walter Benn Michaels (2006), in a book whose title I have borrowed as the title of this section, has argued that the focus on diversity, both within the context of affirmative action and far beyond it, has done a serious disservice to the progressive aim of limiting inequality. Indeed, he turns this concern into a critique of affirmative action itself, which he sees as providing cover to colleges and universities. By being inclusive with respect to race and ethnicity, these institutions need not worry about the fact that they are far from representative when it comes to class. "Race-based affirmative action," he writes, "is a kind of collective bribe rich people pay themselves for ignoring economic inequality" (2006, 86). While I disagree with Michaels's dismissive view of race-based affirmative action, I agree that justifying it by way of diversity undercuts the connection between the policy and inequality.

As Michaels and others, such as Richard Ford (2005), have emphasized, focusing on diversity has a way of converting concerns with race and racial inequality into matters of culture. It therefore subsumes the issue of racial inequality under the more general heading of multiculturalism and directs attention to cultural differences and away from material hardship. It also casts African American applicants and students as the bearers of a distinct black culture and, Ford argues, therefore exaggerates the cultural distance between African Americans and whites. The diversity argument for affirmative action also casts African Americans as a means for the improvement of their white counterparts. It risks sending the message that black students are admitted to selective colleges and universities for the purpose of broadening the horizons of their white (and generally more privileged) fellow students. Concomitantly, what is lost is the sense that African Americans (and other targeted groups) are the intended and legitimate beneficiaries of the policy.

Most important, the diversity rationale both reflects and reinforces the historical amnesia about our racial past that characterizes nearly all public discourse on race in the United States. Diversity provides a fundamentally ahistorical and acontextual justification for affirmative action and therefore decouples the policy from the history of racial injustice that is essential to understand and justify it. Indeed, I strongly suspect (though I cannot prove) that much of the support that affirmative action enjoys rests implicitly on the awareness of the historic injustices that it attempts to address. Though for many, including the courts, diversity is the "official" justification for affirmative action, there is a sense in which this justification is silently parasitic on the compensatory justification that is officially disavowed.

It is reasonable to suspect this because, detached from a specific racial history, the value of diversity cannot plausibly be asked to bear the weight that is asked of it when it is put to work supporting affirmative action. Critics of affirmative action are correct that if diversity is the concern, then all kinds of diversity—ideological, religious, and so on—should be equally valued. If this were the case, then the degree to which affirmative action policies continue to focus on African Americans and a handful of other groups, and the extent to which African Americans are among the primary beneficiaries, could not be justified or even made sense of.

This situation, where diversity is the official justification that nevertheless relies implicitly on a context of historical injustice for additional support, is reflected in Justice Sandra Day O'Connor's majority opinion in the Supreme Court's decision in *Grutter* (2003). In this case the Court upheld its decision in *Bakke*, permitting affirmative action in higher education, because it found diversity to be a constitutionally permissible justification. Yet at the same time, O'Connor seemed to place a time limit on affirmative action, suggesting that the Court's patience with the policy would run out in twenty-five years. If diversity is the rationale for affirmative action, why would this time limit be necessary? Why would diversity become less important in twenty-five years' time? The time frame imposed by O'Connor, I suggest, is an implicit acknowledgment that affirmative action is justified in part, and perhaps in large part, in light of a particular history, a history that she hoped or expected would be more fully overcome within a generation or so. In this O'Connor was no doubt being wildly optimistic, but her comments clearly place affirmative action within a historical trajectory, on a temporal dimension outside of which it would not be justified.

Placing affirmative action in a historical context is important not only for understanding and defending it, but also because of the expressive function that affirmative action performs. As I emphasized in the discussion of reparations in chapter 2, the description under which actions are taken matters a great deal, and the "same" policy described or justified in different ways will convey a very different meaning and significance. Thomas Hill (1991) makes this argument with respect to affirmative action when he focuses on its "message." Hill argues that compensatory and diversity arguments for affirmative action both send the wrong message. The former portrays beneficiaries as being "paid off" for the harms that they have suffered, while the latter rests the policy "on a delicate balance of costs and benefits" (1991, 116). I do not think that the compensatory rationale has the implications that Hill attributes to it, but I agree that the strongest case for affirmative action encompasses both the backward- and forward-looking perspectives in an overall historical narrative. In particular, as I argue below, it is important to convey the message that, in light of our particular history, affirmative action is justified on grounds of justice.

AFFIRMATIVE ACTION AND JUSTICE

The justice-based argument for affirmative action has strong parallels with the justice-based argument for reparations, though it also presents special difficulties that must be confronted. Recall that the case for reparations, understood as public policies that aim to address racial inequality because of its roots in historic injustice, relies on the observation, supported by voluminous evidence, that present-day inequality is the result of past injustice. Similarly, one important argument for affirmative action is backward looking and compensatory: affirmative action aims to compensate present-day individuals for disadvantages that they bear due to past injustice. But the policy is also obviously forward-looking as well. It seeks to create a more just society in the present and the future by creating more equal opportunities and ensuring that the distribution of positions of power, privilege and authority is not shaped by our ugly past. This combination of backward-looking compensatory reasons and forward-looking egalitarian reasons for addressing racial inequality is found in arguments for both black reparations and affirmative action.

There are additional grounds for affirmative action. Perhaps the most important is the fact that affirmative action may be required to combat present-day, ongoing discrimination against African Americans. Particularly in the realm of employment, there is much evidence that African Americans continue to face discrimination. Studies have shown that black job candidates with similar credentials receive calls for interviews at rates much lower than whites (Bendick, Jackson, and Reinoso 1994; Bertrand and Mullainathan 2004). So affirmative action is needed to address not only the differences in opportunities that result from historic injustice, but also those that are a consequence of ongoing antiblack bias.

There are features of affirmative action that distinguish it from the general social policies that would be part of a program of black reparations. The latter are policies that distribute benefits to large numbers of people, and whose costs are widely distributed, usually through taxation. Affirmative action, however, involves more than these broad policies. It entails placing particular individuals into particular positions, whether into a desirable job, or a seat in the entering class of a college, university, or professional school—therefore, according to its critics, denying other particular individuals these positions.

This feature of affirmative action creates special problems but it also is one of its great advantages, according to some advocates. In general social policy, the population is taxed, and the state uses its revenues to support policies that benefit the less well off. This makes it difficult to determine who is paying what, but it also means that money is being taken out of the pockets of some for the benefit of others. Affirmative action, on the other hand, involves taking nothing from anyone, since the goods that it distributes are ones that "no one yet has established a right to and in a way, therefore, [it] imposes no unfair losses on anyone" (Boxill 1978, 266). The truth of this claim depends on an understanding of equality of opportunity. If applicants have a right to be judged solely on the basis of a criterion or set of criteria that does not include race, then this claim is false. If they do not, then it is true. This is the crux of the issue, for many proponents and critics of affirmative action. Opponents claim that applicants are entitled to be judged on their merits, while proponents of affirmative action must take one of two positions: either race can constitute part of merit, or race is a legitimate consideration in awarding positions, even if it is not encompassed by merit.

What, then, is merit? Let us begin with the case of admissions to colleges and universities, because here the view that we know what merit is and how to measure it is most plausible. If it can be shown that the claims about merit made by critics of affirmative action cannot be sustained in this context, it is unlikely that they can be sustained in other contexts, such as job applications and promotions, where it is even more difficult to precisely characterize and measure merit.

In the context of admissions to institutions of higher education, critics of affirmative action often rely on several related claims: there is a particular conception of merit that should determine admission; that we can measure merit according to this conception, and thereby place all applicants along a single continuum of merit; and that admission decisions should be made according to this measurement—that admissions should be granted based on the retrospective judgment of an applicant's past performance rather than a prospective judgment about their potential for academic (and other kinds of) achievement in the future. If these claims are false, then meritocratic objections to affirmative action are defeated. I will argue that all of them are false.

First, there is no single conception of merit that all institutions of higher education are required by justice to utilize in their admissions decisions. Rather, there is a range of possible admissions criteria, and while some criteria (say, whites only) would clearly be unjust, justice does not require some specific criterion, or a particular weighting among a definite set of criteria. This should be obvious upon reflection. Women's colleges admit only women, and so the merit of male applicants is irrelevant under their admissions policies. Some universities have prominent athletic programs, and so athletic abilities constitutes part of merit for the purposes of admission. (Or it constitutes a non-merit-based criterion of admission, in which case the considerations I adduce below would apply.) Some schools have vibrant extracurricular music programs, and so look kindly on applicants with musical ability. Some colleges and universities weigh SAT scores heavily, others less so, and still others not at all. It is implausible to claim that all institutions that depart from a particular conception of merit in their admission process are guilty of injustice.

One of the issues that is sometimes forgotten in the debate over affirmative action is just how important it is for institutions like colleges and universities to be autonomous. A liberal society is liberal in part because power is disbursed among institutions in civil society, and these institutions have some discretion with respect to how they exercise that power. The state, guided by norms of justice, can certainly impose some constraints on these institutions, but it may not dictate specific admissions criteria or procedures. If it were to do so, it would exercise too much control over independent institutions that are diverse in their missions, and would entirely flatten the varied terrain of higher education that is one of its great assets.

Now, one could argue that a critic of affirmative action need not claim that there is a single conception of merit that should determine all admissions criteria, but only that the use of race falls outside of the permissible range. But if this is the claim, it must be shown how race differs from non-merit-based considerations that are widely utilized, such as legacy status, musical or athletic ability, geographic origin, and so on. The most common response to this challenge is to say that race is special: precisely because the use of race has such an ugly history in our society, any further use of it bears a heavy burden of proof—a burden that will usually be unsustainable. This is the thought behind the Supreme Court's use of "strict scrutiny" in examining any racial classification. Yet this reasoning is tortured. If racial classifications have been used to harm African Americans in the past, this increases, not decreases, the case for policies to address the resulting racial inequality. Perhaps policies that disadvantage African Americans should be subject to strict scrutiny, but to treat all use of race in policy as equally suspect defies common sense.

Even if there were a single conception of merit, which included only certain criteria, excluding race, would we be able to rank all applicants according to this conception? There is little reason to think so, for the crucial feature of merit is that it is necessarily *multidimensional*. Some applicants are strong in some respects, but weaker in others. No two candidates are precisely the same, but each brings certain assets and shortcomings that are distinctive of him or her. Some have done extremely well on standardized tests, others are highly ranked in their high school class, or have a high GPA. Again, it is not plausible to maintain that every college or university is required to utilize a specific formula to collapse these measures onto a single dimension. There is no objectively correct way to weight each of the factors, so there is no single continuum on which to place the candidates. The purely meritocratic vision of admissions is a fantasy.

Finally, the notion that admissions decisions should be based purely on past performance is equally implausible. Colleges and universities are entitled to take into consideration prospective judgments about how applicants would benefit from attending their institution, how they would use their degree after they graduate, and what contribution they may make to society. Indeed, it would be bizarre if institutions did not take such things into account. As others have noted, admissions into selective colleges and universities are not merely prizes for past performance. They also legitimately reflect judgments about future contributions. As David Schmidtz (2006) has suggested, one can come to deserve an opportunity in light of what one does after receiving it. Desert is not only retrospective, but prospective as well.

Critics of affirmative action often claim that a particular white student deserves to be admitted into a particular school and is dealt an injustice if denied admission while other candidates with lesser academic credentials are admitted. Courts have accepted these claims and granted standing to rebuffed white applicants when they sue to overturn affirmative action policies. Yet as we saw above, ending affirmative action would only negligibly increase the chances of admission for a white student. White applicants cannot plausibly claim to know that they have been denied admission because of affirmative action. The existence of even one other white applicant with lower credentials who was admitted would seem to defeat the claim that the petitioner was denied admission because of race-based affirmative action. It is difficult to see how white plaintiffs challenging affirmative action can even establish standing to sue, let alone succeed on the merits.

Once one begins to examine and articulate the conception of merit that is implicit in critiques of affirmative action, its implausibility becomes obvious. It crumbles. Historically, the "merit-only" position for admissions to higher education has been invented precisely to argue against affirmative action. Before race-based affirmative action was practiced, there was certainly a trend toward more meritocratic criteria. The SAT test was invented precisely so that applicants other than the sons of the elite could show their merit and gain admission to highly selective institutions. Yet as far as I can tell no one ever argued that *only* considerations of merit should ever have any relevance for admissions—until race came to be used as a factor.

My argument so far has assumed that race is not itself a criterion of merit. But in some contexts it is, and in these instances the case for using race among the selection criteria is only strengthened. So, for example, counseling inner-city black kids may very well be something that an African American applicant, other things being equal, may be in a better position to do successfully. It may be that black doctors, lawyers, and other professionals are more likely to serve underserved communities and are better equipped to do so. It may also be the case that having African American role models in positions of authority is important and has many benefits, and that race is therefore a qualification and does not compete with merit considerations. Now, one could argue that in cases where race constitutes an aspect of merit rather than supplementing or competing with merit, the use of race does not constitute affirmative action. That may be so, but the important substantive point remains: that the use of race, whether conceived of as an aspect of merit, or in addition to merit, is perfectly legitimate.

My argument has also assumed that there is such a thing as merit. Above I called the "purely meritocratic vision" a fantasy, but this does not mean that merit itself is a fantasy. I disagree with Iris Young when she calls merit a "myth" (1990, chap. 7). For any competitive position, there are relevant criteria for selection, and some people are better qualified than others. But our notions of merit, while real, are also vague, difficult to quantify, and, as I've noted, multidimensional. When deciding on whom to hire or whom to admit, there is simply no getting away from a holistic, overall judgment of merit. Those judgments can be good or bad, defensible or less so—and reasonable people can disagree. Merit is real but it is not, and cannot be, the whole story.

CONCLUSION

As I noted at the outset, there is a tension between advocating affirmative action and at the same time advocating support for black institutions. Affirmative action tends to produce integration, but black colleges and universities (for example) can be sites of resistance to integration. While there is a tension, there is no contradiction, for lying beneath both arguments is the requirement to create conditions that support the equality and liberty of African Americans. As I argued in the last chapter, this requires support for black institutions, but it also requires, I have argued in this one, that positions of power and privilege not be distributed in ways deeply marked by our racial past—or the lingering biases, prejudices, and obstacles that remain.

So if there is a vision of integration that emerges from the discussion in this chapter and the last, it is a vision of *uneven* integration. The idea of uneven integration is one that endorses the availability to African Americans of positions in predominantly white institutions. If these positions are genuinely open to them, and if efforts are made to ensure that African Americans are well represented in those positions, there is every reason to think the plenty of them will take advantage of these opportunities. But not all African Americans will want to take this route, certainly under present circumstances, and possibly even under improved circumstances. Some will prefer to attend a historically black college or university, or to work for a black-owned business. As long as this is the case, some white institutions will never be able to reach the point where African American representation within the institution reflects the population at large. This in itself is not an injustice, as long as it results from the aggregation of individual choices that have been made under circumstances that are fair and noncoercive. Needless to say, we are very far from achieving this condition. As things stand now, there is every reason to believe that the underrepresentation of African Americans in positions of power and privilege is a result of structural injustice, not of voluntary choice under fair conditions.

The vision of uneven integration stands against what may be the predominant vision of integration, which holds that the goal of racial justice should be a color-blind society, one in which race is entirely irrelevant. In such a society, we would expect African Americans to be more or less evenly distributed geographically and institutionally. Every college and university, for example, would have roughly the same proportion of students from various racial and ethnic categories. From the perspective of the conception of racial justice I am trying to sketch here, there are at least two problems with this vision: First, it may be the case that this vision can only be achieved through highly coercive means that impose significant costs on African Americans. Second, such a vision holds out the promise—or the threat—that each institution will be essentially the same, in terms of its racial and ethnic makeup, as every other. We are confronted with an inescapable trade-off when it comes to diversity: the drive to make every institution similarly diverse has the implication of eliminating diversity *among* institutions. And diversity among institutions is important for choice. A society in which the demographic profile of every college and university was essentially the same would be a society in which the option of attending a historically black college no longer exists. Now, this may be the society that is eventually achieved, and as I have emphasized, if it comes about through the uncoerced choices of individuals, then the liberal conception of racial justice has nothing to gainsay it. But that would, in some important respects, be a poorer society than the one that we have now, despite the obvious injustices and inequalities that exist today.

6

Justice and Residential Segregation

In chapter 2 I argued that racial inequality today is a case of historic injustice, since present-day patterns are the result of past systematic violations of rights. I also argued that backward-looking considerations of compensatory justice converge with more forward-looking considerations of egalitarian justice, both perspectives requiring public policies that address ongoing structural racial inequality. In chapter 4 I argued that any approach to racial justice must take account of the value that people place on their communities and institutions. Accordingly, the support of predominantly black institutions and communities must be a component of any set of policies focused on racial inequality.

This chapter, focused on racial residential segregation, is an application of both of these lines of thought. It applies the reparations argument in that the patterns of racial segregation that exist today are largely the result of unequal treatment of African Americans during the Jim Crow era, and these patterns do much to perpetuate racial inequality today. Segregation therefore exemplifies the ways in which the compensatory and egalitarian arguments for policies to address racial inequality converge. It applies the second line of thought because black communities created by racial segregation, and the institutions within them, are often deeply valued by their members despite the very adverse conditions in which they exist. Any approach to addressing racial residential segregation must take account of this value, must avoid imposing the costs associated with integrationist strategies, and must instead give pride of place to the liberty and equality of African Americans.

CITIES, SPACE, AND POLITICAL THEORY

In contemporary political theory there is not a robust discourse focusing on space in general or cities in particular. On reflection, this is odd for a couple of reasons. First, as Susan Bickford points out, the roots to which Western political thought is conventionally traced are focused on the city, or city-state (2000, 355). Both Plato and Aristotle argued that the polis is the appropriate site of citizenship and justice. In the modern world, however, citizenship and justice are associated with the larger-scale political communities defined by national borders, and cities have been neglected. As Daniel Weinstock has observed, "Cities have largely been ignored by political philosophers" (2014, 259).

Second, once one begins to think about it, it becomes obvious that spatial arrangements—within cities, between cities and suburbs, and so on—have important implications for the central concerns of normative political theory, including both distributive justice and democracy. How a city is arranged, its infrastructure, the relation between where people live and where they work, how individuals and groups are distributed across the landscape, and many other spatial factors determine to a great extent whether any particular conception of justice can be achieved. As Alan Ryan (1997) has argued, theories of justice have divergent spatial implications, and it may be possible to "read off" of the geography of a city the conception of justice that it embodies. While political theorists are very good at thinking about issues of distributive justice and democracy in the abstract, too few have attended to the spatial implications of their theories, and how spatial factors affect which conceptions are realizable.

One political theorist who has thought quite a bit about cities, space, and justice is Iris Young (1990, chap. 8; 2000, chap. 6). For Young, city life can serve as a normative ideal. She proposes city life as an alternative to the ideal of community, which requires a great deal of mutual identification among members, but also as an alternative to abstract individualism. While cities can be characterized by, and foster, social isolation and alienation, "Contemporary political theory must accept urbanity as a material given for those who live in advanced industrial societies" (1990, 237). Cities are places where people can cluster with others with whom they feel affinity, but also where they can be open to interacting with, or simply sharing space with, those who are different from themselves (1990, 236–41).

Yet this is an idealized version of any actual city, Young acknowledges. Cities are all too often sites of injustice and exclusion (1990, 241). Indeed, by their very nature, including their high population density, cities make inequality and injustice much more visible than they might be otherwise. Many cities have populations that are poor, and the poor are often concentrated in neighborhoods that are characterized by high crime rates and that are avoided by middle- and upper-class residents.

This understanding of cities as having the potential to foster justice, on the one hand, but also embodying and perpetuating deep injustice and inequality, on the other, has informed recent work on the city by political theorists and scholars of urban planning. Loren King (2004a, 2004b) has explored the democratic potential, but also pitfalls, of cities. Bart van Leeuwen (2010) and Richard Dagger (2000) have argued that, even under modern conditions, cities continue to have an important place in fostering, but also undermining, citizenship. Clarissa Hayward and Todd Swanstrom (2011) characterize cities as places of "thick injustice," where the injustice is deeply embedded in physical space, as a result of long-term historical processes, and is reflected in institutional structures and jurisdictional boundaries. Elsewhere Hayward argues that cities are crucial to how race is "made" (2003, 2013). Benjamin Barber is quite bullish on the potential of cities to address deep social problems, if only "mayors ruled the world." While acknowledging the ills of segregation, for example, Barber argues that "the city itself is a form of human community inherently inclined to integration" (2013, 189). All of these scholars are attuned to the potential that cities offer for pursuit of political ideals and for social life more generally, but also to the grim reality of deep inequities that cities almost universally reflect and reproduce.

Yet to date no one has offered a full account of what justice requires when it comes to the spatial distribution of persons, infrastructure, and housing in an urban setting. Some recent contributions by scholars, however, do point in some helpful directions. Susan Fainstein (2010) attempts to identify the criteria by which we can assess the degree to which a city is just or unjust. She assesses the ways in which New York, London, and Amsterdam are relatively just, but her prescriptions are principles to be applied in the urban planning process, not to the overall result. Still, Fainstein is surely correct in arguing that justice applies to the process by which spatial arrangements are changed. In particular, Fainstein highlights the potential for injustice when the state undertakes coercive measures to change the makeup of cities and neighborhoods. As we will see, this aspect of Fainstein's analysis has particular relevance when it comes to the practice of moving the urban poor.

Edward Soja (2010) makes a case for "spatial justice" as an independent dimension of justice, alongside social, economic, and environmental justice. Soja provides a very useful survey of spatial injustices such as apartheid and other forms of racial segregation, but he declines to extend his argument to what justice requires in light of these injustices. Indeed, he criticizes Fainstein for being "normative" rather than "critical" (2010, 29). While Soja is surely right when he concludes that spatial injustice is particularly difficult to address—he notes that "Once spatial injustice is inscribed into the built environment, it is difficult to erase" (2010, 41)—his avoidance of normative analysis means that his work is not very helpful in thinking about appropriate remedies.

Thad Williamson's *Sprawl, Justice, and Citizenship* (2010) engages justice, space and cities when he argues that suburban sprawl is bad for both justice and democracy. In two central chapters Williamson employs an explicitly liberal-egalitarian conception of justice to examine the relation between justice and sprawl (2010, chaps. 4 and 5). Drawing on Rawls, Williamson argues that the built environment and its management play an essential role in achieving both equal basic liberty and fair equality of opportunity. Enforced segregation, for example, is a violation of basic liberties, and if educational and occupational opportunities are unequally distributed spatially, then individuals may not have equality of opportunity (2010, 115–23). Sprawl also undermines individual characteristics important to both liberalism and democracy, such as social trust and tolerance. Williamson concludes that "sprawl is a serious obstacle to Rawlsian liberal egalitarianism" (2010, 172). Since Williamson's focus is on sprawl and therefore on the suburbs, extending his insights to more densely populated city centers would require further argument. But Williamson's analysis of how the spatial layout of a city and its environs advances or retards the prospects of justice has important implications for inner cities and their relation to the rest of the metropolitan areas of which they are a part.

As Soja emphasizes, injustices are often inscribed on the urban landscape and carried out spatially. As Fainstein shows, considerations of justice apply to the mechanisms by which the spatial distribution of individuals is changed, and these mechanisms and processes should avoid imposing unfair costs on already-disadvantaged communities. And as Williamson shows, the built environment itself and how individuals are distributed in it have great implications for the prospects of achieving justice. All of these aspects of spatial (in)justice are borne out in the case of racial residential segregation and what justice requires as a response to it. While we lack a general normative theory of spatial justice, or even of the spatial dimension or requirements of justice (but see Williams 2018), we do have some premises and insights on which to build.

RESIDENTIAL SEGREGATION AS AN ISSUE OF JUSTICE

While racial residential segregation has been declining over the last several decades, the decline has been very slow, and African Americans remain highly segregated. "A majority of African Americans still live in 'hypersegregated' metropolitan areas (such as Detroit), where at least 60% of the African American population would have to move to be evenly spread in the metropolitan area. Ninety-five percent of African Americans live in at least a moderately segregated metropolitan area (such as Kansas City), where 40% of blacks would have to move to achieve integration" (Enos 2012). Even those who have a more sanguine view of segregation trends acknowledge "the obvious persistence of intense segregation in many large cities" (Vigdor 2013).

To understand the importance of racial residential segregation as an issue of justice, one must be aware of both its historical roots and its consequences. The way in which residential segregation came about involved the systematic violation of the rights of African Americans, often actively abetted by federal, state, and local governments, as well as "private" actors such as realtors and banks. Residential segregation of African Americans in the United States is largely a twentieth-century phenomenon. In the Jim Crow South, blacks and whites lived quite interspersed with one another in close proximity. But with industrialization and urbanization, and particularly with the "great migration" of African Americans to northern cities in the first half of the twentieth century, large, overwhelmingly black neighborhoods were created for the first time. "The outlines and form of the modern black ghetto were in place in most northern cities by the outbreak of World War II" (Massey and Denton 1993, 42).

An important aspect of residential segregation is the "direct role that government played not only in maintaining the color line but in strengthening the walls of the ghetto" (Massey and Denton 1993, 42). With the advent of the New Deal in the 1930s, the federal government got into the business of promoting homeownership. Through the Home Owners Loan Corporation (HOLC) and later the Federal Housing Administration (FHA), the government offered very favorable terms for home mortgages—including thirty-year fully amortized mortgages with low down payments and fixed interest rates. The FHA favored new construction, which generally took place in the suburbs (Jackson 1985, 206–7). The underwriting manuals and other instruments make it clear that in this period the FHA had explicit policies against issuing loans in black neighborhoods or in racially mixed ones. In one infamous passage, the underwriting manual counseled: "If a neighborhood is to retain stability, it is necessary that properties shall continue to be occupied by the same social and racial class" (quoted in Jackson 1985, 208). Hence African Americans were denied equal access to these very favorable terms for buying homes and were largely consigned to living in rental property in the inner cities (see also Rothstein 2017).

A similar pattern was exhibited in the housing benefits under the GI Bill (Katznelson 2005, chap. 5). In exchange for their support for the bill, southern members of Congress insisted that the federal benefits available to returning veterans be administered by local boards. The result was that, particularly in the South, but elsewhere as well, black veterans faced discrimination at the hands of white-dominated boards that controlled the application process. Also, like the FHA, the VA favored racially segregated new housing in its loan guarantees, so black veterans were often excluded.

The Fair Housing Act of 1968 was intended to end racial discrimination in housing, but it could do little to reverse the segregation that had already been created, and its enforcement provisions were extremely weak (Massey and Denton 1993, 195–200). Not until it was amended in 1988 did the act have any real teeth, but by then, Massey and Denton write, it was "too late" to make much of a dent in segregation (1993, 211). Furthermore, the Fair Housing Act has not ended racial discrimination in the renting or selling of homes or in mortgage lending. There is ample evidence that racial discrimination continues to occur in these aspects of the housing market, as well as "steering" of minority home-seekers toward predominantly minority neighborhoods (Oh and Yinger 2015; National Community Reinvestment Coalition 2015). All of this contributes to the maintenance of residential segregation.

Hence it cannot plausibly be claimed, as Rockwell (1994, 57, 59) does, that racial segregation is a "natural pattern, a product of rational choice" or that for much of the twentieth century "people have legally been able to live where they wanted to, and that choice has been largely determined by economic considerations." Nor are residential patterns explained by African Americans' preferences. Most African Americans prefer to live in racially mixed neighborhoods, but their modal preference is for neighborhoods that are 50 percent black—far too high for most whites (Massey and Denton 1993, 89; see also Darden 2003, 330). As Thomas Schelling (1969) has shown, segregation, once established, is self-perpetuating, particularly if a significant portion of one population does not wish to live in close proximity to members of another group.

All of this shows that there was deep governmental complicity in creating the racial residential segregation that exists today. This complicity existed at all levels of government—local, state, and federal—and as a result a strong case can be made that compensatory measures are called for. That is, the housing policies of the federal government in particular, which failed to accord African Americans equal protection under the law, create a responsibility to repair the damage that has been done. The history briefly reviewed here can be part of the basis of a case for black reparations (McCarthy 2004; Kaplan and Valls 2007).

While the backward-looking case for compensation is supported by history, a strong forward-looking case for a policy response to residential segregation can be made simply on the basis of segregation's consequences. As William Julius Wilson (1980, 1987, 1996, 2009) and others have documented, racial residential segregation, especially when combined with other developments such as deindustrialization, has had devastating consequences for many African Americans. It has meant limited access to quality education, to employment opportunities, and to services. Residential segregation has created serious obstacles for many African Americans to avail themselves of the resources that are available to many other members of society. On any reasonable conception of fair equality of opportunity, segregation creates serious inequities.

The ways in which long-term residential segregation perpetuates racial inequality is demonstrated by Patrick Sharkey in his recent book *Stuck in Place: Urban Neighborhoods and the End of Progress toward Racial Equality* (2013). Sharkey's analysis of racial inequality and black disadvantage shows that there has been "virtually no improvement over time" (2013, 3). More important for our present purposes, Sharkey traces the lack of progress to the role of place: the persistence of racial inequality can largely be traced to the long-term effects of residential segregation. Even after residents move, the segregated character of their neighborhoods of origin exerts a baleful influence on their prospects for success. Hence, Sharkey argues,

"The story of racial inequality in the current generation must be thought of as a continuation of a story that extends well back in time . . . the story of neighborhoods and race in America is one of enduring, *inherited* inequality" (2013, 7, 9). Sharkey's analysis has important implications for our understanding of the relation between residential segregation, racial inequality, and claims of justice. It strengthens the contention that the history of racial segregation is essential for understanding present-day inequality, and it therefore bolsters claims for compensatory justice based on past governmental policies. But it also, as we will see, has important implications for policy proposals that focus on moving residents out of disadvantaged neighborhoods.

THE DECONCENTRATION STRATEGY

In light of the particularly harmful effects of geographically concentrated poverty, some scholars have advocated deconcentration of the poor as a strategy for addressing inequality. This strategy has been embraced by many who are particularly concerned with racial inequality and segregation. The solution to concentrated urban poverty, especially black urban poverty, is, according to its advocates, mobility—government policies that provide the means and the encouragement to relocate out of poor neighborhoods and into better-off ones. After Hurricane Katrina devastated New Orleans in 2005, for example, over two hundred scholars signed a petition urging the government to respond by dispersing New Orleans' poor black residents out of their former neighborhoods rather than permitting them to return (Imbroscio 2008). The idea was endorsed by David Brooks in the *New York Times* (2005). This deconcentration strategy has been enthusiastically promoted by normatively oriented scholars concerned about racial inequality as well. Most prominently, Owen Fiss and Elizabeth Anderson have advocated giving African Americans, in Fiss's words, "a way out" through housing vouchers and other mechanisms that allow them to escape the ghetto (2003). For Anderson, mobility programs are part and parcel of her overall strategy to integrate African Americans, which, as we saw in chapter 4, she sees as "an imperative of justice" (2010).

Advocates of deconcentration point to two programs as models, the Gautreaux program in Chicago and the Moving to Opportunity program, which provided relocation assistance to the urban poor in five US cities. These programs serve as an inspiration for deconcentration advocates, and scholars like Fiss and Anderson propose to "scale up" these programs to include many more participants in many cities. It is important, therefore, to consider these programs in some detail and to assess both the promise that they hold and their pitfalls and limitations.

The Gautreaux program was the result of a 1966 lawsuit charging the Chicago Housing Authority and the US Department of Housing and Urban Development with engaging in racial segregation in their decisions about where to site public housing. In 1976 the Supreme Court upheld a lower-court ruling, ordering racial integration in public housing across metropolitan Chicago. While the plaintiffs had originally sought the construction of public housing in suburban neighborhoods, the form that relief took was instead the provision of housing vouchers that would allow black families living in public housing to move to privately owned housing in more integrated settings throughout the Chicago area. Participants in the program were carefully screened and were counseled as they made their transitions to predominantly white areas. In this shift from the plaintiff's demand for integrated public housing to the remedy of vouchers for individuals, the Gautreaux program was transformed, according to Andrea Gill: "What began as an attempt to reshape metropolitan housing patterns through the construction of public housing in white suburbs . . . was transformed into a program to relocate select individuals to white communities where they would be racial pioneers and models of 'quality' tenants" (2012, 673). It therefore did not "remediate the racial wrongs" but merely "aid[ed] those who could best make the transition to private market housing" (Gill 2012, 673).

The Gautreaux program had generally positive results, but these often depended on the specific neighborhoods into which participants were placed. Research has found that black women who participated in the program and were placed in integrated neighborhoods with good resources spent less time on public assistance and had higher rates of employment (Mendenhall, DeLuca, and Duncan 2006). Children placed in predominantly white suburbs also benefited from the schools that they attended (Keels 2008a). Boys were less likely to be arrested for drug offenses, though girls were more likely (Keels 2008b). In the longer term, children who participated in the Gautreaux program tended to live in more integrated neighborhoods as adults (Keels 2008c).

Inspired by results like these, the federal government undertook a similar, but larger, program in the 1990s. The Moving to Opportunity (MTO) program provided vouchers to families that lived in high-poverty neighborhoods and were already receiving federal housing assistance. The vouchers were to be used to obtain housing in the private rental market in low-poverty neighborhoods. The program was implemented in five cities (Baltimore, Boston, Chicago, Los Angeles, and New York) and assigned volunteers randomly to one of three groups: the experimental group, which received vouchers to relocate to low-poverty neighborhoods and received counseling to assist their transition; another group that received vouchers with no restrictions on where they could be used and received no counseling; and a control group, which received no vouchers but remained eligible for project-based housing assistance and other benefits (Sanbonmatsu et al. 2011, xiv). The design of the program was intended to minimize selection bias among the participants and therefore to facilitate the study of the effects of the program on those who moved to low-poverty areas.

The results of the MTO program were somewhat more mixed than those of the Gautreaux program, but were still generally positive. Participants in the experimental group ended up living in higher-quality housing and felt safer in their neighborhoods. But they still mostly lived in predominantly minority neighborhoods, and the other indicators of well-being were mixed: the move had little effect on health, for example, and while girls generally did well, boys were in many respects less well off (Sanbonmatsu et al. 2011). Overall, there seems to have been little improvement in academic achievement of children in the program (Sanbonmatsu et al. 2006).

And there was little effect on adults' rate of employment, earnings, or dependence on public assistance (Briggs, Popkin, and Goering 2010, 202). Chetty, Hendren and Katz (2016) find that the program had benefits for young children who participated in the program, but that the effects on teenagers who moved were generally negative.

These mixed results are what one should expect. As Robert Sampson (2012, chap. 11) and Patrick Sharkey (2013) point out, the hope that a change in neighborhood would significantly alter the trajectory of program participants ignores, or at least underestimates, the long-term effects of the neighborhood of origin and other variables that are not affected by such a move. Sampson points out that the neighborhoods to which participants moved, while characterized by lower poverty than their area of origin, were still fairly high in poverty and still overwhelmingly segregated. "Segregation was barely nudged"; participants in Chicago ended up in "areas that were almost 90% black" (2012, 269). Furthermore, as Edward Goetz argues, though the design of the MTO program attempted to address the issue of selection bias, it still relied on volunteers, so there is reason to doubt the generalizability of even its modest results (2003, 76). As Sampson puts it, "MTO has distinct inferential limits" (2012, 283).

Despite these mixed findings and other limitations, and despite similarly mixed results from other mobility programs (Johnson 2012), the strategy of deconcentrating poverty, and poor African Americans in particular, has been held out as a promising route to ameliorating poverty and fostering racial integration. Arguments for such proposals tend to proceed in two steps: they put a positive spin on what are in fact mixed results of the Gautreaux and MTO programs (Imbroscio 2008, 120–21), and then they argue that similar, positive results could be expected from replicating such programs on a larger scale. Hence Own Fiss claims that the Gautreaux program "succeeded admirably" (2003, 41), arguably overstating the case and giving the false impression that overwhelming success is typical of mobility programs. Similarly, Elizabeth Anderson states that "the Gautreaux program dramatically improved the lives of participants who moved to integrated suburbs" (2010, 118), but does not emphasize that those who moved to such suburbs were a subset of the participants in the program. The effects of the program often depended crucially on the specific neighborhood to which participants moved. And while Anderson acknowledges the mixed outcomes of the MTO program, she concludes only that such programs are "not enough." They are not misguided or fundamentally flawed, just insufficient without greater help to participants in "develop[ing] more diverse social networks" after the move (2010, 120).

Scaling up mobility programs as a strategy to deconcentrate poverty and promote racial integration would face a number of practical obstacles. Fiss proposes a program involving three million families, and I focus for the moment on his proposal, because it is very specific. But the considerations adduced below would apply to any large-scale attempt to implement the deconcentration strategy.

One issue that threatens the viability of Fiss's proposal is the possibility that, once poor black residents start moving into a particular (and presumably predominantly white) middle- or upper-class neighborhood, the white residents will start moving out. William Julius Wilson has suggested that the success of mobility programs "is partly a function of [their] relatively small size. Since only a few families are relocated to other housing sites each year, they remain relatively invisible and do not present the threat of mass invasion" (1996, 200). Fiss is aware of this danger but says that the program he envisions "entails moving few enough ghetto residents into each middle- and upper-class neighborhood that the prior residents of those neighborhoods remain" (2003, 43). Yet Fiss offers no analysis to show how his proposal can both operate on the massive scale that he envisions and yet at the same time move small enough numbers of poor black residents into any particular white neighborhood so as not to threaten white flight. Given what we know about the low threshold of black in-migration that triggers white flight, the absence of such analysis is a serious flaw of his argument.

The other reason that small-scale programs might be more successful than a large-scale one has to do with the characteristics of the individuals and families that are likely to participate in the programs. As Goetz (2003, 242) suggests, "Voluntary dispersal efforts have a 'creaming' effect." The participants, as volunteers, are more likely to be those with the wherewithal to do well in their new environment. Accordingly, programs like MTO probably overstate the benefits that would accrue to participants in a more massive mobility policy. And at the same time, skimming off the better-prepared residents would likely leave those who remained in place worse off (Ford 2003).

Hence there are serious obstacles to scaling up an MTO-like program into a national policy. The modest results of MTO should not be over-sold. In particular, the small scale no doubt made the program at least somewhat politically palatable, allowed it to achieve the modestly positive results that it did, and may have helped avoid negative consequences like white flight. There is little reason to think that these results would neces-sarily be reproduced, let alone improved upon, if it were attempted on a more massive scale.

But these are mostly pragmatic and practical concerns. There are deeper, moral problems with the deconcentration strategy.

AGAINST DECONCENTRATION

Deconcentration strategies are deeply problematic on moral grounds for several reasons. First, deconcentration imposes serious costs on many individuals. While participants in the programs may live in better housing in safer neighborhoods and have better employment and edu-cational opportunities, these are not free. The price of obtaining them is to move, which is costly in itself, but also entails leaving behind, or at least attenuating, family and community ties. Furthermore, not all of the participants receive all of the promised benefits. Some of them do no better in terms of educational achievement and employment, and some end up in neighborhoods not much better than the ones that they left. Hence, the record of mobility programs does not guarantee that, even for the participants themselves, the benefits will outweigh the costs.

But what of the residents of poor, inner-city neighborhoods who do not qualify, or who for whatever reason do not participate in mobility programs? As mentioned above, these programs often engage in a certain amount of "creaming." That is, they tend to enroll those who are better pre-pared to meet the challenges of, and to take advantage of the opportunities of, the new neighborhoods to which they would move. This means that their neighborhoods of origin, and those who are left behind, are less well off. These neighborhoods are deprived of some of their residents who have the most ambition and are most capable of taking advantage of opportunities. Advocates of mobility programs often fail to consider the fate of urban residents who do not participate in the programs.

All of these costs, it could be argued, are permissible if they are ac-cepted voluntarily. This brings us to the second serious moral problem with mobility programs: they are sometimes defended as a matter of choice, offering more options, and any costs are therefore voluntarily accepted. Fiss, for example, states that "under my program the choice is vested where it belongs: in the individual family" (2003, 34). But as we have already seen, not all those who are affected by the programs are participants in them. Nonparticipants in the programs who live in the targeted neighborhoods and who remain there after program participants leave may be negatively affected.

But the deeper problem with framing these programs as voluntary is that doing so assumes that, because participants sign up for them, this choice is "free." As I argued in chapter 4, this position neglects the inher-ently coercive nature of the circumstances and the options being offered (see also Imbroscio 2004, 2008). Prospective participants are offered the choice between remaining in their disadvantaged current neighborhood and moving to a neighborhood that is less poor and that often has better schools and more job opportunities. Given this choice, it is not surprising that many volunteer. But this set of options is inherently coercive and unjustly so.

Fiss at least tries to portray mobility programs as voluntary. Anderson does not place much emphasis on this and argues that African Americans must avoid "pervasive self-segregation" and must go through the dis-comfort and stress of integration (2010, 182–83). As we saw in chapter 4, Anderson maintains that African Americans have a duty to integrate, and this duty would seem to extend to their choice of residence. I suggest, to the contrary, that African Americans are under no such duty, particularly since the promised benefits may be quite uncertain and remote (for similar arguments, see Shelby 2016, chap. 2).

The record of involuntary relocation of inner-city black residents in the United States is very ugly. Often done in the name of "urban renewal" or "slum clearance" or of deconcentrating poverty through the destruction of public housing, these efforts involve the breaking up of established communities and social networks, a very serious cost to those affected. It is for this reason that "urban renewal" is often referred to, among African Americans, as "negro removal" (Goetz 2013, 121). Reflecting on this history, Susan Fainstein argues that "households or businesses should not be involuntarily relocated for the purpose of obtaining economic development or community balance" (2010, 172). As I have argued, we should interpret "involuntarily" broadly, to include not only policies that force people to move, but also those that offer moving as a "choice," when the alternatives are so skewed that the decision to move cannot plausibly be seen as voluntary. Fiss, Anderson, and the whole "dispersal consensus" (Imbroscio 2008) place themselves in a long and problematic tradition in American urban policy.

The third and final problem with deconcentration that I wish to focus on concerns its implications for democratic citizenship and political power. Both Fiss and Anderson acknowledge that dispersal of African American urban residents threatens their political power by undermining the geographic concentration that enables them to elect representatives through majority-minority districts. But they both also argue that this threat is worth the potential benefits. "We may simply have to run the risk of altering established and all too familiar patterns of political representation," Fiss (2003, 33) says. Similarly, Anderson argues that "recent shifts in the willingness of whites to vote for black candidates suggest that the time has come to foster interracial coalition politics more broadly. This would involve shifting the principle for districting away from the majority-minority formula to one that favors coalitional districts" (2010, 133). Both Fiss and Anderson, then, are willing to countenance the threat to black representation posed by residential deconcentration.

For Anderson, though, there is a deeper democratic imperative behind deconcentration. She argues that deconcentration is necessary for the creation of a national identity shared by blacks, whites, and other racial and ethnic groups. Integration, she argues, is necessary for democratic citizenship (2010, chap. 5). Yet Anderson arguably overstates the extent to which a shared identity is necessary for democratic politics and underestimates the extent to which democratic citizenship may be enhanced by racial residential clustering. Robert Putnam (2007), for example, reports that more diverse neighborhoods tend to exhibit lower levels of social trust and solidarity, and less social capital (see also Oliver 2010). This, in turn, may undermine rather than enhance democratic participation. In any case, advocates of deconcentration do not take seriously enough the extent to which it poses a threat to black political representation and power. While geographic representation is problematic in many ways, as long as we are stuck with it geographic concentration serves to enhance the representation of distinct communities of interest.

As others have pointed out (see Williamson 2010, 116; Stanley 2014), Iris Young offers an alternative account of the injustice of residential segregation and of what justice requires as a remedy. Young recognizes the injustice of residential segregation, yet she resists the position that racial or ethnic clustering of residences is in itself bad or wrong and offers a sustained and multipronged critique of the ideal of integration that underlies deconcentration strategies. Young argues that integration plans "tend to leave the dominant group relatively undisturbed while requiring significant changes from members of excluded groups." Integration also "rejects the validity of people's desire to live and associate with others for whom they feel particular affinity." Integrationist programs also are often met with resistance and failure, and when they fail, the blame is placed on members of the disadvantaged group. If a plan fails, "Blame [is placed on] the subordinate group members who cannot or will not integrate" on the terms offered. Finally, Young argues, the ideal of integration focuses on the "wrong issue," on the residential clustering itself rather than on the disadvantages that contingently flow from it (2000, 216–18).

As a counterpoint to the integrationist ideal, Young offers what she calls the ideal of differentiated solidarity. This ideal accepts, indeed it embraces, the common phenomenon of racial and ethnic residential clustering, and it accepts the tendencies and preferences that may partly cause this. Young's position is that segregation or "clustering" is not necessarily unjust or bad, but only contingently so. Though the process that created black neighborhoods entailed many wrongs, these neighborhoods and the communities and institutions in them have come to be valued by many of their residents. Maintaining existing communities, and devoting resources to improving them, should be an option open to residents. Differentiated solidarity recognizes, in effect, the legitimacy of the claim to have the kinds of choices that deconcentration advocates reject.

LIBERTY, EQUALITY, AND SEGREGATION

Anderson and Fiss portray deconcentration as an imperative of justice. Only this strategy, they argue, can overcome the ills of racial residential segregation and combat its role in perpetuating racial inequality. Yet, as I noted in chapter 4, there is some ambiguity about how to interpret this claim. It could be that it simply reflects their diagnosis of what is likely to be effective in achieving racial equality. In this case, deconcentration would be an imperative of justice only because a large number of contingent facts limit other possibilities and enhance the prospects of deconcentration as the best strategy. If this is the claim, then their respective discussions of the social science literature on segregation and inequality make sense: a thorough review of the empirical questions involved is essential to arriving at the recommendation of deconcentration. But both Fiss and Anderson seem to be claiming more than this: it is not just that deconcentration is the most promising strategy, but that it is (at least partly) constitutive of justice. For both, justice requires the deconcentration and integration of African Americans, not because this is contingently necessary to achieve racial equality, but because residential concentration by its very nature violates the requirements of a racially just society. In the end, it may be their commitment to racial integration as a conception of racial justice, rather than their reading of the social-scientific literature, that underwrites Fiss's and Anderson's stronger claims about the connection between deconcentration and justice.

This is the vision of racial justice against which I have argued in chapter 4 and throughout this book. Racial segregation as it presently exists is an injustice, I have argued, for two specific reasons: it was brought about through systematic injustice, and it plays a central role in perpetuating ongoing injustice. But addressing the legacies of past discrimination and combating segregation's ongoing role in maintaining racial inequality do not necessarily require deconcentration. It may be possible to pursue racial justice through other strategies, and indeed there are good reasons, grounded on justice, not to pursue racial justice through a single-minded focus on integration.

These reasons are the ones I attempted to elucidate in chapter 4, and it is worthwhile to recall them now and apply them to the specific context of residential segregation. There are two sets of considerations that argue against integration as the sole route to racial equality, one pertaining to considerations of equality, and the other to liberty. The equality considerations are these: As Iris Young points out, integration, and residential deconcentration specifically, imposes high costs on its intended beneficiaries, and does not impose similar costs on others—in particular whites, who as a whole have benefited materially from the injustices perpetrated upon African Americans. These costs include the loss of community and social ties, the undermining of black institutions, and severe dislocation. These are serious costs indeed. Whites, on the other hand, are asked to make few changes, beyond "tolerating" a few African Americans in their midst. Hence deconcentration imposes its heaviest costs on those who have already paid much for the injustice imposed on them, while asking little or nothing of those who have benefited from residential segregation. This can hardly be an equitable way to distribute costs and benefits between victims and beneficiaries of injustice.

The even weightier considerations, however, are those related to liberty. Deconcentration is highly coercive. No one leaves his or her home, neighborhood, or community lightly. Certainly, the involuntary removal of African Americans, as often takes place under the heading of "urban renewal," is plainly coercive. But even "voluntary" mobility programs are coercive in terms of the alternatives that they offer: stay in your very disadvantaged neighborhood or take a voucher to move to a more promising neighborhood with better schools and better employment prospects. It is not surprising that many would choose the latter, but this does not mean that the programs are not coercive. The very nature of the options that they offer creates a coercive condition.

The alternative, I have suggested, is not to focus on a particular end-state of the spatial distribution of residences, whether an integrated one or a clustered one. Rather, the focus should be on the conditions under which individuals make their choices about where to live. These conditions should uphold the liberal values of liberty and equality. That is, the choices African Americans make about where to live should not be associated with heavy costs that others do not face. And they should be genuine choices, not ones driven by dramatically disparate options. The imperative of justice in the context of residential segregation is not integration, but securing fair conditions under which African Americans, and all others, can make choices about place of residence consistent with their equality and liberty.

What does this mean in practice? This view requires that the neighborhoods where poor, inner-city African Americans now live must be the target of substantial funds so that they are no longer sites of concentrated disadvantage. This takes us back to the idea of a "domestic Marshall Plan" advocated by some civil rights leaders decades ago. At that time, the main argument was compensatory: the idea was to compensate for the disadvantages that had accumulated in black communities over the many generations of Jim Crow. But the rationale is also forward looking: to achieve justice now and in the future, the neighborhoods, schools, and other institutions to which African Americans are attached must not be sites of disadvantage. They must be comparable to their predominantly white counterparts in terms of their resources and the opportunities that they create for those who participate in them.

This redistribution of resources is a requirement of justice for several reasons. I have already mentioned two: it is justified on compensatory grounds and on grounds of forward-looking equity and fairness. But there is another reason, related to the coercive nature of deconcentration. The implication of the observation about the coercive nature of the options offered by "voluntary" mobility programs is this: a necessary condition for such programs to be considered voluntary is that the choice of remaining in place is not much more costly than taking the voucher. Mobility programs, if they are to be pursued, must be accompanied by efforts to improve the neighborhoods that they target—and, indeed, all poor neighborhoods.

This conclusion converges with the recommendations of Patrick Sharkey, who points out that, while we have much evidence about the impact of mobility programs, there is no comparable body of evidence about the results of improving urban neighborhoods—in part because there has been no comparable effort to do so (2013, 151). Sharkey considers mobility programs and the difficulties of attempting to implement them on a wider scale and concludes: "On the basis of the evidence available on the likely impact of large-scale residential mobility, and given the political realities of urban America, it is time to discard the idea that moving large numbers of families out of the ghetto can be a primary solution to concentrated poverty" (2013, 175). Enhancing mobility may very well be an important part of pursuing racial equality, but it must be a subordinate part, with the greater emphasis on improving the lives of urban residents where they already live.

The conception of racial justice of which this prescription is a part is agnostic about what should be the ultimate spatial distribution of residences along racial lines. It may be that, over time, African American residents will choose to move to more integrated neighborhoods. Or it may be that, under improved conditions, many will choose to remain where they are, or move to other predominantly black neighborhoods. The view I have sketched takes no position on what the right mix is, or the degree of racial clustering that is desirable. It focuses instead on the conditions under which individuals make the choices that result in whatever the overall pattern turns out to be. As long as these individual choices are made under fair conditions, conditions that support the liberty and equality of those making them, the resulting pattern is compatible with justice.

The preceding argument is not meant to suggest that all strategies of deconcentrating poverty and decreasing racial residential segregation are equally objectionable. On the contrary, the history of public housing in dense inner cities, away from more affluent parts of the city and its suburbs, should dispel any idealized picture of overwhelmingly poor and black neighborhoods. When poverty is concentrated its effects are exacerbated, so mixed-income housing, and placing new public housing in more affluent areas, may be one way to advance racial equality. The objections I have made to deconcentration policies apply mainly to policies that are highly coercive in terms of the set of options that they offer, that impose serious costs on their intended beneficiaries, and that neglect the value and importance of predominantly black institutions and communities. Policies that aim to provide more housing options to the urban poor but that do not do these things may very well be a desirable part of an overall approach to addressing the injustices associated with, and reproduced by, racial residential segregation.

CONCLUSION

The focus in this chapter has been on state policies that attempt to move poor black city residents without also improving the neighborhoods where they already live. Hence I have not argued against housing vouchers per se, but rather against their use to the exclusion of additional policy measures. Indeed, a strong case can be made for a significant expansion of the use of housing vouchers, as Matthew Desmond argues in his book *Evicted* (2016, 308–13). There is also a strong case for expanding the housing alternatives available to African Americans through more vigorous enforcement of antidiscrimination laws in the sale and renting of houses and in mortgage lending. In short, policy should expand the number of good housing options available to all urban residents. Public policy should not focus on moving urban residents out of impoverished neighborhoods, offering no other options and doing nothing for those left behind.

Often, one of the consequences of improving impoverished neighborhoods is gentrification, and gentrification can create its own coercive pressures that essentially force urban residents to move. This pressure comes not solely from the state but from market mechanisms that raise rents, taxes, and other costs. Longtime residents and businesses frequently cannot afford these higher prices and therefore move to other, often poor, neighborhoods. Gentrification involves not only the displacement of individuals, but also a change in the character of a neighborhood, with black residents and black-owned businesses being replaced by white residents with more money and the businesses that cater to their budgets and tastes. This process has been taking place in my own city of Portland, Oregon (see Hern 2016; *Priced Out* 2017) and in many other cities across the country.

Any view that places value on individuals' ability to continue to live in communities where they have strong ties of affinity must confront the threats to those communities posed not just by state efforts to break them up but also by market pressures that do essentially the same thing. An implication of the view developed here, then, is that public policies that combat and constrain the effects of market transactions may be necessarily to address gentrification. There are strong parallels between policies that do this, such as limits on the rate at which rents may rise, and other restrictions on market transactions. It is widely recognized that structural features of some markets threaten the conditions necessary for voluntary transactions, as in the case of monopolies or the disparity in bargaining power held by large corporations on the one hand and individual workers on the other. Liberal egalitarianism is committed to policies and institutions that maintain conditions in which individuals do not face undue coercive pressures in the market, such as by adopting redistributive policies, wage policies, protection of collective bargaining rights, and so on. So too do we need policies to address the coercive pressures exerted by the market that threaten the stability of communities and the individual lives lived within them. In addition, housing subsidies and policies that require developers to provide affordable housing alongside market-rate housing may also allow neighborhoods to continue to be accessible to poorer residents.

A liberal view must strike a balance. From the perspective that I have sketched here, the goals of policy in this area should include both the protection of black institutions and communities from destruction by external forces, and also the freedom of individuals to choose where they live and with whom they associate. This does pose a challenge: how do we protect the character of black neighborhoods while also protecting the freedom of their residents to move out and the freedom of others to move in? There is an irresolvable tension in any view that values both individual autonomy and also communities of affinity. Public policy cannot preserve the character of communities indefinitely, but it can slow the pace of change and protect residents from some of the effects of that change.

7

Racial Justice and Criminal Justice

The criminal justice system in the United States ensnares a very large portion of the population. Over two million people are behind bars and about another four million are on probation or parole (National Research Council 2014, 33, 40). Vulnerability to imprisonment is not evenly distributed across the population. Entanglement with the criminal justice system is strongly (and negatively) correlated with socioeconomic status and educational attainment (Western 2006, 111). It is also strongly correlated with race: 40 percent of those behind bars are African Americans, making the ratio of black to white incarceration rates eight to one (Western 2007, 514; Husak 2008, 4).

These numbers are anomalous both historically and cross-nationally. In the five decades ending in the mid-1970s, the incarceration rate in the United States was fairly low and stable, at about one in a thousand, but in the four decades that followed incarceration grew rapidly to five times that rate. Compared to other democracies, the criminal justice system in the United States stands out. Sentences are longer, and the overall rate of incarceration much higher, than in other Western democracies (and indeed all other countries) (Clear and Frost 2014, chap. 1; Pettit 2012, 9–18; Tonry 2007, 353; Western 2007, 510–11; National Research Council 2014, 34–43). No other country locks up its own citizens at nearly the same rate as the United States.

By any standard, the American criminal justice system is unjust—to a great many people, but particularly to African Americans. As Douglas Husak (2008) has argued, it locks up too many people for too long, and often for offenses that either should not be criminalized at all or should be treated as minor infractions. As Christopher Wellman (2017) puts it, "No one defends the status quo." Yet while it is true that few would defend the overall system and patterns of punishment that presently prevail, many of the specific practices that contribute to these patterns do have their defenders. Racial profiling certainly does have defenders, as do capital punishment and life sentences without the possibility of parole—despite strong arguments that these practices are necessarily unjust, and despite the racial patterns in how they are applied. So while many observers— politicians as well as scholars, across partisan, ideological, and theoretical lines—deplore the current state of affairs, there is genuine disagreement over the propriety and justice of the individual factors that produce the overall patterns in the criminal justice system.

The prospects for criminal justice reform are enormously consequential to the prospects for racial justice overall. The ways in which police, prosecutors, judges and juries, prisons, and parole boards do their jobs affects not only the treatment of the individuals subject to their decisions. The massive presence of African American men in the criminal justice system also has profound implications for their families and communities, as well as for their own life prospects once they are out of that system. The overrepresentation of African Americans in the criminal justice system contributes mightily to the overall disadvantages under which black communities labor, so it is an essential factor in the maintenance of racial inequality. No adequate conception of racial justice, then, can ignore the issues raised by current patterns of crime and punishment or can fail to address the question of what justice demands in relation to these facts.

CRIMINAL JUSTICE AND LIBERAL THEORY

One of the primary purposes of the state is to protect people from harm by others. The way that the state has come to fulfill this function is to (among other things) criminalize certain behaviors and punish individuals who engage in them. From a classical liberal point of view, the state takes over the function of punishment from individuals who would otherwise have to do it for themselves. It is preferable to have an institutionalized third party play this role, rather than have victims, or posses or vigilantes, impose punishment. The state announces ahead of time, through its laws, what actions it will punish and how severely, and it establishes procedures for determining guilt or innocence in particular cases. All of this should diminish the biases and uncertainties that would be involved in having victims or their partisans determining guilt and punishment.

For liberals, however, punishment would seem to be somewhat problematic. For one thing, punishment often involves the severe limitation of liberty—a core liberal value. Indeed, liberty is so fundamental for some liberals that it raises the question of whether its severe restriction by punishments like incarceration can ever be justified at all. Rawls's answer is that punishment is grounded on the value of liberty itself. He reasons that if social cooperation is to be possible, some reassurance that others will abide by its terms is necessary. Punishment serves this purpose and therefore plays a role in fostering the scheme of social cooperation that is itself necessary for liberty (1999, 211–12).

Yet, as Nathan Hanna (2009) points out, it is one thing to say that social cooperation requires some (threat of) coercion, but it is another to say that it requires punishment. Punishment is a particular kind of coercion. It is the purposeful infliction of suffering that is accompanied by the denunciation or condemnation of the act that is punished—or what Douglas Husak (2008, 92) calls "hard treatment and censure." It is therefore to be distinguished from mere penalties, which can serve to deter certain kinds of actions, but which can also be seen as a mere tax on them rather than entailing condemnation. There is a difference in the message that the state sends when it issues a parking or speeding ticket and when it imprisons someone convicted of rape or murder (Feinberg 1970).

Because punishment involves state condemnation, and not just coercion, there are other grounds on which to argue that a truly liberal state may not punish. Punishment is often thought to condemn not only the criminal act but also the person who perpetrates it. In punishing, the liberal state risks going beyond its public functions by judging the character of individuals. That is, it risks violating its neutrality or impartiality with respect to what constitutes the appropriate moral character for members of society. Rather than merely upholding justice, it engages in moral judgments that should be private and that inevitably go beyond justice and into the realm of comprehensive conceptions of the good. Hence, some argue, the liberal state may not punish, at least not in a manner consistent with a prevalent understanding of what punishment is (see Brubaker 1988; Hanna 2009).

Most theorists reject these arguments, however, and affirm that the liberal state may punish—but they acknowledge that liberal principles limit what may be criminalized, and what form punishment may take (Duff 2001). Liberalism requires the rejection of "legal moralism," the idea that the law may prohibit and punish an act just because the state, or a portion of the population, judges it to be immoral or vicious. The state may not criminalize and punish for perfectionist reasons, but only for reasons related to harm to others (Matravers 2013; Feinberg 1987). Though punishment involves coercion that would be impermissible in the absence of a criminal act, the right not to be punished is forfeited, or overridden, or justly infringed in cases where one is guilty of an act that is properly criminalized (Bennett 2006; Husak 2008; Wellman 2012, 2017).

The liberal-democratic character of a political regime arguably imposes other, broader constraints on punishment. The fact that prospective convicts are our fellow citizens (as well as our fellow human beings) means that the acts punished and how they are punished must be justifiable even to those on the receiving end of punishment (Brettschneider 2007). This means that the system of punishment must take the interests of the convicted themselves into account, and should generally be characterized by reluctance to punish and by lenience in the severity of punishment (Kateb 2007). Punishment should never "treat the criminal as irredeemable" (Kateb 2007, 280), and it must not harm his or her future capacities for agency and citizenship (Jacobs 2013, 2014).

RACE AND MASS INCARCERATION

There are many things that are disturbing about the American criminal justice system, but two of them are the sheer number of people in prison and the racial disparities in the prison population. These two concerns are certainly related, as we will see, but they are also distinct. That is, even if there were no racial disparities in who gets locked up, mass incarceration would still be deeply troubling. And if American incarceration rates were more in line with historical and international norms, but exhibited significant racial disparities, then here too we would have reason to be concerned. Despite being analytically distinct, mass incarceration and the racial disparities that it manifests are difficult to disentangle in practice. In myriad ways, race and mass incarceration are intertwined, though exactly how is sometimes a matter of debate.

In her book *The New Jim Crow* (2012), Michelle Alexander argues that mass incarceration is largely driven by race. In her account, the tough sentencing laws that were passed in the 1970s and 1980s were motivated by racial animus, as a way to re-establish racial caste after the civil rights movement (2012, chap. 1). Alexander argues that the war on drugs is largely responsible for mass incarceration, and the way that that war has been waged is largely responsible for the racial disparities in incarceration rates (2012, chap. 2). She highlights the racial biases at each stage of the criminal justice system, arguing that the use of discretion—by police, prosecutors, and others—produces systematic racial disparities in incarceration (2012, chap. 3). Finally, Alexander focuses on the similarities between ways in which a criminal record operates and the way race worked under Jim Crow. Many forms of discrimination that were legal on the basis of race under Jim Crow are now legal on the basis of a criminal record. Hence having a criminal record now operates much as race once did, as a proxy that permits discrimination in housing, employment, and other areas (2012, chap. 4).

Alexander's analysis has come under considerable scrutiny by other scholars. Prominent among them is John Pfaff (2017), who argues that many of the factual premises of Alexander's argument do not hold up.

Pfaff focuses on Alexander's emphasis on the war on drugs as the primary driver of mass incarceration. While it is true that drug offenders constitute a high proportion of prisoners in federal prisons, the vast majority of prisoners in the United States are in state prisons, where nonviolent drug offenders are only about 20 percent of the population (2017, 31–35). Releasing all nonviolent drug offenders would free some two hundred thousand inmates but would certainly not end mass incarceration. Most prisoners are serving time for property crimes or violent crimes, a fact that Alexander does not adequately account for, Pfaff argues. Furthermore, the war on drugs cannot account for the racial disparities in incarceration because "there simply aren't enough drug offenders in prison to have much of an impact" (2017, 46).

Scholars have also argued that Alexander's historical account of the rise in incarceration is flawed because she downplays the fact that there was a significant spike in crime rates in the 1960s and 1970s. This point has been made forcefully by James Forman Jr. (2012), who argues that this rise in crime may help explain both the rise in incarceration rates and the public's support for harsher criminal penalties. Forman emphasizes that even among African Americans there is significant support for tough-on-crime measures—not quite as high as among whites, but still a majority (2017, 9). This is in part because while a disproportionate number of offenders caught up in the criminal justice system are African American, the victims of crime are also disproportionately African American. Forman examines the case of Washington, DC, "the nation's only majority-black jurisdiction that controls sentencing policy" (2012, 117), and finds that its incarceration rate and racial disparities do not differ markedly from the rest of the country. The complex politics around crime policy within the African American community, Forman argues, undermine the notion that mass incarceration is the new Jim Crow.

Finally, Marie Gottschalk (2015, chap. 6) echoes and elaborates some of these criticisms. Gottschalk argues that the role of race in sentencing disparities is "grossly overstated, especially for serious and violent crimes" (2015, 123) and that African Americans "disproportionately commit the types of crimes that usually draw a long prison sentence" (2015, 125).

While Gottschalk acknowledges that "Drug cases present the most compelling evidence of the disparate treatment of blacks in the criminal justice system," (2015, 126), she also suggests that "the racial gap in the war on drugs is narrowing" (2015, 128). Hence, like Pfaff, Gottschalk argues that the war on drugs cannot explain racial disparities in incarceration.

Yet as one astute observer puts it, "When Alexander calls our criminal-justice system 'the new Jim Crow,' she is drawing an imperfect parallel that tells us more about what this system does than about why it exists" (Sanneh 2015). What the system does is to help perpetuate racial inequality and sanction discrimination against ex-prisoners, who are disproportionately black. While Alexander may be wrong about some of the historical and explanatory claims that she makes, she is surely right about the devastating consequences of mass incarceration—particularly for African Americans. These consequences and their racial disparities should trouble us, even if some of the particulars of Alexander's argument do not stand up to scrutiny.

I suggest that we should be concerned about racial disparities in the criminal justice system for at least three reasons. First, these disparities reflect racial inequality in the society at large. That is, even if there were no racial discrimination within the criminal justice system, we would still expect to see racial disparities in crime and punishment simply because African Americans are overrepresented among those who are exposed to conditions that foster crime (Krivo and Peterson 1996). "For reasons of social disadvantage, neighborhood residence, and limited life chances that disproportionately affect them, blacks relative to whites have been more involved in violent crime and are more frequently arrested for such crimes" (National Research Council 2014, 96). Hence, racial disparities within the criminal justice system reflect, and provide additional reason to be concerned about, racial inequality more generally.

Second, racial disparities in the criminal justice system may also provide evidence of discrimination within the system itself. If African Americans are being treated unfairly by that system, marked out for particularly bad or harsh treatment, then that is a serious injustice. As we will see, there is some debate among scholars about the precise role of racial bias within the criminal justice system in producing racial disparities in incarceration rates, but it is clear that it does play some role. Regardless of the relative importance of rates of offending and racial bias within the system in explaining the overall racial disparities in incarceration rates, then, we should find these disparities deeply troubling. These disparities either reflect unjust social conditions or they reflect different treatment by the criminal justice system—or, most likely, both.

Third, as I will try to show in the last section of this chapter, incarceration plays a large role in perpetuating racial inequality. Being in prison has serious consequences not only for those imprisoned, but for their families and communities. Upon release, there are significant barriers to re-entry into society, and to finding housing and employment. Given the racial disparities in the criminal justice system, these costs fall disproportionately on African American individuals and communities. Even if it is unhelpful to think of mass incarceration as the new Jim Crow, then, there is good reason to be concerned about both mass incarceration and the racial disparities that characterize it.

RACIAL BIAS AND RACIAL PROFILING

We have already seen that there is some debate about what explains the racial disparities in incarceration rates. The two obvious candidates are differences in rates of offending and differences in how African Americans and whites are treated by the criminal justice system. In the case of drug crimes, the evidence suggests that it is differences within the criminal justice system that explain much of racial disparity. While African Americans are no more likely than whites to buy, sell, or use drugs, they are much more likely to be arrested and sentenced to prison for these offenses (Tonry 2011, chap. 3; National Research Council 2014, 97; Pfaff 2017, 48). The racial disparities among those serving time for drug offenses reflect police practices more than they do disparities among groups in activities that may lead to arrest. As Michael Tonry suggests, it may simply be easier to catch black drug dealers than white ones because the former are more likely to deal drugs in more public places. "Police can arrest inner-city street-level drug dealers almost at will, meaning that arrests are more a measure of police activity than of criminality" (2011, 40). In the case of violent crime, African Americans may commit these offenses at higher rates than whites, but the rate of black violent crime has been going down, both in absolute terms and relative to the white violent crime rate—and yet the racial disparities among those serving time for these offenses have not diminished as much (National Research Council 2014, 59–60).

One classic analysis found that racial disparities in imprisonment for most types of crime can be explained by reference to racial disparities in arrests rather than by racial bias in the criminal justice system post-arrest (Blumstein 1982). However, Michael Tonry (2011, chap. 2), using more recent data and different indicators for bias, finds a greater role for racial bias in explaining racial disparities in incarceration rates. Tonry also argues that while the data do not show significant racial differences in sentencing, African Americans are more likely to be arrested and convicted for crimes that carry long sentences (2011, 49).

In sorting all of this out we are limited by the available data, and sometimes, even with the same data, scholars disagree how about to interpret the results. As the authoritative report by the National Research Council states, "Disentangling in detail the respective roles of [offending patterns and case processing] is difficult" (2014, 94). The report states that "racial disparities in imprisonment have worsened substantially over time since the early 1990s relative to patterns of involvement in serious crimes" (2014, 94). The cause of this is "straightforward: severe sentencing laws enacted in the 1980s and 1990s greatly increased the lengths of prison sentences mandated for violent crimes and drug offenses for which blacks are disproportionately often arrested" (2014, 96). After arrest, racial bias also contributes to the disparities in incarceration. These disparities "result partly from small but systematic racial differences in case processing, from arrest through parole release, that have a substantial cumulative effect" (2014, 103).

Some of the racial bias that contributes to disparate treatment by the criminal justice system may be unconscious. But some practices that use race to the detriment of African Americans are not unconscious at all—they are a matter of policy, and they have their defenders among policymakers and scholars. There is overwhelming evidence that police use race in determining whom to subject to stops, a practice known as racial profiling. Racial profiling does much to perpetuate mistrust between police and African Americans, and it means that many African Americans are often subjected to unfounded police harassment.

Comprehensive data on the extent of racial profiling does not exist, but some cases are well documented. Two of these are the use of "stop and frisk" in New York City and the use of race in determining whom to stop along the Interstate 95 corridor in Maryland. In the former case, the New York Police Department made 4.4 million stops from 2004 to 2012, and more than half of these were stops of African Americans, who constitute only 23 percent of the New York population (*Floyd v. City of New York* 2013). In the case of Maryland highway stops, the Maryland State Police routinely stop cars on I-95 because it is a primary route for drug trafficking. Under a court order, troopers recorded data on every stop that resulted in a vehicle search, and these data were analyzed by Gross and Barnes (2002). From 1995 to 2000, state troopers engaged in over eight thousand searches, about 60 percent of which were of cars driven by African Americans. Gross and Barnes conclude that African Americans were about twice as likely to be stopped and more than five times as likely to be searched as whites (2002, 666; see also Epp, Maynard-Moody, and Haider-Markel 2014).

In the academic literature on racial profiling two issues predominate: is racial profiling effective, and is it justified? For racial profiling to be effective—or "rational"—it would have to achieve some goal more efficiently than some other (any other?) method. Many analyses of racial profiling assume that the goal is maximizing the number of arrests, but as Bernard Harcourt (2007, 123) points out, it is unclear why this should be the goal of any police practice. Surely, he suggests, the goal of police work should be to minimize the social costs of crime, not maximize arrests. Maximizing arrests may not decrease overall crime rates or the social costs of crime. Yet even if we accept maximizing arrests as the goal of searches, the evidence does not support profiling. If racial profiling were efficient, the "hit rate" (the rate at which contraband is found) among African Americans and other targeted groups would be as high or higher than among nontargeted groups. Yet most analyses of hit rates show the opposite: the hit rate among whites is often higher than that for African Americans (Gross and Barnes 2002, 668; Harcourt 2007, chap. 4; LaFraniere and Lehren 2015).

Racial profiling has other negative consequences. While it may or may not deter crime among targeted groups, it decreases deterrence for nontargeted groups and may therefore actually increase the overall crime rate (Harcourt 2007, chap. 4; Glaser 2015, chap. 5). It is difficult to sort out all of these effects, but the bottom line is that the case for the effectiveness of racial profiling is very weak.

Even if racial profiling were "rational," it would not be justified. After all, racial profiling involves police officers stopping people who are walking down the street or driving down the road, usually with no reasonable suspicion that they have done anything illegal. This can be done on the thinnest of pretexts or with no pretext at all. Officers may ask those being questioned to "consent" to being searched, without informing them that they may refuse (Cole 1999, chap. 1).

It is surprising that the courts have allowed this. The Fourth Amendment to the US Constitution prohibits "unreasonable searches," which the courts have interpreted to mean searches conducted without "probable cause"—that is, a reason to believe that a crime has been committed. The Supreme Court has held that police officers may stop people based on something less than probable cause, applying a weaker standard of "reasonable suspicion." This turns out to be a very open-ended standard, providing no protection against being stopped and questioned by police for no reason. The practice of pretextual stops and "consensual" searches arguably violates the presumption of innocence (DeAngelis 2014), and, as some judges have found, many such stops violate the Constitution's protection against government intrusion (*Floyd v. New York* 2013). Most fundamentally, it violates what Louis Brandeis called "the right to be let alone" (Warren and Brandeis 1890), surely a fundamental value for a liberal society.

All of this would be morally and legally objectionable even if it were not conducted in a racially discriminatory way, but the use of race makes it all the more problematic. Many African Americans report being stopped repeatedly, whether walking down the street or driving down the road— "driving while black," as the well-known phrase has it. Racial profiling countenances a society in which a racially marked group, already disadvantaged in many ways, is subjected to the further humiliation of repeated scrutiny by law enforcement. It is simply not plausible to suggest, as some defenders of racial profiling have, that the practice does not contribute to the oppression of minority groups (see Risse and Zeckhauser 2004; Boonin 2011). Rather, as Supreme Court Justice Sonia Sotomayor has recently written in a passionate dissent, racial profiling treats members of targeted groups as "second-class citizens. . . . It implies that you are not a citizen of a democracy but the subject of a carceral state" (*Utah v. Strieff* 2016).

The bottom line is that racial profiling involves a practice that should be highly suspect in a liberal society that values protection from government intrusion. And the use of race to target some people for scrutiny exacerbates and reproduces the harms and indignities of racial injustice. Racial profiling contributes to racial disparities in arrest and conviction rates and thereby helps to create the very facts that are then used to justify the practice, creating a "self-fulfilling prophesy" (Glaser 2015, 10). It "oversamples" the targeted group, leading to the overrepresentation of that group among the incarcerated. "This disproportion produces a distortive effect on our carceral populations and has a tendency to perpetuate itself," thereby reinforcing the association of blackness with criminality (Harcourt 2007, 149). Crucially, this overrepresentation results from racial profiling whether or not the initial justification of profiling holds true. That is, whether or not African Americans commit certain crimes at higher rates, racial profiling leads to an overrepresentation of African Americans among those who are found to have committed crimes. The practice should be abandoned.

SENTENCING

One of the perennial debates among theorists of punishment takes place around the question of what the appropriate end, or goal, of punishment is. The main contenders are that punishment serves as retribution for crime; that it deters future crime; that it incapacitates the criminal; and that it rehabilitates him or her. Engaging this debate would take us too far afield here, but there is broad consensus, compatible with all of these views, that punishment should be limited in its severity and in the form that it takes. Punishment should be proportional to the crime and to the individual's degree of culpability, and it should be parsimonious— that is, as lenient as possible while still performing its function (National Research Council 2014, 324–27). While it is difficult, if not impossible, to make these broad principles determinate (see von Hirsh and Ashworth 2005), we can use historical and cross-national comparisons to arrive at reasonable inferences about what constitutes just punishment. The fact that the United States uses much more severe punishments than it used to, and much more severe punishments than nearly all other countries, strongly suggests that punishment in the United States is neither proportional nor parsimonious.

Most thoughtful observers agree that the punishments meted out by the American criminal justice system are too severe. As discussed above, the current state of mass incarceration is due in part to changes in criminal laws in the direction of increased severity of punishment. Many states and the federal government have enacted laws such as stiff mandatory minimum sentences, three-strikes laws, and laws that criminalize the possession of certain drugs. Douglas Husak (2008) describes all of this as "overcriminalization." We criminalize too much and punish too severely. Husak focuses his attention on areas of criminal law where what is prohibited are actions that arguably do no harm in themselves, such as drug possession, and his main argument focuses on what is criminalized more than on how severely crimes are punished. This focus may make sense with respect to drug laws, but it provides little guidance for thinking about how severely acts that are properly criminalized should be punished. This is important because, as I noted above, nonviolent drug offenses do not account for most cases of incarceration. Rather, most people serving time in US prisons are there because of either violent crime or property crime—things that are, in principle, properly criminalized.

Hence, while part of the solution to mass incarceration is to decriminalize acts that do no harm, part of it must also involve rethinking the appropriate severity of punishment. These changes are required by any plausible theory of justice in punishment, quite apart from the racial disparities in punishment. However, inevitably, race also factors into sentencing, and therefore this is a concern for racial justice as well. As we have seen, research shows that African Americans tend to be treated more severely at many stages of the criminal justice process and tend to be somewhat more severely punished for similar crimes. While the differences are sometimes small, the racial disparities at each stage have a "cumulative effect" (National Research Council 2014, 97–101). Some studies show a significant difference in sentence length between African Americans and whites, when other factors are controlled for. For example, a recent report by the US Sentencing Commission (2017) found that in the federal system, African American men received sentences 19 percent longer than white men in similar cases.

From the point of view of any reasonable theory of justice in punishment, then, justice requires a thoroughgoing reform of American sentencing policies. I agree with Husak that many acts, such as drug possession, should be decriminalized, but the severity of punishment for property and even violent crime should also be carefully reviewed. Severe mandatory minimum sentences should be reconsidered, even for the most serious crimes, and three-strikes laws, which often require lengthy sentences for a third offense, even if the offense is not in itself very serious, should be abolished. A thoroughgoing effort at sentencing reform is badly needed (Clear 2007, chap. 8; Clear and Frost 2014, chap. 7; Tonry 2016, chap. 6). Alternatives to incarceration should also be expanded, and the conditions of incarceration must also be improved. Prisons must cease to be places where convicts are subject to routine humiliation and violence, and practices such as the widespread use of solitary confinement must also end (see Gibbons and Katzenbach 2006). Punishment, in terms of both its form and its severity, should reflect the idea that those being punished are fellow citizens and fellow human beings, and one of the goals of punishment should be to prepare those being punished for active and productive participation in the society, economy, and polity once they are released. It should also reflect the fact that some prisoners are innocent of the crimes for which they have been convicted. The Innocence Project has used DNA evidence to exonerate many prisoners convicted of crimes that they did not commit—though usually after they have served many years (McPhate 2016).

Two forms of punishment require separate treatment: life sentences without the possibility of parole, and the death penalty. The Supreme Court has ruled that imposing a life sentence without parole on juveniles in nonhomicide cases is unconstitutional (*Graham v. Florida* 2010), and that mandatory life sentences for juveniles in homicide cases are also unconstitutional (*Miller v. Alabama* 2012). The latter ruling leaves open the possibility of juveniles being sentenced to life without parole, but this must be based on an assessment of the facts in a particular case. In 2008 Human Rights Watch reported that in the United States there were nearly twenty-five hundred persons serving life-without-parole sentences for crimes they committed under the age of eighteen (Human Rights Watch 2008, 1). Here as elsewhere in the realm of criminal justice, the United States is "an international anomaly," as the only country in the world where youth offenders are serving life sentences without the possibility of parole (2008, 8). And, again, here are elsewhere, substantial racial disparities exist. The majority of people serving life without parole sentences for crimes committed as youths—60 percent—are African American (Human Rights Watch 2008, 2).

The case for prohibiting the imposition of this kind of sentence on children is strong. Indeed, it is difficult to see what legitimate purpose such sentences serve. Regardless of one's preferred rationale for punishment, life without parole for children is excessively harsh (Human Rights Watch 2008, 9–11). The idea that one must remain in prison for the rest of one's life, without even the possibility of parole, as punishment for an act committed as a youth suggests that even as a child one can mark himself as being utterly irredeemable. The fact is that most people "age out" of crime, especially violent crime (Pfaff 2017, 190–94), so holding people into their forties or fifties—or beyond—for a crime that they committed as a teenager makes little sense from the point of view of any reasonable theory of punishment.

If the case against life without parole for children is strong, I would suggest that the case against this sentence for *anyone* is nearly as strong. In the United States, about forty-nine thousand prisoners were serving life without the possibility of parole in 2012, and nearly half of these were African American (The Sentencing Project 2013, 13, 1). Again, this is anomalous historically, with the corresponding figure in 1992 being only 12,453, and it places the United States far outside of international human rights norms. For example, the European Court of Human Rights has ruled that life without parole violates the European Convention on Human Rights (*Vinter and Others v. United Kingdom* 2013).

Many of the same considerations that weigh in favor of abolishing this sentence for juveniles also favor its abolition for all. The main difference is that part of the rationale for eliminating life without parole for youths is that the young are less culpable for their crimes due to immaturity and consequent reduced capacity. But this is only part of the argument in the case of juveniles. The other reasons for eliminating life without parole are perfectly general: it is incompatible with the idea of rehabilitation and redemption and it is excessively harsh, regardless of whether punishment is thought to deter, exact retribution, or serve some other goal (see generally Ogletree and Sarat 2012).

If life without parole is problematic, the death penalty is more so. Among philosophers, political theorists, and legal thinkers, capital punishment has both defenders (see Aspenson 2013; Blumenson 2007; Cooper and King-Farlow 1989; Lenta and Farland 2008; Pojman 2005; Sunstein and Vermeule 2005) and critics (see Cholbi 2006; Londono 2013; McDermott 2001; Nathanson 2014; Steiker 2005; Wilson 2012). The arguments on both sides of the issue tend to be either substantive (addressing whether the death penalty in itself is morally permissible or required) or procedural (addressing whether the death penalty is, or can be, fairly administered). In these debates, opponents of the death penalty would seem to have an advantage, since they must show only that capital punishment fails in one of these respects, whereas defenders must show that it satisfies both substantive and procedural requirements (Stitcher 2014). I am persuaded that capital punishment is impermissible on substantive grounds, but for the purposes of the present discussion I focus on how it is administered.

Many of the problems with the death penalty are set out by Supreme Court Justice Stephen Breyer in his dissent in *Glossip v. Gross* (2015). Breyer's arguments are cast in constitutional terms, but the issues he raises are issues of justice as well. Breyer cites evidence that the procedures that lead to the imposition of the death penalty are unreliable: innocent people have been executed, and others sentenced to death have later been found to be innocent (2015, 3–9). The death penalty is also arbitrarily imposed: an examination of murder convictions shows that the death penalty is not utilized in the most heinous cases. Rather, whether it is imposed depends on such arbitrary factors as the county in which the crime was committed (2015, 12–14). As currently practiced, then, the death penalty makes a mockery of justice: similar cases are not treated similarly, and punishments are not proportional.

Justice Breyer makes a more fundamental argument, one that suggests that these procedural problems cannot be fixed. He points out that capital punishment, if it is to be reliable, requires extensive procedural protections, where those sentenced to death have ample opportunity to challenge their sentence. Yet these necessary procedural protections ensure that the imposition of the death penalty will always be long delayed (2015, 32). Hence, the procedural problems with the death penalty are not ones that can be remedied: if the death penalty is to be carried out, we must either cut short opportunities for appeals (hence increasing the risk of executing innocent persons and others who do not deserve it) or the punishment must be long delayed, undercutting any deterrent that the sentence carries and inflicting additional cruelties on those convicted.

Race also plays a role in the death penalty's arbitrariness. Many studies have shown that the race of both the perpetrator and the victim can play a role in whether the death penalty is imposed. It is more likely to be used in cases where the victim is white, and also more likely to be used when the perpetrator is African American (Shatz and Dalton 2013; Cholbi 2006). One such study (Baldus, Pulaski, and Woodworth 1983) became the basis of a constitutional challenge to the death penalty, but the Supreme Court, in *McCleskey v. Kemp* (1987), rejected the argument that racial disparities make the death penalty unconstitutionally arbitrary.

Finally, as Justice Breyer points out, the use of the death penalty places the United States outside of international human rights norms. No country in Europe uses the death penalty any longer, and most nations in the world have abolished it either formally or in practice.

So while it is difficult to determine what constitutes a fair or proportionate punishment for a given crime, sentencing in the United States fails to satisfy the most minimal standards of justice. Judged by historical and comparative norms, sentences are excessively harsh. There is little pretense of rehabilitating convicts or preparing them for reentry into society. And race plays an important role in sentencing, as it does in other aspects of the criminal justice system.

COLLATERAL CONSEQUENCES

Most prisoners are eventually released, and having been in prison entails a whole new set of negative consequences, not only for the ex-prisoners themselves, but also for their loved ones and communities. As John Pfaff (2017, 74–76) has emphasized, there is a "flow" of people in and out of prison, many serving short sentences, yet the long-term consequences of even a short prison sentence are very severe. The consequences are a function of the way in which policies beyond the criminal justice system treat those who have been convicted of a crime and have served time. They are not necessary consequences of incarceration, but a result of policy choices that impose additional serious costs on ex-prisoners, make their reintegration into society more difficult, and exacerbate racial inequality.

Ex-prisoners face significant obstacles in obtaining gainful employment, as well as the education and training necessary to compete for jobs. Many of those going into prison are high school dropouts and have little job training, and their time in prison does little to advance their education (Alexander 2012, 150; Clear and Frost 2014, 102; Western 2006, 113). In addition, most private employers are disinclined to hire someone with a criminal conviction, even when the conviction is unrelated to the job to which the person is applying (Alexander 2012, 149). Indeed, most states allow public and private employers to deny employment on the basis of an arrest that did not even lead to a conviction (Legal Action Center 2009, 10). In addition, many states allow occupational licensing agencies to deny certification on the basis of a criminal record, so many occupations that require a professional license are off limits to ex-prisoners. Of course some employers may have reasonable concerns about hiring those with certain kinds of convictions, especially those related to the work for which they would be hired. But barring ex-prisoners from whole professions and allowing unfettered public access to criminal records (Legal Action Center 2009, 2) hardly constitute a careful balancing among the legitimate interests involved and hardly serve to advance the imperative of reintegrating ex-prisoners into society.

All of this, inevitably, is exacerbated by race. African Americans already face employment discrimination (Bendick, Jackson, and Reinoso 1994; Bertrand and Mullainathan 2004), and having a criminal record makes it extremely difficult to find work in the "primary" job market. In her experimental audit study of employers in Milwaukee, Devah Pager (2003, 2007) finds that blacks and whites with comparable qualifications get called back at significantly different rates, and that the impact of a criminal record is greater for blacks than it is for whites. African Americans without a criminal record get called back 14 percent of the time, but with a criminal record this rate drops nearly two-thirds to 5 percent. Whites without a criminal record, on the other hand, get called back 34 percent of the time, and with a criminal record this rate is cut in half, to 17 percent (2007, 91). This shows that whites with a criminal record get called back at a higher rate than African Americans without one and suggests that the combination of being black and having a criminal record has a devastating impact on one's ability to find a job (see also Pager and Shepherd 2008; Mueller-Smith 2015).

Ex-prisoners, then, are often forced into the secondary job market, which offers less job security, fewer benefits, and lower pay. Bruce Western (2006, chap. 5) shows that while those who end up in prison generally had low incomes to start with, after prison they earn even less than before. In terms of wages, employment, and annual earnings, ex-prisoners almost always see a significant decline.

If being unable to find a job were not bad enough, ex-prisoners face more obstacles, and many of these are directly due to public policy decisions. For example, public housing authorities can deny housing to those with a criminal record (Alexander 2012, 144–48; Clear and Frost 2014, 104–9). As Nicholas Turner (2016) has argued, this policy can be extremely counter-productive, since it hinders many ex-prisoners' ability to be reunited with their families and their ability to simply have a place to live. Turner points out, relying on a study by Peterson (2016), that homeless ex-prisoners, like homeless people more generally, are at increased risk of being (re)arrested and sent back to prison. Most states also deny certain public benefits, such as food stamps, to those with some felony drug convictions, and some impose a lifetime ban (Legal Action Center 2009, 11). Many states also suspend or revoke driver's licenses for some drug convictions (Legal Action Center 2009, 9). Hence ex-prisoners face the very real prospect of having no place to live, few job opportunities, no ability to drive to a job or a job interview, and no public assistance. Far from encouraging ex-prisoners to reintegrate into society, public policy seems to be aimed at preventing them from doing so.

These consequences are borne not only by the ex-prisoners themselves, but also by their families and loved ones. Not surprisingly, the marriage rate is lower and the divorce rate higher for those who go to prison (Western 2006, chap. 6). Millions of children have fathers who are in prison, or who have been, and these children are at increased risk for behavioral and mental health problems, infant mortality, homelessness, and poverty (Wakefield and Wildeman 2014). And the racial disparities are "stark." The rate of parental imprisonment for black children is 25.1 percent, whereas for white children it is 3.6 percent (Wakefield and Wildeman 2014, 152).

The effects of mass imprisonment also have devastating consequences for whole communities, especially black communities. Todd Clear (2007) has argued that the geographic concentration of those subject to mass incarceration has important implications for all who live in their neighborhoods. Clear emphasizes that large-scale incarceration means that there is "a reentry cycle, involving both removal and return, and often more than once" (2007, 75). This weakens the social ties, and therefore the social networks and social capital that play an important role in informal social control. Clear cites many empirical studies that support the hypothesis that high incarceration rates have significant negative effects on both the families and communities of those in prison (2007, 118–19). He also argues that, in undermining the stability of these communities, mass incarceration may actually increase rather than decrease crime rates (2007, chap. 6). While aspects of Clear's argument are somewhat speculative, his analysis strongly suggests that mass incarceration has negative effects that ripple through whole communities that are disproportionately subject to it. This includes, of course, many black communities.

All of this suggests that mass incarceration is a major contributor to racial inequality (Western 2006, 2007). As we have seen, African Americans are subject to social conditions that foster certain crimes, they are targeted by racial profiling, and they are sentenced to longer prison terms. For these reasons, African Americans constitute a vastly disproportionate share of the prison population, and therefore also of the population of ex-prisoners. Upon release, they face the dual barriers to employment of being black and having a criminal record and are denied many other public benefits. Their families and children also pay a heavy price, and the cycle of disadvantage continues.

Indeed, Becky Pettit (2012) argues that mass incarceration not only reproduces racial inequality but also leads social scientists to underestimate it. Many studies of inequality rely on surveys of households, which exclude both prisoners and those (including many ex-prisoners) who are not members of stable households. Given the overrepresentation of

African Americans among these groups, estimates may significantly understate the degree of racial inequality. Once all prisoners and ex-prisoners are included in the data, racial inequality is revealed to be greater than is often thought.

One final consequence of imprisonment must be discussed, and this regards the right to vote. All but two states (Maine and Vermont) bar prisoners from voting while they are incarcerated, and most states bar some ex-prisoners from voting—either while they are on probation or parole or for some specified period after release. Four states impose a lifetime ban on voting for convicted felons. As of 2016, over 5.8 million people were disenfranchised because of these policies, and the impact disproportionately falls on African Americans: one in thirteen African Americans is disenfranchised, as opposed to one in fifty-six nonblacks (The Sentencing Project 2016a, 2016b). As with other policies related to criminal justice, these facts place the United States well outside the norms that characterize other democracies. Many European countries allow prisoners to vote, and many more restore voting rights immediately upon release. As Michelle Alexander states, "No other country in the world disenfranchises people who are released from prison in a manner even remotely resembling the United States" (2012, 158; see also Manza and Uggen 2006, 38). Race plays an important role in explaining this divergence. Manza and Uggen present statistical analysis that shows that "when African Americans make up a larger proportion of a state's prison population, that state is significantly more likely to adopt or extend felon disenfranchisement" (2006, 67).

The case for disenfranchising prisoners while in prison is somewhat stronger than for disenfranchising ex-prisoners (see Altman 2005; Ramsay 2013). Prisoners are usually not really a part of the community in which their prison happens to be situated. Yet these communities get to count prisoners as residents of their legislative district, thereby increasing the electoral power of districts with prisons (Pfaff 2017, 172–73). Pfaff suggests changing the laws that govern legislative districts so that these communities may not count prisoners for this purpose. An alternative would be a policy that says that if prisoners are counted for this purpose, then they must also be able to vote. Another option is that prisoners could be permitted "to adopt as their voting residence the last place they lived prior to their imprisonment" and to vote in elections there (Lippke 2001, 579n). Regardless of how the issue of voting in local elections is handled, prisoners remain members of the national community, so the case for allowing them to vote in presidential elections and perhaps congressional (or at least Senate) elections may be stronger than for allowing them to vote in local elections.

The case for disenfranchising ex-prisoners is very weak. The main argument to justify this is based on the idea that those who have violated the law have also violated the social contract, placing themselves outside of the political community. It is thus appropriate to deny them the vote (for discussions see Kleinig and Murtagh 2005; Reiman 2005). Duff (2005) characterizes this as the "exclusionary" view of punishment, in which the law-abiding "us" is sharply distinguished from the law-violating "them." There are many problems with this view, beginning with the fact that most of "us" violate the law too. But a deeper problem is that the argument assumes that the social contract is itself just. If it is not, or if it is sufficiently unjust, then there would seem to be little warrant for excluding from citizenship those who have been treated unjustly by the de facto social contract (Lippke 2001; Munn 2011). Their crimes may be reasonable and justifiable, or at least excusable—especially if they violate conventional rules of justice (like those regulating property) rather than natural duties against, say, cruelty and violence (Shelby 2007, 2016).

In addition, even if (in the case of those serving their sentences) it is reasonable to see prisoners as (temporarily) excluded from membership in the political community, continuing to exclude those who have been released is counterproductive because it inhibits the reintegration of ex-prisoners into society, much as other policies do. It promotes distrust in government among African Americans and suppresses political participation that might otherwise bolster political legitimacy (Lerman and Weaver 2014).

Ex-prisoner disenfranchisement is unjust since it denies the vote to people who must live under the laws and who have the same interest in voting as everyone else. It is also unjust because it compounds the injustices and disadvantages that African Americans already face. Indeed, ex-prisoner disenfranchisement must be seen in the context of the long history of African American voter suppression that continues to this day (Manza and Uggen 2006, chap. 2). This voter suppression has an impact on election outcomes. Manza and Uggen (2006, chap. 8) offer analysis to suggest that if ex-prisoners had been permitted to vote in the 2000 presidential election, Al Gore would have won Florida by about eighty thousand votes, and hence would have been elected president (but see Burch 2012). Disenfranchisement may also have decided the outcome of some congressional races (Manza and Uggen 2006, chap. 8). The disenfranchisement of ex-prisoners contributes significantly to the political disempowerment of the black community as a whole (Burch 2013).

CONCLUSION

The criminal justice system, combined with other policies that exacerbate the consequences of a criminal record, reflects, perpetrates, and reproduces racial inequality. Because of concentrated urban poverty, African Americans commit certain types of crime at higher rates, and they are disproportionately targeted by police even for crimes, like drug crimes, that they do not commit at higher rates. Once in the system, African Americans are treated more harshly, and upon release, like all ex-prisoners, they face serious obstacles to employment and other preconditions for a decent and stable life. While all ex-prisoners face these barriers, black ex-prisoners confront the combined effects of racial discrimination and the mark of a criminal record. The overrepresentation of African Americans in the criminal justice system also has serious and damaging effects not only on the prisoners and ex-prisoners themselves, but also on their children, families, and communities at large. Mass incarceration therefore plays a devastating role in the reproduction of racial inequality.

Addressing mass incarceration and its racial disparities therefore requires both reforms in the criminal justice system and also reforms beyond that system. Since poverty, lack of education, and lack of job opportunities breed crime, addressing the concentration of black poverty is a prerequisite for addressing the disproportionate representation of African Americans in prisons. Within the criminal justice system, racial profiling must end, more subtle forms of racial bias must be combated, and the system must be made less punitive for everyone. Prisoners must be seen as fellow citizens who, upon release, are able to rejoin society on equal terms. Policies that make it difficult for ex-prisoners to participate in the society and pursue a decent life must also be reformed.

Some observers would find these normative conclusions too limited. Advocates of "prison abolition" argue that there is a fairly direct line of descent from slavery, through Jim Crow, to current conditions of mass imprisonment. This lineage calls into question the practice of incarceration, and so these advocates argue for the abolition of the prison system itself (see Davis 2003). Although I agree with much of the abolition movement's assessment of the criminal justice system as it operates today, I find its prescription unpersuasive. It is true that the problems with the American criminal justice system are profound and that prisons are vastly overutilized. Alternatives to incarceration should certainly be expanded. Yet without a plausible alternative to prisons for even the most serious offenders, calling for abolition is unrealistic. Still, the prison abolition movement is surely right that racial injustice undermines the authority of the state to punish. This authority depends on the state's establishing both a reasonably just society and a reasonably just criminal justice system (Shelby 2016, chap. 8). Until these conditions are met, the criminal justice system will continue to function primarily as a tool of oppression.

8

Common Schools and Black Schools

The experience of three generations of an African American family in Tuscaloosa, Alabama, exemplifies the state of school desegregation in the United States today. James Dent, born in 1950, attended segregated schools and, after a brief stint in the military, spent his working life mixing cement. His daughter, Melissa, born in 1969, attended school at the height of federal court supervision over the public schools in Tuscaloosa and therefore attended a high-achieving, integrated school. She graduated from high school and then college. She works at the Mercedes-Benz factory just outside of town. Melissa always assumed that her daughter, D'Leisha, would do even better than she has, but by the time D'Leisha attended high school, Tuscaloosa had been released from court supervision and its high schools had resegregated. D'Leisha attended a school that resembled the one that her grandfather attended far more than it resembled the one attended by her mother (Hannah-Jones 2014).

Over the last twenty years or so, hundreds of school districts have been released from federal court supervision after being certified as having overcome the legacy of de jure segregation. This certification has often meant, in practice, that the district is free to resegregate, as happened in Tuscaloosa (Reardon et al. 2012; Orfield and Frankenberg 2014). It seems plausible to think that, decades or centuries from now, the 1970s and 1980s will be seen as a brief interlude when the United States achieved a significant degree of racial integration in its public schools. This period may come to be seen as merely an interruption in the basic pattern of racial segregation that persisted until the 1960s under Jim Crow and has reasserted itself in the post-civil rights era.

The courts have played an important role in this, of course. As I detail below, resegregation has been abetted by the restricted and convoluted ways in which the courts have approached these issues. Under current Supreme Court doctrine, once a school district has been released from court supervision, it is prohibited from taking the race of individual students into account in making school assignments in order to maintain racial integration. It requires color-blindness, even if this results in resegregation. In the view of the majority on the Court, our constitutional principles ban the use of race, even to achieve integration.

At the same time, a very different consensus seems to have emerged among scholars. In the view of one prominent group of scholars, racial integration is required by justice, and they understand integration to mean not just the absence of de jure segregation (that is, desegregation), but the actual mixing of African American and white students (was well as Asians, Latino/as, and others) within schools and within classrooms. Though there are different versions of this integrationist argument, they converge in concluding that integration is a necessary condition for equal educational opportunity. Hence we have a very sharp divergence between the courts and scholars: what one believes is absolutely necessary the other holds to be prohibited—unless it can be achieved through color-blind means, which is often difficult or impossible.

I believe that both the courts and proponents of integration are wrong. I argue that justice does not require integration, and that the costs of and alternatives to integration should be carefully weighed before it is undertaken. But I also argue that where school integration seems to be a promising route to racial equality, then it is certainly permissible. Contextual factors, such as whether sufficient numbers of students of different races live within a given geographic area, will largely determine which means are most viable. But if it turns out that racially diverse schools cannot be created without significant costs to minority students, then justice, prudence, and common sense demand that we focus on ensuring that all students get an equal and adequate education. None of this is to deny that there are many factors that weigh in favor of integration, factors that integration advocates have delineated. But there are other considerations involved as well, I hope to show, ones that advocates of integration too often ignore.

LIBERALISM AND EDUCATION

It will help place my argument in its proper context if we briefly consider the relation of education to liberal theory. Education clearly has an important role to play in fostering a just, liberal, and democratic society. This is so for many reasons, but I emphasize two: First, from the point of view of justice, education plays a crucial role in creating fair equality of opportunity. Only if everyone has access to an adequate education can it be said that each individual has the opportunity to achieve all that her talents and ambitions make possible. If, on the other hand, a child's educational opportunities are shaped by the neighborhood in which she lives, or her parents' economic status, then fair equality of opportunity cannot be secured. Education therefore has an important role in establishing distributive justice and helps individuals achieve the "private" good of career satisfaction and economic success. Second, education also "creates citizens" (Callan 1997). It inculcates the values and beliefs necessary for a liberal society to persist, and it creates a sense of common citizenship and national membership. It also should convey the message that all citizens are of equal moral worth, and the way that it frames the narrative of the nation's history is crucial to performing all of these functions. Hence education is important to achieving the two dimensions of racial justice that I have emphasized throughout this book: distributive justice, which requires that African Americans not be overrepresented among the less well off, and equal citizenship, which requires that the equal moral worth of all be affirmed, and that the past be acknowledged and memorialized in certain ways.

There are a number of lively debates about what, more specifically, liberal theory requires of an educational system. I will highlight two of them because they are particularly relevant to the arguments below. First, there is a debate about the appropriate distribution of educational resources and the principles that should guide this. Very roughly, the debate is between those who advocate equality as the basis of distribution and those who argue for a standard of educational adequacy (Reich 2013). Advocates of an adequacy standard argue that it is sufficient if each student's education meets some minimum standard, even if others receive a better education or more educational resources, whereas advocates of equality would require educational quality or resources to be equalized among students.

The demand for equal education has a long pedigree that includes the Supreme Court's declaration in *Brown v. Board of Education* (1954) that if the state offers public education, it must do so "on equal terms." But in its *San Antonio Independent School District v. Rodriguez* (1973) decision, the Court held that equality does not necessarily mean equal funding. It ruled that there is no constitutional violation when states apportion educational resources so that wealthier school districts have more money (as happens when schools are financed on the basis of local property taxes). Since the *Rodriguez* case, however, much litigation on this issue has taken place at the state level, and many state courts have ruled that under state laws and constitutions, school financing must be substantially equal statewide.

While conceptually distinct, the adequacy and the equality standards often converge in practice, especially if the threshold of adequacy is sufficiently high. In a society such as ours, where the education received by many students (including many African American students) is both very unequal and woefully inadequate, fully implementing either the equality or the adequacy requirement would be a vast improvement. Under prevailing nonideal conditions, then, this debate may be largely irrelevant. Indeed, even at a philosophical level, advocates of one position have difficulty resisting the claims of the other. Elizabeth Anderson (2007, 2012) and Debra Satz (2007, 2012) are generally viewed as proponents of an adequacy standard, yet their arguments contain strong egalitarian elements.

There is also the question of what, exactly, is to be equalized or made adequate. As Rob Reich suggests, the three obvious candidates are "inputs, opportunities, or outcomes" (2013, 52). Reich suggests that equality is usually thought of in the context of inputs, while adequacy comes to the fore when the focus is outcomes. Again, it may be that the two principles are not opposed but are better thought of as working together. Perhaps more equal funding is required to achieve adequate outcomes for all students. More likely, an unequal distribution, with less well-off students getting more and better educational resources, will be required to achieve more equal and adequate outcomes. I do not engage these important debates directly, but instead will speak generically of an equitable distribution of educational resources. I hope that by doing so I can sidestep the significant issue of what exactly an equitable distribution of resources would look like, but I assume that it would involve poor and minority schools getting more resources than they do now, and perhaps more resources than schools in better-off areas, which do not have the same obstacles to student achievement to overcome.

The other debate among liberal theorists regarding education concerns the content of the curriculum and the goals of education. Specifically, there has been a great deal of debate about whether, or the extent to which, liberal theory requires that the curriculum in public schools be "neutral" with respect to moral and religious doctrines. Such neutrality is sometimes thought of as the hallmark of liberal-egalitarian thought, and the implications of this for schooling might seem to be direct and straightforward: if liberalism requires the state to be neutral among different moral and religious views, then state-sponsored education must be so as well.

But this line of thought contains two important errors. First, it reflects a misunderstanding of what is meant by "neutral" in this context. As Rawls (2005, 190–95) emphasizes, political liberalism is neutral in the sense that it is not based upon a more comprehensive doctrine such as utilitarianism or Christianity. But it is not neutral in its implications: it rules out, for political purposes, doctrines that are fundamentally inegalitarian (such as ones that consign women to traditional or subordinate roles). Second, the requirement of neutrality among adult citizens and their comprehensive doctrines does not necessarily apply to children. Indeed, one of the issues at stake in debates about the content of public education curricula, perhaps the main issue, is what kind of people children will turn out to be. To some extent, parents have special claims over their children in terms of how they will be educated and the comprehensive doctrines that will be inculcated in them. But the claims of parents are limited. They must be balanced with the interests of the children themselves, as well as the claims of the rest of us—the fellow citizens of schoolchildren, who have a stake in the kind of citizens the students will turn out to be. Hence public education in a liberal society legitimately teaches certain virtues, attitudes, and beliefs that are appropriate to (indeed, necessary for) democratic citizenship. And it rules out inculcating beliefs and attitudes that are antithetical to equal citizenship, such as ideas about racial superiority. In short, public education for a liberal and democratic society cannot be neutral and should not try to be. A liberal society requires the creation of citizens who have attitudes, beliefs, and knowledge that are appropriate for democratic citizenship in general and for citizenship in their particular society (see Costa 2011; Gutmann 1999; Levinson 1999; Macedo 1995, 2000).

While both of these issues inform the arguments that follow, the main debate that I engage revolves around the question of whether justice, under conditions that presently exist in the United States, requires or permits public schools to be racially integrated. I frame this issue as it concerns the two goals of education that I highlighted above: creating equality of opportunity and creating democratic citizens who see each other as civic equals. This is a complex issue, and its various strands must be disentangled. I begin by reviewing the legal aspects of the debate and the way in which Supreme Court decisions have shaped it, for good and ill, from *Brown* onward.

FROM *BROWN* TO *PARENTS INVOLVED*

What, exactly, is the evil of segregation in education, and what is the appropriate remedy? These questions have been bequeathed to us by *Brown*.

Today, as I will argue in subsequent sections, it remains a point of contention whether predominantly black schools are, in and of themselves, an injustice, requiring integration as a remedy. This is a question that *Brown* largely evades, or at least is ambiguous about, leaving plenty of material for opposing sides to draw upon.

While in public memory *Brown* enjoys unquestioned moral stature, among scholars the Court's opinion in the case has come under withering critique from an array of perspectives. It is worthwhile, then, to pause for a moment and dwell on the opinion's virtues. One of these virtues is that the Court emphasized the importance of education for two aspects of justice, the same two that I have already noted: education, the Court held, is essential to "our democratic society . . . [and] is the very foundation of good citizenship." It also prepares children for "later professional training" and is essential for "succe[ss] in life." Since the opportunity to get an education is a prerequisite for future opportunities, the Court held, it "must be made available to all on equal terms." The Court thereby recognized the role of education in ensuring equality of opportunity and for preparing children for democratic citizenship.

Another virtue of the opinion is that the Court recognized, if implicitly, the importance of the expressive dimension of the law. It distinguished between "tangible" and "intangible" factors that may make different schools equal or unequal to each other, and it held that racially segregated schools are "inherently" unequal, even if they are equal in terms of their tangible aspects. The Court emphasized that segregation, "when it has the sanction of the law," conveys a certain message, "denoting the inferiority of the negro as a group" and that this message is constitutionally impermissible.

Unfortunately, however, the Court conflated the message of state-sanctioned segregation and its psychological effects, and it thereby created confusion about the sense in which racially segregated schools are "inherently" unequal. Intertwined with its discussion of what segregation "denotes" the Court relies on social-scientific evidence about the effects of segregation on the development of African American children. This raises the question of whether the constitutional violation is the message of segregation itself or the harmful effects that it has on black students and on

African Americans more generally. Also left unanswered is whether the inherence is entirely dependent on the de jure nature of the segregation, or whether de facto segregated schools might also carry this same message or have the same damaging psychological effects. If so, do de facto segregated schools also violate the Constitution?

In his opinion, Chief Justice Earl Warren opted for a brief, powerful statement of principle that is restricted to a limited question: whether de jure segregated public schools are unconstitutional. This may very well have been, on balance, a wise and prudent course. But it meant that many questions were left unanswered, giving much ammunition to those who want to argue for differing visions of *Brown*'s meaning and legacy. For not only is the precise nature of the wrong, or constitutional violation, left ambiguous, but so too is the appropriate remedy. The year after the landmark decision, the Court infamously ordered, in *Brown v. Board of Education* II (1955), that desegregation should proceed "with all deliberate speed," which ended up meaning that southern school districts got an additional ten-plus years to remain segregated. It was only in the late 1960s and early 1970s that the Court lost patience and ordered segregation to be eliminated "root and branch" and endorsed bussing as a means to achieve actual integration. In cases during this period, it became clear that policies that eliminated de jure segregation but did not achieve actual integration would not be tolerated. This shift in emphasis from desegregation (eliminating de jure segregated schools and assignment based on race) to integration (actual mixing of students of different races within schools) indicates another tension in *Brown* and its progeny: was integration the original goal of *Brown* or was it added later (Minow 2010, chap. 1)? Perhaps a better way of framing this question is to ask, how should we think of these issues today? Should the goal be integration, or is mere desegregation, often resulting in de facto segregation, permissible? And if integration is the goal, what means are permissible to achieve it?

In the *Parents Involved v. Seattle* (2007) case, a narrow majority of the Court addressed these questions. The case involved the use of race as one factor among several in assigning students to schools to achieve racial integration in Seattle, Washington, and Louisville, Kentucky. In his majority

opinion, Chief Justice John Roberts stated that this use of race was incompatible with precedent (including *Brown*), with the Constitution, and
with Supreme Court doctrine—which subjects any use of race in public
policy to "strict scrutiny." He argued that this use of race failed to meet
that high standard because it served no "compelling state interest." The
two candidates for such an interest that he dismissed were the promo-
tion of diversity in schools and overcoming a history of past discrimination. In arguing against the former, Roberts had to sharply distinguish
between higher education and K-12 schools. Just a few years before this
case, the Court had reaffirmed, in *Grutter*, that diversity is a compelling
state interest—but, Roberts insisted, only in higher education. This left
the Court in the awkward position of holding that diversity is a compelling state interest in higher education but not in primary and secondary
schools.

The other possible state interest served by the school integration plans
was overcoming a history of de jure segregation. Here Roberts emphasized
that the Seattle district had never been found by a court to have practiced
de jure segregation, and Louisville had been certified as having achieved
"unitary" status in 2000, meaning that it had been judged to have overcome its history of de jure segregation—so there was no longer a need to
overcome that history.

The upshot of the majority decision in *Parents Involved* is that such
districts are forbidden to take race into account, even for the purpose of
achieving integration. But there is a caveat to this, which is that Justice
Kennedy did not join the whole of the majority opinion. Contrary to the
rest of the majority in the case, Kennedy maintained in his concurrence
that diversity in K-12 schools can be a compelling state interest, and he
suggested that many policies to achieve it are constitutionally permissible.
He distinguished between policies that assign children to schools based on
an individualized assignment to a racial category, on the one hand, and,
on the other, those that use aggregate demographic data to help determine the location of new schools or the drawing of district lines. So while
the plurality rejected diversity as a legitimate end and any use of race as a
means, Kennedy sees diversity as potentially a legitimate compelling state

interest and would allow some, though not all, uses of race to pursue it. Still, Kennedy joined the majority in the result of the case, striking down plans that use race as one factor among others in determining school assignments when this use of race involves placing individual students in racial categories.

The most powerful opinion in the case is Justice Breyer's dissent. Breyer points out that, while it is true that Seattle had never been declared by a court to have practiced de jure segregation, this is because it settled out of court with the NAACP and entered into a voluntary desegregation plan. He also points out that Louisville, like other districts, was released from court supervision because of its good-faith efforts to achieve integration. Breyer persuasively argues that the majority's position is untenable: the very efforts to integrate schools that are required while a district is under court supervision become prohibited the moment it is declared to have achieved unitary status and is released from supervision. Once a district achieves integration, on this view, it is virtually required to resegregate.

Justice Breyer also argues that the majority relies far too heavily on the distinction between de jure and de facto segregation—a distinction that loses much of its cogency when examined closely. While the distinction was no doubt important in the *Brown* era, under contemporary circumstances it means little. Across the country, racial segregation in schools is to a large extent a byproduct of residential segregation, and residential segregation, as we saw in chapter 6, is the product of many factors, but significant among these are explicit governmental policies that encouraged and abetted it. When the courts speak of de jure segregation in schools, they mean only explicit governmental policies to separate races in education. They ignore other areas of public policy where segregation was created through government action that contributed to the patterns of residential segregation that we see today. Hence, as Richard Rothstein argues, "Current residential patterns of racial isolation are unconstitutional products of state action" (2013, 174).

Both Roberts and Breyer claim to be the true exponents of the spirit and letter of the *Brown* decision. For Roberts, *Brown* was about ending de jure segregation and race-consciousness in public policy, all forms of which he equates with racial discrimination. For Breyer, this is an impoverished and extremely limited way of looking at the issue. For him, *Brown* and its progeny are about ending racial subordination and inequality.

From the point of view propounded throughout this book, the Roberts majority is wrong on these issues. It is a mistake to equate all uses of race-consciousness with racial discrimination, and wrong to suggest that all uses of race in public policy, even those aimed at promoting racial equality, are suspect. (Of course, I have not made a constitutional argument to this effect, but there is substantial overlap between the constitutional and normative issues.) As I have argued, race-blindness in the context of a society deeply shaped by a history of racial hierarchy is a recipe for continued subordination.

While the Roberts Court is mistaken on these matters, proponents of integration are also mistaken in some of their claims. As I now try to show, its advocates sometimes overstate the case for integration and ignore the benefits of its alternatives.

THE TROUBLE WITH INTEGRATION

During the civil rights movement, the appeal of integration as an ideal was obvious: it was the antithesis of racial segregation, which separated black and white students and thereby denied the former access to the educational resources enjoyed by the latter. Integration was also appealing because, in contrast to desegregation, integration suggested a positive, inspiring ideal. While desegregation implied the (often grudging) cessation of legal separation, integration came to be associated with Martin Luther King Jr.'s idea of a "beloved community," where diversity is valued and where citizens genuinely accept each other rather than merely tolerate each other.

However, in the post-civil rights era, and as a guide to policymaking, the single-minded pursuit of integration faces many obstacles, both practical and philosophical. As we have already seen, the courts have made it much more difficult to achieve integrated schools. But the deeper problems are the philosophical and principled ones. While doubtless appealing, integration as a focus of policy and as the sole, or even primary, route to racial equality in education simply cannot bear the weight that integrationists wish to place on it. So while the courts have been wrong to limit integration policies as strictly as they have, integrationists are also wrong to place so much hope in it.

What are some of the rationales that have been offered for integration in schools? First, integrated education has been said to be essential to democratic citizenship. For example, Amy Gutmann argues that de facto segregated schools are incompatible with a functioning democracy because they perpetuate a "damaging cycle of discrimination" (1999, 162). While we must regret the intrusion into local politics that is often required to achieve integration, Gutmann argues, on balance this intrusion is necessary for the future well-being of American democracy (1999, 160–70). Similarly, Elizabeth Anderson argues that integrated schools are essential to creating a sense of common citizenship and a diverse "elite" that is competent to run the major institutions of society (2010). And Lawrence Blum (1998, 2002) argues that integrated education is necessary for preparing students to function as citizens in a multicultural and multiracial society.

In addition to being important for democratic citizenship, it is often argued that integrated schools enhance the academic achievement of black students and also their long-term career prospects. There may be many causal factors contributing to the connection between integrated schooling and one's success in life, but one of these, emphasized by Elizabeth Anderson, is that integrated education reduces the social isolation of African Americans and may enhance their access to the informal networks and dominant cultural norms that contribute to future success.

Both of these arguments focus on the direct benefits for black and, to a lesser extent, white students from being in the same schools and the same classrooms together. Some arguments for integration, however, take a different approach. They focus on the more contingent and strategic connections between integration on the one hand and academic achievement and life outcomes on the other. Chief among these arguments is that "green follows white." Here the argument is that predominantly white schools will inevitably have more and better educational resources, so the best way to provide access to those resources for African American students is to place them in these schools. This seems to be the implicit, and sometimes explicit, assumption of Gary Orfield, whose Civil Rights Project provides indispensable documentation and analysis of segregation trends in its periodic reports. As Larry Blum has noted, Orfield's analysis is characterized by "a tendency to assume both that racial separation can virtually never be anything other than inequality-producing, and also that inequality (of opportunity) is the only thing wrong with racially separated schools" (2002, 392). Indeed, Orfield explicitly characterizes the drive for integration as a fight "for access to the opportunities concentrated in White schools" (Orfield 2007, 1). Elsewhere, Frankenberg and Orfield observe that "segregated schools often have fewer key resources that are important for students' learning: a high-quality, experienced, and stable faculty and a challenging curriculum" (2012, 18).

It should be readily acknowledged that advocates of integration have had no trouble marshaling evidence of its benefits. Ever since the Coleman Report (Coleman 1966), evidence has accumulated that integration can, under favorable conditions and when implemented well, enhance the academic achievement of black students. These benefits occur, presumably, because of the combination of factors highlighted by the arguments I described above: integration both places African American students in schools with better facilities and also places them in classrooms where the backgrounds of the students promote greater academic achievement.

But this is not a conclusive argument for integration. Take the "green follows white" argument. While it is true that black students can get access to good teachers and other important educational resources by attending predominantly white schools, the normative implication of this is not self-evident. From the fact that predominantly white schools have better resources than predominantly black schools, one could just as easily conclude that justice requires the equalization of these resources rather than the integration of black students into white schools. The integrationist conclusion, then, seems to be based upon a political or pragmatic assumption that the only way, or the best way, to get these resources to black students is to place them in predominantly white schools. Yet I know of no reason to think that this proposal is any likelier to succeed than a proposal to redistribute educational resources. Indeed, in light of the fierce opposition that integration plans often confront, there is more reason to think that a redistribution of resources would be more politically viable.

What of the other benefits of integration, those related to democratic citizenship and equality of opportunity? Advocates of integration can point to much evidence of its benefits, but then they sometimes mistakenly suggest something that does not follow: that these benefits can be had *only* through integrated schools. They slide from observing that, properly implemented, integration is sufficient for achieving its benefits to claiming that it is necessary for achieving them—or they equivocate on this important issue. Hence from the evidence that she cites about the benefits of integration, Anderson concludes that it is "indispensable" and a "necessary condition for a racially just future" (2010, 180, 189). And Blum argues that the benefits of integration "can either be provided *only* in ethnoracially plural settings, or that such settings are *much more likely* than monoracial ones to provide them." These benefits, Blum writes, are "virtually unattainable without, or greatly facilitated by, racial and cultural plurality in the student bodies of our schools" (2002, 397, 411).

Finally, in pointing to its (potential) benefits, advocates of integration often ignore or downplay its costs. As I have argued elsewhere (Valls 2002), the actual record of integration shows that it sometimes has very serious costs for black students. More often than not, it is African Americans who are integrated into predominantly white schools, rather than vice versa. Many black students took long bus rides into hostile territory. Integration as it actually proceeded in the aftermath of the civil rights movement often had the effect of closing many traditionally black schools, and many black teachers and administrators lost their jobs, while whole black communities lost an important institution. One could argue that these effects are not inevitable, and that is true. But some costs of integration may be inevitable, such as the loss of community control over schools and curriculum. Integration places African American students into schools where blacks are a minority and hence deprives them of the benefits of being in a predominantly black school. For many students, this trade-off might very well be worth it. But for others it may not.

The bottom line is that any argument for integration must be explicit about what the alternatives are and what, realistically, can be achieved. Since integration is not analytically required by justice, any argument for it is contingent and comparative. We must be explicit about what integration is being compared to, and what are the costs and benefits of each of the alternatives. Too often arguments for integration seem to assume that its only alternative is the (obviously unjust) status quo—but this is not the case. Hence any assessment of integration must reckon with the benefits of predominantly black schools.

THE CASE FOR BLACK SCHOOLS

It is perhaps best to begin with a few words about what I mean by "black school." A school may be "black" in a variety of ways and in varying degrees. It may have a predominantly black student body. It may have a predominantly black faculty and staff. It may have a curriculum focused on black history and culture, and it may employ a pedagogy thought to be appropriate for black students. When I write of "black schools" or "predominantly black schools," I do not have a single model in mind. At a minimum, though, I assume that any school worthy of these descriptors will have a predominantly African American student body. I have in mind K-12 schools that are already predominantly black, usually by virtue of being situated in a geographic area, often an inner city but also some suburbs and even rural areas, that have a predominantly black population. But we may include in this category also private, magnet, and charter schools. In addition, one dimension of the "blackness" of a school may be the extent to which it embraces a self-image and mission, and also a curriculum, that reflects its demographics. In other words, I would include in the category of "black schools" those that just happen to be predominantly black as well as schools that embrace their demographic character and use it to define their identity, mission, and/or curriculum. This means that the schools I want to discuss are a heterogeneous lot that may differ in important ways. I should also state at the outset that the schools I have in mind are not "racially or ethnically exclusive" (Macedo 2000, 273). They would not deny whites or others admission on the basis of their race. Nor are these schools necessarily cases of "voluntary" separation (see Brooks 1996; Merry 2013). They may be voluntary, as in cases of charter or magnet schools. But they may also simply be neighborhood schools that happen to be predominantly black and whose students do not have much of a choice but to attend them.

The argument for black schools is partly pragmatic and partly principled, and it is partly negative and partly positive. The negative argument focuses on the problems with integration that I emphasized above. While integration sometimes provides important benefits to students, especially black students, it also often involves serious costs. These costs may exceed the benefits for these students, and in these cases it may make more sense to focus on enhancing the education of black students where they are— which is, often, in predominantly black schools.

The positive case for black schools, however, must show that (at a pragmatic level) they entail acceptable trade-offs and can serve the essential functions of public education in a liberal and democratic society. And to be just (or not unjust), they must be compatible with liberal and democratic principles. Addressing these issues will inevitably involve considerations of curriculum, especially since some black schools embrace an Afrocentric curriculum that, in some of its variants, may run afoul of these principles. However, I wish to distinguish the case for black schools as defined by their student bodies and personnel from issues raised by Afrocentric curricula, because a predominantly black school need not have an Afrocentric curriculum but may nevertheless be worth defending. It is a mistake, that is, to ground the defense of black schools on the premise of black cultural distinctiveness or on the basis of a curriculum that a predominantly black school may or may not have (see Merry 2013, chap. 6).

So can black schools provide an acceptable trade-off between costs and benefits, and are they compatible with liberal theory? I think that the answer to both of these questions is yes. To answer the first one, we must examine both the costs and the benefits of predominantly black schools. The costs that advocates of integration would emphasize have already been mentioned: predominantly black schools may reproduce the social isolation of African Americans and often concentrate poor students who do not benefit from being among peers whose social and family backgrounds incline them to value academic pursuits. Integration policies often improve the academic performance and long-term career prospects of black students. As I mentioned earlier, however, these improvements involve a comparison to the status quo, which includes poorly resourced black schools—so the evidence fails to show that integration itself provides these benefits, as opposed to the increased educational resources that black students have access to by virtue of being at a predominantly white school. Still, we can grant that integration can provide important benefits and that under favorable conditions it may be a practicable strategy for advancing racial equality.

But what advantages can black schools provide? In an earlier essay (Valls 2002) I emphasized two: predominantly black schools can protect and promote black culture, and they can provide a refuge in a racist world, a place where African Americans form a majority and exercise some control over an important institution. I am now much more wary of relying on an unproblematic or essentialized notion of "black culture" to justify predominantly black institutions, including schools. Whether there is a distinct black culture, wherein its distinctiveness lies, and to what extent it should be preserved are all deeply contested questions. But as I argued in chapter 4, these are questions that African Americans are entitled to debate under conditions that do not unduly favor certain outcomes. In the case of schools, within liberal limits African Americans can engage in what Eamonn Callan (2005, 498) calls "quasi-nation building." Liberal theory does not guarantee the success of that project, but it should ensure that those who undertake it are able to do so under fair conditions.

Black schools, as well as other predominantly black institutions, still provide a refuge in an often hostile and racist society. Black schools, like schools for girls and women's colleges, help prepare members of a disadvantaged group to compete in the wider world. A predominantly black school, especially one that defines its identity and its mission in these terms, tends to affirm the message that African Americans are capable of achievement. Its curriculum is likely to highlight African American, and more generally black, accomplishments and contributions. This is a very different set of messages, or at least a very different emphasis, from what a black student in a predominantly white school is likely to receive.

If enhanced self-esteem comes at the cost of academic achievement, then black schools would involve a sacrifice in terms of providing equality of opportunity. If there is a trade-off between equality of opportunity on the one hand and self-respect on the other, then we are faced with some difficult choices (Brighouse 2007). But there is no evidence of such a trade-off. There is no reason to believe that a predominantly black school, with adequate resources, cannot provide an excellent education. In fact, research suggests that predominantly black schools may have some advantages in this regard. For example, the problem of 'acting white,' where black students who achieve academically are penalized by their peers, seems to be much more of a problem in integrated schools than in black schools. Where African Americans are a minority, the pressure toward group solidarity increases in ways that may harm motivation to achieve. But in predominantly black schools, academic achievement is not as strongly associated with "acting white," and it does not carry the same penalties. So black schools, and peer relations among students in them, may be more conducive to academic achievement (Fryer 2006; Fryer and Torelli 2010).

Even if black schools can provide a good education and foster academic achievement, they may still fail to provide fair equality of opportunity in life prospects if they exacerbate, or fail to address, the problem of social isolation and the barriers to academic achievement associated with concentrated poverty, as Elizabeth Anderson emphasized. I acknowledge that this is a serious issue, but overcoming social isolation by itself cannot bear the whole weight of justifying integration as a single-minded strategy, nor is there any reason to think that social isolation can be overcome only in and through schools. Integrating schools is neither a necessary nor a sufficient condition for addressing the problem, and (again) in many metropolitan areas integration is either not a viable option or would involve such high costs as to not be worth the benefits. So we have to think about other ways of addressing social isolation beyond integrating schools.

The problems for schooling posed by concentrated poverty and social isolation point to the importance of addressing education as one component in an overarching approach to racial justice. Education alone cannot overcome racial inequality, and it is impossible to address all of the problems associated with (equal and adequate) schooling within the schoolhouse itself. If the policies I have advocated in previous chapters were adopted, then the disadvantages of living in a predominantly black neighborhood and attending a predominantly black school would be greatly diminished. The transportation, public services, job training, infrastructure, and so forth, of these neighborhoods would be much better than they are. As I argued in chapter 6, the disadvantages of living in a predominantly black neighborhood can and should be addressed without destroying those neighborhoods and dispersing their inhabitants. If the problems plaguing many inner-city black neighborhoods were aggressively addressed, then the disadvantages of the schools located within them would also be greatly diminished.

But if these schools can provide quality education and equality of opportunity, can they also provide education for democratic citizenship? There are good reasons to think that they can. While predominantly black schools may tend to suffer from what Meira Levinson (2012) calls a "civic empowerment gap," whereby students are not well trained to engage their wider society as equal citizens, there is no reason to think that this gap can only be addressed through integration and not through reforms within the predominantly black schools themselves. Indeed, as Levinson's account of her time as a teacher in predominantly black middle schools in Atlanta and Boston attests, much can be done through pedagogical and curricular reform to address this gap. One of the striking features of Levinson's book is the virtual absence of integration as a topic—let alone any reliance on it as a solution to the problems she identifies. Rather, Levinson takes de facto segregation in schools more or less as a given, and proceeds to think very fruitfully about how black children can be prepared for active and effective citizenship. Levinson is quite bullish on the prospects for this, despite acknowledging the depth of the problems and the seriousness of the obstacles.

More generally, as Callan (1997, chap. 7) as argued, "separate" schools may nevertheless be common schools in the sense that much of what they teach is similar to what is taught in other schools. Despite their "separateness," they may teach respect and tolerance toward other groups and may prepare their students for citizenship in the wider community. Of course, whether predominantly black (or white) schools will be common schools in this sense depends crucially on the curriculum that they offer.

CURRICULUM IN BLACK AND WHITE

As I have already noted, some authors assume that a "black school" is best understood and justified in terms of its distinctive curriculum. This is a mistake: a predominantly black school may have a very traditional curriculum and may employ a very traditional pedagogy. But it remains the case that one of the things that worries critics of black schools is that their curriculum may teach the "wrong" values and may inhibit rather than facilitate black students' entry into the institutions and culture of the wider society. This is a legitimate concern from the point of view of liberal theory. As discussed at the outset, one function of education, particularly public education, is to open up future opportunities for children, not only so that they may pursue different careers, but also so that they can reflect upon and decide on their conception of the good life. This is why the *Wisconsin v. Yoder* (1972) decision, which allowed the Amish to pull their children out of public schools at an early age, is so problematic from a liberal point of view. It places priority on parental rights and the perseveration of the Amish as a group over the interests of the children in their own education and autonomy.

Among advocates of black schools, and of a distinctively black curriculum, there is disagreement on this very issue: whether the goal is to enhance the opportunities of students by preparing them to participate in a multiethnic and multiracial (though still white-dominated) society.

For some, "The overriding concern is to prepare African-Americans to compete in a society that is currently dominated by institutions controlled by the white population" (Steele 1993, 595; see also powell 1993, 681–82; Leake and Leake 1992, 785). For others, however, this is an "outdated goal" (Rockquemore 1997, 190). From a liberal point of view, it is deeply problematic for a group to limit the opportunities, both for economic advancement and for self-development, in the interest of maintaining or promoting group cohesion. Hence any school curriculum must be compatible with the requirement that it does not limit students' prospects in these ways.

The kind of curriculum that most worries critics of black schools is often called "Afrocentrism" (see Asante 1987, 1988). Afrocentrism is a loose collection of doctrines, generally placing Africa and its culture(s) at the center of the curriculum, and emphasizing the unity of all people of African descent. According to one critic, three strands of thought are prominent in Afrocentric thought (Sewall 1996, 55–56). First, Afrocentrism portrays Africa, and in particular Egypt, as the source of much of ancient Greek culture, and by extension portrays much of Western civilization as having its origins in Africa. Second, Afrocentrism "operates on a particular theory of cultural inheritance and continuity" (1996, 56) such that all black people, regardless of their location or socialization, have an essential nature that is tied to Africa and its culture (the latter of which is also essentialized). Third, Afrocentrism involves a rejection of "Western values and modes as deeply flawed, even evil" (1996, 56).

So described, Afrocentrism raises a number of concerns on the part of its critics. First, Afrocentrism may teach things that simply are not true. According to Sewall, "In Afrocentric education, the ordinary tests of historical proof are suspended" (1996, 55). It presents "dubious claims . . . as facts" (Schlesinger 1992, 78; see also Lefkowitz 1997). Second, and perhaps even more important, Afrocentrism may be incompatible with one traditional goal of public education: the creation of a sense of nationality and common bonds. According to Amy Gutmann, "The inaccuracy of Afrocentrism is only part of what makes it problematic as an educational movement. The chief problem with Afrocentric education from a democratic perspective is not inaccuracy but *discrimination*. Its cultivation of a reverse racial mythology and sense of racial superiority makes Afrocentrism an uncivic ideology" (1996, 158).

These critics may be right about the version(s) of Afrocentrism that they are discussing and that have been prominent in public debates. But, following Lawrence Blum, we can distinguish between "moderate" and "extreme" forms of Afrocentrism. According to Blum, we should think of moderate Afrocentrism as involving "a special and distinct concern with the problems of African-American students and a desire to ensure a recognition of the character, historical importance, and contributions of both African-Americans and African civilizations." Extreme Afrocentrism, for Blum, is the strand that claims that "European civilizations hold nothing of cultural or ethical worth but only oppression to members of the African diaspora" (1996, 48n). While extreme Afrocentrism may be incompatible with liberal and democratic education, moderate Afrocentrism is compatible. Indeed, as some advocates of Afrocentrism make clear, an Afrocentric curriculum should be provided in addition to, not instead of, the common curriculum that is prescribed to all schools (Sanders and Reed 1995, 96). In other respects as well, Afrocentrism can and should be made compatible with the constraints on education that have been discussed above: it should teach the truth as far as this can be discerned and should teach liberal values and democratic citizenship. All of this is compatible, however, with a special focus on the history, experiences, and contributions of Africa and people of African descent. As in many other cases of educational curricula with a particular focus, it is compatible with the ideal of the common school and common curriculum.

We should not leave the topic of curricula without at least a brief consideration of the demands of racial justice for the common curriculum itself, particularly as it is taught in predominantly white schools. All schools, as I have said, should teach mutual respect among citizens and convey the idea that all are civic and moral equals. But more than this, as I argued in chapter 3, racial justice has implications for how the past is remembered and memorialized. This has important implications for curricula, since it is in schools that citizens often learn first and best the history of their society. So how American history is taught, and particularly its racially charged events, is important for racial justice.

In this respect, much progress has been made in recent decades, particularly in the South, but that progress has sometimes been partial, incomplete, and uneven. According to one study that examined the history curricula in all fifty states (Stern and Stern 2011), while some southern states have revised their curriculum to reflect most historians' understanding of events, others continue to soft-pedal some episodes in American history, particularly with respect to the Civil War and the civil rights movement. One example of improvement is Alabama, where, according to the study, "The decisive role of slavery in the coming of the Civil War is candidly acknowledged . . . [and] slavery and its aftermath are dealt with openly and honestly. The course makes no effort to either glorify or conceal the role of Alabama in the antebellum period" (2011, 21). By contrast, Texas fares very poorly in the report, which highlights how "complex historical issues are obscured with blatant politicizing." Slavery is "largely missing. . . . Sectionalism and states' rights are listed before slavery as causes of the Civil War, while the issue of slavery in the territories—the actual trigger for the sectional crisis—is never mentioned at all. During and after Reconstruction, there is no mention of the Black Codes, the Ku Klux Klan, or sharecropping; the term 'Jim Crow' never appears. Incredibly, racial segregation is only mentioned in a passing reference to the 1948 integration of the armed forces" (2011, 142; see also Southern Poverty Law Center 2018).

Of course textbooks and prescribed curricula are one thing, and how a teacher teaches the material—with what additions, emphases, and omissions—is something else. Even where the official curriculum passes muster, there may be reason to be concerned about what is actually taught in many classrooms on issues where race is salient. As one historian has remarked, "The way courses are taught depends on the teacher, and changes in textbooks can only go so far." There is anecdotal evidence that, particularly in the South, what is taught about the Civil War in particular is deeply concerning from the point of view of racial justice (Strauss 2010).

HBCUs

A useful way to bring together many of the themes of the argument that I have been making throughout this book is to focus on historically black colleges and universities (HBCUs). These institutions were mainly created to provide education to freed slaves and, later, to give African Americans access to higher education at a time when almost no predominantly white institutions would admit blacks. Under Jim Crow, HBCUs helped to create the black middle class and produced many of the teachers who taught in segregated schools. Many HBCUs, such as Morehouse College, have a storied place in African American history. Generations of African Americans have attended these schools, and they have provided a pathway for many into professional life.

In the post-civil rights era, however, HBCUs have struggled. The roughly one hundred HBCUs, some public, some private, still collectively produce about 20 percent of all black college graduates in the United States (Fryer and Greenstone 2010, 116). But they must now compete with many predominantly white colleges and universities that aggressively recruit the top black high school graduates. Some ask, why do HBCUs still exist? What is their mission? Are they not an anachronism, a holdover from a bygone era (Riley 2010)?

Yet HBCUs continue to serve a vital function for African Americans, and attempts to integrate them have done much harm and little good. The existence of predominantly black colleges and universities should not be seen as a failure of integration, but rather as evidence of a continuing need that they serve, and they should be looked on as a means to expand the opportunities for African Americans. Like women's colleges, they provide a place where a disadvantaged group is in control and is served by the particular environment that is thereby created. At HBCUs African Americans are the majority, and the mission of these institutions is to combat the racism of the wider society and to bolster the achievement of African American students. Countless graduates, such as Ta-Nehisi Coates (2013), attest to the important role that an HBCU played in their development.

The social-scientific evidence on the benefits of attending an HBCU is mixed, however. Some studies find that black students attending them report "better academic performance, greater social involvement, and higher occupational aspirations than Black students who attended predominantly White institutions" (Allen 1992, 39). But a more recent analysis suggests that students who attend HBCUs may pay a penalty in terms of their future earnings, perhaps because predominantly white institutions have gotten better at fostering success among their black students (Fryer and Greenstone 2010). The mixed record of HBCUs may be partly due to the fact that they tend to enroll students who are less well prepared and from lower socioeconomic backgrounds than African American students who attend predominantly white colleges and universities (Fryer and Greenstone 2010, 125). But the situation is made worse by the fact that HBCUs have small endowments and that the public ones are often underfunded by the state. One recent report found that ten states provide fewer funds to their HBCUs than is required by law (Kelderman 2013a).

An even greater threat to HBCUs may be the integrationist perspective that has animated legal doctrine and public policy with respect to them. A prime example of this is the Supreme Court's decision in *United States v. Fordice* (1992). In this case, plaintiffs brought suit against the State of Mississippi, arguing that it continued to maintain two unequal systems of higher education by providing disparate funding to its predominantly white and predominantly black colleges and universities. What the plaintiffs sought was increased funding for the state's black institutions. The Court refused to order this, instead ordering program duplication between the two sets of institutions to be eliminated. This created pressure on the HBCUs in the system to integrate by attracting more white students (Johnson 1993). Only by doing so could the HBCUs obtain additional resources (Sum, Light, and King 2004, 3). Hence much of the burden of overcoming segregation in the system was placed on the HBCUs, and the remedy was transformed from improving the HBCUs, as the plaintiffs had sought, to using carrots and sticks to get the HBCUs to integrate. This approach has been repeated elsewhere. In Maryland, for example, public

HBCUs have been required to meet a specific quota of white students before they can gain access to additional funding (Hebel 2001; Kelderman 2013b).

This approach has therefore led to the perverse situation where black colleges and universities are using much more aggressive forms of affirmative action for white students, including quotas, than is permitted for predominantly white institutions recruiting black applicants. It also places the burden on the HBCUs themselves. Rather than providing additional funds that would enhance their programs, and that may (or may not) attract more white students—but that in any case would enhance the education of the black students attending the schools—these institutions are told that unless they become more integrated, the additional funds will be withheld. Of course integrating HBCUs is more easily said than done, particularly because of the perceptions of white students and their families (Sum, Light, and King 2004). The racial attitudes of whites have the effect of increasing the incentives that black schools must offer to attract white students.

A more sensible, and more just, approach would be to give the plaintiffs in the *Fordice* case what they sought: additional funding for public HBCUs, not conditional on integration, but unconditionally. Increased funding should not be used to attempt to attract more white students to the schools, but should enhance the education of the students who already attend them. Furthermore, the range of options available to college-bound black students is enhanced by the existence of HBCUs. Unlike K-12 schools, where choice is not always available, higher education provides a realm in which genuine choice is possible.

As I argued in chapter 5, the impulse to make each college and university "diverse" in more or less the same way has the effect of reducing diversity among institutions. Rather than pursuing this path, we should make room for diversity both within and among institutions. Supporting HBCUs is one important way to do this. This is why I argued for a conception of "uneven" integration. Predominantly white colleges and universities should engage in affirmative action to try to attract black students. But this should not mean that the demographic profile of each school should be the same as every other. Rather, for now at least, HBCUs have a valuable and legitimate role to play, and they should be allowed to compete with other schools for black students. But the competition must be fair, meaning that HBCUs must not be handicapped by a long history, and current practice, of unequal funding.

This does not guarantee the long-term survival of HBCUs as predominantly black institutions. If it turns out that, under conditions of fair competition, African Americans abandon the colleges and universities that many of their parents and grandparents attended, this may be reason for regret, but it is no injustice. When it comes to HBCUs, as with other black institutions, liberal principles do not guarantee indefinite survival, but they do require that the conditions under which their fate is decided are fair.

CONCLUSION

It is a mistake to think that racial justice requires integration in schools. Justice requires, not integration, but an equitable distribution of educational resources and, crucially, a policy of assigning students to schools that does not impose undue costs on black students and families. Where possible, providing a choice between, say, a predominantly black school and a more integrated one would be desirable. But under the conditions that exist in many geographic areas, particularly many urban areas, making such a choice available is not a viable option because of residential segregation. In this case, ensuring that a good-quality education is available at a local, neighborhood school may be the most sensible approach.

There are, no doubt, conditions under which integration is the best option for ensuring quality education for black students, and under these conditions (say, where residential segregation is not too severe), integration should be seen as one viable option to pursue. In such cases, black students may have little choice but to attend an integrated school even if they would prefer not to. I have not argued that black students have a right to attend a predominantly black school, any more than they have a right to attend an integrated one. What they have a right to is an adequate and equal set of educational opportunities, and schooling that respects the demands of liberal and democratic education.

9

Conclusion

What is the conception of racial justice that follows from the foregoing considerations? One way to answer this question is simply to summarize the main normative conclusions for which I have argued. On the account offered here, racial justice requires reparations, understood as a set of policies to address racial inequalities with respect to income, wealth, and opportunities; appropriate acknowledgment and collective memory, which affirms the moral and civic equality of African Americans; support for black institutions and communities; aggressive affirmative action policies; dramatic improvement of conditions in poor black neighborhoods (a domestic Marshall Plan rather than deconcentration); reform of the criminal justice system to reduce rates of incarceration, eliminate racial biases, and improve the prospects of ex-prisoners; and improvement of the educational opportunities of black students where they live, whether in predominantly white or predominantly black schools.

The underlying theme that unites all of these prescriptions is a commitment to the liberty and equality of all, particularly African Americans. Placing the emphasis on liberty and equality, I have argued, leads to policies that improve the lives and opportunities of African Americans without coercion in the service of integration. This entails supporting black neighborhoods, black schools, black colleges and universities, and other black institutions, on the one hand, while ensuring that African Americans are also welcome and free to participate in settings where they are a minority. It demands that all Americans have accurate factual information about our racial past and its impact on the present, and the moral and civic equality of all must not only be reflected in the substance of policy but must also be publicly affirmed—both to express the values of the political order and to rebut the views of citizens who remain nostalgic for the old order.

Another theme underlying all of the arguments offered here is the importance of giving due attention to the distinctiveness of black claims. The arguments in this book have not been those of high theory, ideal or otherwise. This is because determining what justice demands, here and now, for a specific group in a specific society involves deep engagement with the history and circumstances concerning that particular case. The book also does not offer a general theory that applies to all racialized minorities, all postemancipation societies, or all multiethnic, multinational, or multicultural societies. As I noted at the outset, other groups have their distinctive claims, and other societies have their own histories that may raise issues similar to those treated here. I certainly hope that the arguments offered in the preceding chapters provide some inspiration for others confronting similar issues. But I have made no attempt to extend my arguments to other contexts, preferring to first develop, as fully as I can, an account of racial justice as it applies to African Americans.

One thing that I hope this single-minded focus has allowed me to do is to place the issues in their proper historical and empirical (and not just theoretical) context. In exploring what justice requires in a case like this, facts matter. History matters. It matters a great deal whether present-day racial inequality is the product of a fair competition or the result of unrectified systemic injustice. Of course, liberal egalitarians are right to point out that we have good reasons to address racial inequality quite apart from the history that brought it about, but the tenor of the debate changes when the emphasis is placed on generic egalitarian principles outside of any historical context. The debate becomes about whether liberal-egalitarian principles are the right ones, and if so, what their implications are. To be sure, I have appealed to universalist liberal-egalitarian principles, but I hope that emphasizing the history and context has enabled me to offer arguments that that will be persuasive to a variety of philosophical and ideological perspectives. Placing the issues of race and racial justice in a historical context shifts the debate from the merits and implications of universalist principles to the terrain of clear injustice (even on more limited views of what justice requires) and what is required to address its legacies. Even those who are not liberal egalitarians can recognize the injustices of the past as injustices, and given the way that these have shaped the distribution of resources and opportunities in the present, those with less egalitarian views nevertheless should be able to endorse at least some of the arguments offered in the preceding chapters.

At the same time, the conception of racial justice developed here converges with many of the demands of movements, both within and outside of the academy, that are sometimes thought of as radical and are understood in contradistinction to liberalism. Some of the arguments that I have presented resonate with those offered by scholars affiliated with critical race theory, who support policies such as reparations and affirmative action while rejecting integration and assimilation as the primary route to racial justice. Indeed, my perspective on racial justice has been shaped by critical race theory, and in particular its view of racial injustice as deeply embedded in American society and its resulting pessimism (or at least "realism") about the prospects of overcoming racial inequality. While many critical race theorists see their outlook as an alternative to liberalism, I have been spurred by their arguments, particularly those of Gary Peller (1995, 2012), to show that in fact liberal political theory can endorse many of the positions associated with their perspective.

Similarly, it is striking the extent to which the issues I have focused on, and the conclusions I have reached, converge with those of the Movement for Black Lives (2017). An examination of the website of the organization shows that many of the demands of the movement are essentially the same as the conclusions that I have reached: reparations, criminal justice reform, support for black communities and neighborhoods, and so forth.

The fact is, I would suggest, that many of the demands of "radical" movements such as the Movement for Black Lives are also the demands of liberalism. Liberal values of liberty and equality have great emancipatory potential, and much of the work of social movements is to show that these values have unrecognized implications. Many political conflicts involve arguments about the meaning and implications of liberal values, and these values have proven to be sufficiently expansive to support progressive change. Much of the social and legal progress that has taken place in American history has been advanced by breathing new life into these simple values and using them to point to ways in which the status quo fails to live up to them.

This is not to say that liberal political theory, as it has been expounded by scholars, is always as helpful as it could be. Too little attention has been given to issues that, despite their intrinsic philosophical interest and their political importance, fall outside of what seems to be considered the core concerns of liberal political theory. This is particularly the case regarding the issues that were discussed in chapter 3, on acknowledgment, memorialization, and collective memory. While some work has been done on these matters, they merit much more attention, particularly in light of the current conflicts surrounding them in contemporary American politics.

In the end, then, liberal political theory has far-reaching implications for racial justice as it pertains to African Americans. But the case of African Americans has much to teach us about the state of political theory. The persistence of racial inequality in the United States, in all of its manifestations, is in part due to a failure to enact what justice clearly requires. But it may be partly due to a genuine uncertainty about what is to be done. Racial inequality raises issues where what justice requires is not immediately obvious. Engaging with real-world injustice is one fruitful way to explore the resources and implications of liberal values.

This book makes its appearance in the year that marks the fiftieth anniversary of the assassination of Martin Luther King Jr. With the assassination of King and the passage of the Fair Housing Act soon thereafter, 1968 is often thought of as the closing chapter of the civil rights era. Nothing said in this book is meant to deny that much progress on issues of race has been made in those fifty years, but what is even more striking is how much more progress needs to be made. Deep inequality persists, and in many ways the current era perpetuates the racial patterns created under slavery and Jim Crow. To a great extent, continuity, not rupture and repudiation, characterizes the relation of the present to our racial past. Much of the population responds to racial inequality (when it is aware of it at all) with indifference, and attempts at further progress are often greeted with outright opposition and hostility. The current resurgence of white nationalism and white supremacy in mainstream American political discourse merely exposes racial attitudes that attentive observers have known to be there all along.

The indifference, hostility, and entrenched interests that help to perpetuate racial inequality make it nearly impossible to be optimistic about further progress. I had hoped to conclude this book on a positive note, but, particularly in this moment, that would be disingenuous. Any progress on issues of race will likely be difficult, uneven, and precarious, and indeed there is always the danger of backsliding and regression. One thing is certain: further progress toward racial justice will not take place on its own. Racial inequality, in all of its manifestations, is stubbornly durable. I fear that fifty, or even one hundred, years from now American society will be confronted with many of the same issues of race that it faces today. Indeed, without a renewed sense of urgency and commitment to the pursuit of racial justice, that outcome is virtually guaranteed.

BIBLIOGRAPHY

Adams, Mason. 2016. "How the Rebel Flag Rose Again—and Is Helping Trump." Available at http://www.politico.com/magazine/story/2016/06/2016-donald-trump-south-confedcrate-flag-racism-charleston shooting 213954. Accessed June 16, 2016.

Ahmad, Muhammad. 2007. *We Will Return in the Whirlwind: Black Radical Organizations, 1960-1975*. Chicago: Charles H. Kerr.

Alderman, Derek H. 2006a. "Street Names as Memorial Arenas: The Reputational Politics of Commemorating Martin Luther King, Jr. in a Georgia County." In Renee C. Romano and Leigh Raiford, eds., *The Civil Rights Movement in American Memory*. Athens: University of Georgia Press, 67–95.

Alderman, Derek H. 2006b. "Naming Streets for Martin Luther King Jr.: No Easy Road." In Richard H. Schein, ed., *Landscape and Race in the United States*. New York: Routledge, 213–36.

Alderman, Derek H. 2008. "Martin Luther King, Jr. Streets in the South: A New Landscape of Memory." *Southern Cultures* 14: 88–105.

Alexander, Michelle. 2012. *The New Jim Crow: Mass Incarceration in the Age of Colorblindness*. Rev. ed. New York: New Press.

Allen, Jonathan. 1999. "Balancing Justice and Social Utility: Political Theory and the Idea of a Truth and Reconciliation Commission." *University of Toronto Law Journal* 49: 315–53.

Allen, Walter R. 1992. "The Color of Success: African-American College Student Outcomes at Predominantly White and Historically Black Public Colleges and Universities." *Harvard Educational Review* 62: 26–44.

Alter, Torin. 2000a. Review of George Schedler, *Racist Symbols and Reparations: Philosophical Reflections on Vestiges of the American Civil War. Social Theory and Practice* 26: 153–71.

Alter, Torin. 2000b. "Symbolic Meaning and the Confederate Battle Flag." *Philosophy in the Contemporary World* 7: 1–4.

Altman, Andrew. 2005. "Democratic Self-Determination and the Disenfranchisement of Felons." *Journal of Applied Philosophy* 22: 263–73.

America, Richard. 1972. "A New Rational [*sic*] for Income Redistribution." *Review of Black Political Economy* 2: 3–21.

Anderson, Elizabeth. 2004. "Racial Integration as a Compelling Interest." *Constitutional Commentary* 21: 15–40.

Anderson, Elizabeth. 2007. "Fair Opportunity in Education: A Democratic Equality Perspective." *Ethics* 117: 595–622.

Anderson, Elizabeth. 2010. *The Imperative of Integration*. Princeton: Princeton University Press.

Anderson, Elizabeth. 2012. "Race, Culture, and Educational Opportunity." *Theory and Research in Education* 10: 105–29.

Anderson, Terry H. 2004. *The Pursuit of Fairness: A History of Affirmative Action*. Oxford: Oxford University Press.

Appiah, Anthony and Amy Gutmann. 1996. *Color-Conscious: The Political Morality of Race*. Princeton: Princeton University Press.

Asante, Molefi Kete. 1987. *The Afrocentric Idea*. Philadelphia: Temple University Press.

Asante, Molefi Kete. 1988. *Afrocentricity*. Trenton: Africa World Press.

Aspenson, Steve. 2013. "The Rescue Defense of Capital Punishment." *Ratio* 26: 91–105.

Ayres, Ian and Richard Brooks. 2005. "Does Affirmative Action Reduce the Number of Black Lawyers?" *Stanford Law Review* 57: 1807–54.

Baldus, David C., Charles Pulaski, and George Woodworth. 1983. "Comparative Review of Death Sentences: An Empirical Study of the Georgia Experience." *Journal of Criminal Law and Criminology* 74: 661–753.

Balfour, Lawrie. 2008. "Act and Fact: Slavery Reparations as a Democratic Politics of Reconciliation." In Will Kymlicka and Bashir Bashir, eds., *The Politics of Reconciliation in Multicultural Societies*. Oxford: Oxford University Press, 94–113.

Banaji, Mahzarin R. and Anthony G. Greenwald. 2012. *BlindSpot: Hidden Biases of Good People*. New York: Delacorte Press.

Barber, Benjamin R. 2013. *If Mayors Ruled the World: Dysfunctional Nations, Rising Cities*. New Haven: Yale University Press.

Baraka, Amiri. 1997. "Speech to the Congress of African Peoples." In William L. Van Deburg, ed., *Modern Black Nationalism: From Marcus Garvey to Louis Farrakhan*. New York: New York University Press, 145–57.

Barkan, Elazar. 2000. *The Guilt of Nations: Restitution and Negotiating Historical Injustices*. New York: Norton.

Barkan, Elazar. 2007. "Introduction: Reparation: A Moral and Political Dilemma." In Jon Miller and Rahul Kumar, eds., *Reparations: Interdisciplinary Inquiries*. Oxford: Oxford University Press, 1–19.

Barsalou, Judy and Victoria Baxter. 2007. "The Urge to Remember: The Role of Memorials in Social Reconstruction and Transitional Justice." Stabilization and Reconstruction Series No. 5. United States Institute of Peace.

Bassett, C. Jeanne. 1994. "House Bill 591: Florida Compensates Rosewood Victims and Their Families for a Seventy-One-Year-Old Injury." *Florida State University Law Review* 22: 503–23.

Bedau, Hugo Adam. 1972. "Compensatory Justice and the Black Manifesto." *Monist* 56: 20–42.

Bendick, Marc, Jr., Charles W. Jackson, and Victor A. Reinoso. 1994. "Measuring Employment Discrimination through Controlled Experiments." *Review of Black Political Economy* 23: 25–48.

Bennett, Christopher. 2006. "State Denunciation of Crime." *Journal of Moral Philosophy* 3: 288–304.

Bermanzohn, Sally Avery. 2007. "A Massacre Survivor Reflects on the Greensboro Truth and Reconciliation Commission." *Radical History Review* 97: 102–109.

Bertrand, Marianne and Sendhil Mullainathan. 2004. "Are Emily and Greg More Employable Than Lakisha and Jamal? A Field Experiment on Labor Market Discrimination." *American Economic Review* 94: 991–1013.

Bhargava, Rajeev. 2000. "Restoring Decency to Barbaric Societies." In Robert I. Rotberg and Dennis Thompson, eds., *Truth v. Justice: The Morality of Truth Commissions*. Princeton: Princeton University Press, 45–67.

Bickford, Susan. 2000. "Constructing Inequality: City Spaces and the Architecture of Citizenship." *Political Theory* 28: 355–76.

Bittker, Boris I. 1973. *The Case for Black Reparations*. Boston: Beacon Press.

Blackmon, Douglas A. 2008. *Slavery by Another Name: The Re-enslavement of Black Americans from the Civil War to World War II*. New York: Anchor Books.

Blatz, Craig W., Karina Schumann, and Michael Ross. 2009. "Government Apologies for Historical Injustices." *Political Psychology* 30: 219–41.

Blinder, Alan. 2016. "Momentum to Remove Confederate Symbols Slows or Stops." *New York Times*, March 13. Available at http://nyti.ms/22e4TEN. Accessed March 14, 2016.

Blinder, Alan and Richard Fausset. 2017. "Nearly 8 Decades Later, an Apology for a Lynching in Georgia." *New York Times*, January 26. Available at http://nyti.ms/2k9gMii. Accessed January 27, 2017.

Bloom, Joshua and Waldo E. Martin Jr. 2016. *Black against Empire: The History and Politics of the Black Panther Party*. New ed. Berkeley: University of California Press.

Blum, Lawrence. 1996. "Antiracist Civic Education in the California History-Social Science Framework." In Robert K. Fullinwider, ed., *Public Education in a Multicultural Society: Policy, Theory, Critique*. Cambridge: Cambridge University Press, 23–48.

Blum, Lawrence. 1998. "'Racial Integration' Revisited." In Joram G. Haber and Mark S. Halfon, eds., *Norms and Values: Essays on the Work of Virginia Held*. Lanham: Rowman and Littlefield, 205–29.

Blum, Lawrence. 2002. "The Promise of Racial Integration in a Multicultural Age." In Stephen Macedo and Yael Tamir, eds., *NOMOS XLIII: Moral and Political Education*. New York: New York University Press, 383–424.

Blumenson, Eric. 2007. "Killing in Good Conscience: What's Wrong with Sunstein and Vermeule's Lesser Evil Argument for Capital Punishment and Other Human Rights Violations?" *New Criminal Law Review* 10: 210–38.

Blumstein, Alfred. 1982. "On Racial Disproportionality of the United States' Prison Populations." *Journal of Criminal Law and Criminology* 73: 1259–81.

Blustein, Jeffrey. 2008. *The Moral Demands of Memory*. Cambridge: Cambridge University Press.

Boettcher, James. 2009. "Race, Ideology, and Ideal Theory." *Metaphilosophy* 40: 237–59.

Bonner, Robert E. 2002. *Colors and Blood: Flag Passions of the Confederate South.* Princeton: Princeton University Press.

Boonin, David. 2011. *Should Race Matter? Unusual Answers to the Usual Questions.* Cambridge: Cambridge University Press.

Booth, W. James. 2006. *Communities of Memory: On Witness, Identity, and Justice.* Ithaca: Cornell University Press.

Boraine, Alex. 2000. "Truth and Reconciliation in South Africa: The Third Way." In Robert I. Rotberg and Dennis Thompson, eds., *Truth v. Justice: The Morality of Truth Commissions.* Princeton: Princeton University Press, 141–57.

Bowen, William G. and Derek Bok. 1998. *The Shape of the River: Long-Term Consequences of Considering Race in College and University Admissions.* Princeton: Princeton University Press.

Bowen, William G., Matthew M. Chingos, and Michael S. McPherson. 2009. *Crossing the Finish Line: Completing College at America's Public Universities.* Princeton: Princeton University Press.

Boxill, Bernard R. 1972. "The Morality of Reparation." *Social Theory and Practice* 2: 113–23.

Boxill, Bernard R. 1978. "The Morality of Preferential Hiring." *Philosophy and Public Affairs* 7: 246–68.

Boxill, Bernard R. 1992. *Blacks and Social Justice.* Rev. ed. Lanham: Rowman and Littlefield.

Boxill, Bernard R., ed. 2001. *Race and Racism.* Oxford: Oxford University Press.

Branch, Taylor. 1998. *Pillar of Fire: America in the King Years, 1963–65.* New York: Simon and Schuster.

Brendese, P. J. 2014. *The Power of Memory in Democratic Politics.* Rochester: University of Rochester Press.

Brettschneider, Corey. 2007. "The Rights of the Guilty: Punishment and Political Legitimacy." *Political Theory* 35: 175–99.

Brettschneider, Corey. 2012. *When the State Speaks, What Should It Say? How Democracies Can Protect Expression and Promote Equality.* Princeton: Princeton University Press.

Briggs, Xavier de Souza, Susan J. Popkin, and John Goering. 2010. *Moving to Opportunity: The Story of an American Experiment to Fight Ghetto Poverty.* Oxford: Oxford University Press.

Brighouse, Harry. 2007. "Equality of Opportunity and Complex Equality: The Special Place of Schooling." *Res Publica* 13: 147–58.

Brooks, David. 2005. "Katrina's Silver Lining." *New York Times,* September 8. Available at http://www.nytimes.com/2005/09/08/opinion/katrinas-silver-lining.html. Accessed November 11, 2017.

Brooks, Roy L. 1996. *Integration or Separation? A Strategy for Racial Equality.* Cambridge: Harvard University Press.

Brooks, Roy L., ed. 1999. *When Sorry Isn't Enough: The Controversy over Apologies and Reparations for Human Injustice.* New York: New York University Press.

Brooks, Roy L. 2004. *Atonement and Forgiveness: A New Model for Black Reparations.* Berkeley: University of California Press.

Brooks, Roy L. 2009. *Racial Justice in the Age of Obama*. Princeton: Princeton University Press.

Brophy, Alfred L. 2002. *Reconstructing the Dreamland: The Tulsa Riot of 1921. Race, Reparations, and Reconciliation*. Oxford: Oxford University Press.

Brown, Michael K. 1999. *Race, Money, and the American Welfare State*. Ithaca: Cornell University Press.

Brown, Robert A. and Todd C. Shaw. 2002. "Separate Nations: Two Attitudinal Dimensions of Black Nationalism." *Journal of Politics* 64: 22–44.

Browne, Robert S. 1968. "The Case for Two Americas—One Black, One White." *New York Times Magazine*, August 11, 12–13, 50–51, 56, 60–61.

Browne, Robert S. 1972. "The Economic Basis for Reparations to Black America." *Review of Black Political Economy* 2: 67–80.

Brubaker, Stanley C. 1988. "Can Liberals Punish?" *American Political Science Review* 82: 821–36.

Bruyneel, Kevin. 2013. "The Trouble with Amnesia: Collective Memory and Colonial Injustice in the United States." In Gerald Berk and Dennis C. Galvan, eds., *Political Creativity: Reconfiguring Institutional Order and Change*. Philadelphia: University of Pennsylvania Press, 236–57.

Bruyneel, Kevin. 2014. "The King's Body: The Martin Luther King Jr. Memorial and the Politics of Collective Memory." *History & Memory* 26: 75–108.

Burch, Traci. 2012. "Did Disfranchisement Laws Help Elect President Bush? New Evidence on the Turnout Rates and Candidate Preferences of Florida's Ex-Felons." *Political Behavior* 34: 1–26.

Burch, Traci. 2013. *Trading Democracy for Justice: Criminal Convictions and the Decline of Neighborhood Political Participation*. Oxford: Oxford University Press.

Bush, Rod. 1999. *We Are Not What We Seem: Black Nationalism and Class Struggle in the American Century*. New York: New York University Press.

Callan, Eamonn. 1997. *Creating Citizens: Political Education and Liberal Democracy*. Oxford: Oxford University Press.

Callan, Eamonn. 2005. "The Ethics of Assimilation." *Ethics* 115: 471–500.

Carcieri, Martin. 2010. "Rawls and Reparations." *Michigan Journal of Race & Law* 15: 267–316.

Cave, Damien and Christine Jordon Sexton. 2008. "Florida Legislature Apologizes for State's History of Slavery." *New York Times*, March 27. Available at http://www.nytimes.com/2008/03/27/us/27florida.html. Accessed November 11, 2017.

Celermajer, Danielle. 2009. *The Sins of the Nation and the Ritual of Apologies*. Cambridge: Cambridge University Press.

Chambers, David L., Timothy T. Clydesdale, William C. Kidder, and Richard O. Lempert. 2005. "The Real Impact of Eliminating Affirmative Action in American Law Schools." *Stanford Law Review* 57: 1855–98.

Chapman, Audrey R. and Hugo van der Merwe, eds. 2008. *Truth and Reconciliation in South Africa: Did the TRC Deliver?* Philadelphia: University of Pennsylvania Press.

Chetty, Raj, Nathaniel Hendren, and Lawrence Katz. 2016. "The Effects of Exposure to Better Neighborhoods on Children: New Evidence from the Moving to Opportunity Experiment." *American Economic Review* 106: 855–902.

Cholbi, M. 2006. "Race, Capital Punishment, and the Cost of Murder." *Philosophical Studies* 127: 255–82.

Clark, John A. 1997. "Explaining Elite Attitudes on the Georgia Flag." *American Politics Quarterly* 25: 482–96.

Clear, Todd R. 2007. *Imprisoning Communities: How Mass Incarceration Makes Disadvantaged Neighborhoods Worse.* Oxford: Oxford University Press.

Clear, Todd R. and Natasha A. Frost. 2014. *The Punishment Imperative: The Rise and Failure of Mass Incarceration in America.* New York: New York University Press.

Coates, Ta-Nehisi. 2013. "Homecoming at Howard." *New York Times,* October 30. Available at http://www.nytimes.com/2013/10/30/opinion/coates-homecoming-at-howard.html. Accessed November 11, 2017.

Coates, Ta-Nehisi. 2014. "The Case for Reparations." *The Atlantic,* June. Available at https://www.theatlantic.com/magazine/archive/2014/06/the-case-for-reparations/361631/. Accessed November 12, 2017.

Cochran, David Carroll. 1999. *The Color of Freedom: Race and Contemporary American Liberalism.* Albany: State University of New York Press.

Cohen, Andrew I. 2017. "Vicarious Apologies and Moral Repair." *Ratio* 30: 359–73.

Cohen, G. A. 2011. "How to Do Political Philosophy." In *On the Currency of Egalitarian Justice, and Other Essays in Political Philosophy.* Princeton: Princeton University Press, 225–35.

Cole, David. 1999. *No Equal Justice: Race and Class in the American Criminal Justice System.* New York: New Press.

Cole, David. 2016. "Trouble at Yale." *New York Review of Books,* January 14.

Coleman, James S. 1966. *Equality of Educational Opportunity.* Washington, DC: Government Printing Office.

Collins, Daisy G. 1970. "The United States Owes Reparations to Its Black Citizens." *Howard Law Journal* 16: 82–114.

Conley, Dalton. 1999. *Being Black, Living in the Red: Race, Wealth, and Social Policy in America.* Berkeley: University of California Press.

Cooper, Christopher A. and H. Gibbs Knotts. 2006. "Region, Race, and Support for the South Carolina Confederate Flag." *Social Science Quarterly* 87: 142–54

Cooper, W. E. and John King-Farlow. 1989. "The Case for Capital Punishment." *Journal of Social Philosophy* 20: 64–76.

Coski, John M. 2000. "The Confederate Battle Flag in Historical Perspective." In J. Michael Martinez, William D. Richardson, and Ron McNinch-Su, eds., *Confederate Symbols in the Contemporary South.* Gainesville: University of Florida Press, 89–129.

Coski, John M. 2005. *The Confederate Battle Flag: America's Most Embattled Emblem.* Cambridge: Harvard University Press.

Costa, Victoria M. 2011. *Rawls, Citizenship, and Education.* New York: Routledge.

Cowen, Tyler. 1997. "Discounting and Restitution." *Philosophy and Public Affairs* 26: 168–85.

Cowen, Tyler. 2006. "How Far Back Should We Go? Why Restitution Should Be Small." In Jon Elster, ed., *Retribution and Reparation in the Transition to Democracy.* Cambridge: Cambridge University Press: 17–32.

Crocker, David A. 1999. "Reckoning with Past Wrongs: A Normative Framework." *Ethics and International Affairs* 13: 43–64.

Cruse, Harold. 1967. *The Crisis of the Negro Intellectual: From Its Origins to the Present*. New York: Morrow.

Cunningham, Michael. 1999. "Saying Sorry: The Politics of Apology." *Political Quarterly* 70: 285–93.

D'Orso, Michael. 1996. *Like Judgment Day: The Ruin and Redemption of a Town Called Rosewood*. New York: Putnam.

Dagger, Richard. 2000. "Metropolis, Memory, and Citizenship." In Engin F. Isin, ed., *Democracy, Citizenship, and the Global City*. New York: Routledge, 25–47.

Daniel, Pete. 1973. *The Shadow of Slavery: Peonage in the South, 1901–1969*. Oxford: Oxford University Press.

Darden, Joe T. 2003. "Residential Segregation: The Causes and Social and Economic Consequences." In Curtis Stokes and Theresa Meléndez, eds., *Racial Liberalism and the Politics of Urban America*. East Lansing: Michigan State University Press, 321–44.

Davis, Angela. 2003. *Are Prisons Obsolete?* New York: Seven Stories Press.

Davis, Darren W. and Ronald E. Brown. 2002. "The Antipathy of Black Nationalism: Behavioral and Attitudinal Implications of an African American Ideology." *American Journal of Political Science* 46: 239–53.

Davis, F. James. 1991. *Who Is Black? One Nation's Definition*. University Park: Pennsylvania State University Press.

Davis, Paul. 2002. "On Apologies." *Journal of Applied Philosophy* 19: 169–73.

Dawson, Michael C. 1994. *Behind the Mule: Race and Class in African-American Politics*. Princeton: Princeton University Press.

Dawson, Michael C. 1995. "A Black Counterpublic? Economic Earthquakes, Racial Agenda(s), and Black Politics." In The Black Public Sphere Collective, ed., *The Black Public Sphere*. Chicago: University of Chicago Press, 199–227.

Dawson, Michael C. 2001. *Black Visions: The Roots of Contemporary African American Political Ideologies*. Chicago: University of Chicago Press.

DeAngelis, Peter. 2014. "Racial Profiling and the Presumption of Innocence." *Netherlands Journal of Legal Philosophy* 43: 43–58.

De Greiff, Pablo. 2006a. "Introduction." In Pablo De Greiff, ed., *The Handbook of Reparations*. Oxford: Oxford University Press, 1–18.

De Greiff, Pablo. 2006b. "Justice and Reparations." In Pablo De Greiff, ed., *The Handbook of Reparations*. Oxford: Oxford University Press, 451–77.

De Greiff, Pablo. 2008. "The Role of Apologies in National Reconciliation Processes: On Making Trustworthy Institutions Trusted." In Mark Gibney, Rhoda E. Howard-Hassmann, Jean-Marc Coicaud, and Nicklaus Steiner, eds., *The Age of Apology: Facing Up to the Past*. Philadelphia: University of Pennsylvania Press, 120–36.

Desmond, Matthew. 2016. *Evicted: Poverty and Profit in the American City*. New York: Broadway Books.

Deveaux, Monique. 2006. *Gender and Justice in Multicultural Liberal Societies*. Oxford: Oxford University Press.

Doppelt, Gerald. 2009. "The Place of Self-Respect in a Theory of Justice." *Inquiry* 52: 127–54.

Draper, Theodore. 1970. *The Rediscovery of Black Nationalism*. New York: Viking Press.

Duff, R. A. 2001. *Punishment, Communication, and Community*. Oxford: Oxford University Press.

Duff, R. A. 2005. "Introduction: Crime and Citizenship." *Journal of Applied Philosophy* 22: 211–16.

du Toit, André. 2000. "The Moral Foundations of the South African TRC: Truth as Acknowledgment and Justice as Recognition." In Robert I. Rotberg and Dennis Thompson, eds., *Truth v. Justice: The Morality of Truth Commissions*. Princeton: Princeton University Press, 122–40.

Dwyer, Owen J. 2002. "Location, Politics, and the Production of Civil Rights Memorial Landscapes." *Urban Geography* 23: 31–56.

Dwyer, Owen J. 2004. "Symbolic Accretion and Commemoration." *Social & Cultural Geography* 5: 419–35.

Dwyer, Owen J. 2006. "Interpreting the Civil Rights Movement: Contradiction, Confirmation, and the Cultural Landscape." In Renee C. Romano and Leigh Raiford, eds., *The Civil Rights Movement in American Memory*. Athens: University of Georgia Press, 5–27.

Dwyer, Owen J. and Derek H. Alderman. 2008. *Civil Rights Memorials and the Geography of Memory*. Chicago: Center for American Places at Columbia College Chicago.

Dye, R. Thomas. 1996. "Rosewood, Florida: The Destruction of an African American Community." *Historian* 58: 605–23.

Dye, R. Thomas. 1997. "The Rosewood Massacre: History and the Making of Public Policy." *Public Historian* 19: 25–39.

Dyzenhaus, David. 2000. "Justifying the Truth and Reconciliation Commission." *Journal of Political Philosophy* 8: 470–96.

Edgemon, Erin. 2015. "Nathan Bedford Forrest Bust Back in Alabama Cemetery." Available at http://www.al.com/news/index.ssf/2015/05/nathan_bedford_forrest_bust_ba.html. Accessed October 26, 2017.

Eisenberg, Avigail and Jeff Spinner-Halev, eds. 2005. *Minorities within Minorities: Equality, Rights and Diversity*. Cambridge: Cambridge University Press.

Ellsworth, Scott. 1992. *Death in a Promised Land: The Tulsa Race Riot of 1921*. Baton Rouge: Louisiana State University Press.

Enos, Ryan D. 2012. "The End of Nothing." *Boston Review*, February 9. Available at http://www.bostonreview.net/ryan-d-enos-manhattan-institute-segregation. Accessed November 11, 2017.

Epp, Charles R., Steven Maynard-Moody, and Donald P. Haider-Markel. 2014. *Pulled Over: How Police Stops Define Race and Citizenship*. Chicago: University of Chicago Press.

Eskew, Glenn T. 2001. "From Civil War to Civil Rights: Selling Alabama as Heritage Tourism." *International Journal of Hospitality and Tourism Administration* 2: 201–14.

Eyal, Nir. 2005. "'Perhaps the Most Important Primary Good': Self-Respect and Rawls's Principles of Justice." *Politics, Philosophy, and Economics* 4: 195–219.

Fainstein, Susan S. 2010. *The Just City*. Ithaca: Cornell University Press.

Farrington, David P., Patrick A. Langan, and Michael Tonry, eds. 2004. *Cross-National Studies in Crime and Justice*. Washington, DC: Bureau of Justice Statistics.

Fausset, Richard. 2016. "As Trump Rises, So Do Some Hands Waving Confederate Battle Flags." *New York Times*, November 18. Available at http://nyti.ms/2f7OU7G. Accessed November 21, 2016.

Fears, Darryl. 2008. "House Issues an Apology for Slavery." *Washington Post*, July 30, A3.

Feinberg, Joel. 1970. "The Expressive Function of Punishment." In *Doing and Deserving: Essays in the Theory of Responsibility*. Princeton: Princeton University Press.

Feinberg, Joel. 1987. "Some Unswept Debris from the Hart-Devlin Debate." *Synthese* 72: 249–75.

Finan, Eileen. 1995. "Delayed Justice: The Rosewood Story." *Human Rights* 22: 8–30.

Fiss, Owen. 2003. *A Way Out: America's Ghettos and the Legacy of Racism*. Ed. Joshua Cohen, Jefferson Decker, and Joel Rogers. Princeton: Princeton University Press.

Fogg-Davis, H. 2003. "The Racial Retreat of Contemporary Political Theory." *Perspectives on Politics* 1: 555–64.

Foner, Philip S. 1974. *Organized Labor and the Black Worker, 1619–1973*. New York: Praeger.

Foner, Philip S., ed. 1995. *The Black Panthers Speak*. New York: Da Capo Press.

Ford, Richard. 2003. "Down by Law." In Joshua Cohen, Jefferson Decker, and Joel Rogers, eds., *A Way Out: America's Ghettos and the Legacy of Racism*. Princeton: Princeton University Press, 47–50.

Ford, Richard Thompson. 2005. *Racial Culture: A Critique*. Princeton: Princeton University Press.

Forman, James. 1969. "The Black Manifesto." In Robert S. Lecky and H. Elliott Wright, eds., *Black Manifesto: Religion, Racism, and Reparations*. New York: Sheed and Ward, 114–26.

Forman, James, Jr. 1991. "Driving Dixie Down: Removing the Confederate Flag from Southern State Capitols." *Yale Law Journal* 101: 505–26.

Forman, James, Jr. 2012. "Racial Critiques of Mass Incarceration: The New Jim Crow." Yale Law School Faculty Scholarship Series. Available at http://digitalcommons.law.yale.edu/fss_papers/3599/. Accessed November 17, 2017.

Forman, James, Jr. 2017. *Locking Up Our Own: Crime and Punishment in Black America*. New York: Farrar, Straus and Giroux.

Fortin, Jacey. 2017. "Florida Apologizes for 'Gross Injustices' to Four Black Men, Decades Later." *New York Times*, April 27. Available at http://nyti.ms/2qbz2rE. Accessed April 28, 2017.

Foster, Gaines M. 1987. *Ghosts of the Confederacy: Defeat, the Lost Cause, and the Emergence of the New South, 1865–1913*. Oxford: Oxford University Press.

Frankenberg, Erica and Gary Orfield. 2012. "Why Racial Change in the Suburbs Matters." In Erica Frankenberg and Gary Orfield, eds., *The Resegregation of Suburban Schools: A Hidden Crisis in American Education*. Cambridge: Harvard Education Press, 1–25.

Fredrickson, George M. 1995. *Black Liberation*. Oxford: Oxford University Press.

Freeman, Michael. 2002. "Past Wrongs and Liberal Justice." *Ethical Theory and Moral Practice* 5: 201–20.

Freeman, Michael. 2007. "Back to the Future: The Historical Dimension of Liberal Justice." In Max DuPlessis and Stephen Pete, eds., *Repairing the Past? International Perspectives on Reparations for Gross Human Rights Abuses*. Oxford: Intersentia, 29–51.

Freeman, Michael. 2008. "Historical Justice and Liberal Political Theory." In Rhoda E. Howard-Hassmann, Jean-Marc Coicaud, and Niklaus Steiner, eds., *The Age of Apology: Facing Up to the Past*. Philadelphia: University of Pennsylvania Press, 45–60.

Fryer, Roland G. 2006. "Acting White." *Education Next* 6: 53–59.

Fryer, Roland G. and Michael Greenstone. 2010. "The Changing Consequences of Attending Historically Black Colleges and Universities." *American Economic Journal: Applied Economics* 2: 116–48.

Fryer, Roland G., Jr., and Paul Torelli. 2010. "An Empirical Analysis of 'Acting White.'" *Journal of Public Economics* 94: 380–96.

Garcia, Jorge L. A. 1996. "The Heart of Racism." *Journal of Social Philosophy* 27: 5–45.

Gibbons, John J. and Nicholas de B. Katzenbach. 2006. *Confronting Confinement: A Report of the Commission on Safety and Abuse in America's Prisons*. Vera Institute of Justice. Available at https://www.vera.org/publications/confronting-confinement. Accessed August 11, 2016.

Gibney, Mark, Rhoda E. Howard-Hassmann, Jean-Marc Coicaud, and Niklaus Steiner, eds. 2008. *The Age of Apology: Facing Up to the Past*. Philadelphia: University of Pennsylvania Press.

Gibney, Mark and Erik Roxstrom. 2001. "The Status of State Apologies." *Human Rights Quarterly* 23: 911–39.

Gibson, James L. 2004. *Overcoming Apartheid: Can Truth Reconcile a Divided Nation?* New York: Russell Sage.

Gill, Andrea M. K. 2012. "Moving to Integration? The Origins of Chicago's Gautreaux Program and the Limits of Voucher-Based Housing Mobility." *Journal of Urban History* 38: 662–86.

Gill, Kathleen. 2000. "The Moral Functions of an Apology." *Philosophical Forum* 31: 11–27.

Glaser, Jack. 2015. *Suspect Race: Causes and Consequences of Racial Profiling*. Oxford: Oxford University Press.

Glaude, Eddie S., Jr. 2002. "Introduction: Black Power Revisited." In Eddie S. Glaude Jr., ed., *Is It Nation Time? Contemporary Essays on Black Power and Black Nationalism*. Chicago: University of Chicago Press, 1–21.

Glynn, Patrick. 1997. "Beyond Apologies: Can Religion Work Where Politics Has Failed?" *Responsive Community* 7: 35–44.

Goering, John. 2001. "An Assessment of President Clinton's Initiative on Race." *Ethnic and Racial Studies* 24: 472–84.

Goetz, Edward G. 2003. *Clearing the Way: Deconcentrating the Poor in Urban America*. Washington, DC: Urban Institute Press.

Goetz, Edward G. 2013. *New Deal Ruins: Race, Economic Justice, and Public Housing Policy*. Ithaca: Cornell University Press.

Goldberg, David and Trevor Griffey, eds. 2010. *Black Power at Work: Community Control, Affirmative Action, and the Construction Industry*. Ithaca: Cornell University Press.

Goodin, Robert E. 1991. "Compensation and Redistribution." In John W. Chapman, ed., *NOMOS XXXIII: Compensatory Justice*. New York: New York University Press, 143–77.

Gottschalk, Marie. 2015. *Caught: The Prison State and the Lockdown of American Politics*. Princeton: Princeton University Press.

Govier, Trudy and Wilhelm Verwoerd. 2002. "The Promise and Pitfalls of Apology." *Journal of Social Philosophy* 33: 67–82.

Green, Leslie. 1995. "Internal Minorities and Their Rights." In Will Kymlicka, ed., *The Rights of Minority Cultures*. Oxford: Oxford University Press, 256–72.

Gross, Samuel R. and Katherine Y. Barnes. 2002. "Road Work: Racial Profiling and Drug Interdiction on the Highway." *Michigan Law Review* 101: 653–754.

Gutmann, Amy. 1996. "Challenges of Multiculturalism in Democratic Education." In Robert K. Fullinwider, ed., *Public Education in a Multicultural Society: Policy, Theory, Critique*. Cambridge: Cambridge University Press, 156–79.

Gutmann, Amy. 1999. *Democratic Education*. Princeton: Princeton University Press.

Hall, Raymond L. 1978. *Black Separatism in the United States*. Hanover: University Press of New England.

Hamber, Brandon. 2001. "Does the Truth Heal? A Psychological Perspective on Political Strategies for Dealing with the Legacy of Political Violence." In Nigel Biggar, ed., *Burying the Past: Making Peace and Doing Justice after Civil Conflict*. Washington, DC: Georgetown University Press, 131–48.

Hanna, Nathan. 2009. "Liberalism and the General Justifiability of Punishment." *Philosophical Studies* 145: 325–49.

Hannaford, Ivan. 1996. *Race: The History of an Idea in the West*. Baltimore: Johns Hopkins University Press.

Hannah-Jones, Nikole. 2014. "Segregation Now . . ." *The Atlantic*. Available at https://www.theatlantic.com/magazine/archive/2014/05/segregation-now/359813/. Accessed November 11, 2017.

Harcourt, Bernard E. 2007. *Against Prediction: Profiling, Policing, and Punishment in an Actuarial Age*. Chicago: University of Chicago Press.

Harris, Leonard, ed. 1999. *Racism*. Amherst, NY: Humanity Books.

Harris, William H. 1982. *The Harder We Run: Black Workers since the Civil War*. Oxford: Oxford University Press.

Harter, L. M., R. J. Stephens, and P. M. Japp. 2000. "President Clinton's Apology for the Tuskegee Syphilis Experiment: A Narrative of Remembrance, Redefinition, and Reconciliation." *Howard Journal of Communication* 11: 19–34.

Harvey, J. 1995. "The Emerging Practice of Institutional Apologies." *International Journal of Applied Philosophy* 9: 57–65.

Hayner, Priscilla B. 2002. *Unspeakable Truths: Facing the Challenge of Truth Commissions*. New York: Routledge.

Hayward, Clarissa Rile. 2003. "The Difference States Make: Democracy, Identity, and the American City." *American Political Science Review* 97: 501–14.

Hayward, Clarissa Rile. 2013. *How Americans Make Race: Stories, Institutions, Spaces*. Cambridge: Cambridge University Press.

Hayward, Clarissa Rile and Todd Swanstrom, eds. 2011. *Justice and the American Metropolis*. Minneapolis: University of Minnesota Press.

Hebel, Sara. 2001. "A New Push to Integrate Public Black Colleges." *Chronicle of Higher Education*, June 8.

Hern, Matt. 2016. *What a City Is For: Remaking the Politics of Displacement*. Cambridge: MIT Press.

Hill, Herbert. 1977. *Black Labor and the American Legal System I: Race, Work, and the Law.* Washington, DC: Bureau of National Affairs.

Hill, Renee A. 2002. "Compensatory Justice: Over Time and between Groups." *Journal of Political Philosophy* 10: 392–415.

Hill, Thomas E. 1991. "The Message of Affirmative Action." *Social Philosophy and Policy* 8: 108–29.

Hirsch, James S. 2002. *Riot and Remembrance: The Tulsa Race War and Its Legacy.* New York: Houghton Mifflin Harcourt.

Hochschild, Jennifer, Vesla Weaver, and Traci Burch. 2012. *Creating a New Racial Order: How Immigration, Multiracialism, Genomics, and the Young Can Remake Race in America.* Princeton: Princeton University Press.

Hough, Joseph C., Jr. 1968. *Black Power and White Protestants: A Christian Response to the New Negro Pluralism.* Oxford: Oxford University Press.

Human Rights Watch. 2001. "An Approach to Reparations." Available at http://www.hrw.org/legacy/campaigns/race/reparations.htm. Accessed October 26, 2009.

Human Rights Watch. 2008. "The Rest of Their Lives: Life without Parole for Youth Offenders in the United States in 2008." Executive Summary. Available at https://www.hrw.org/sites/default/files/reports/us1005execsum.pdf. Accessed August 11, 2016.

Husak, Douglas. 2008. *Overcriminalization: The Limits of the Criminal Law.* Oxford: Oxford University Press.

Imbroscio, David. 2004. "Fighting Poverty with Mobility: A Normative Policy Analysis." *Review of Policy Research* 21: 447–61.

Imbroscio, David. 2008. "'[U]nited and Actuated by Some Common Impulse of Passion:' Challenging the Dispersal Consensus in American Housing Policy Research." *Journal of Urban Affairs* 30: 111–130.

Innis, Roy. 1997. "From Separatist Economics: A New Social Contract." In William L. Van Deburg, ed., *Modern Black Nationalism: From Marcus Garvey to Louis Farrakhan.* New York: New York University Press, 176–81.

Inwood, Joshua F. J. 2009. "Contested Memory in the Birthplace of a King: A Case Study of Auburn Avenue and the Martin Luther King Jr. National Park." *Cultural Geographies* 16: 87–109.

Inwood, Joshua F. J. and Derek Alderman. 2016. "Taking Down the Flag Is Just a Start: Toward the Memory-Work of Racial Reconciliation in White Supremacist America." *Southeastern Geographer* 56: 9–15.

Jackson, Kenneth T. 1985. *Crabgrass Frontier: The Suburbanization of the United States.* Oxford: Oxford University Press.

Jacobs, Jonathan. 2013. "The Liberal Polity, Criminal Sanction, and Civil Society." *Criminal Justice Ethics* 32: 231–46.

Jacobs, Jonathan. 2014. "Punishing Society: Incarceration, Coercive Corruption, and the Liberal Polity." *Criminal Justice Ethics* 33: 200–19.

James, Michael. 2016. "Race." *Stanford Encyclopedia of Philosophy.* Available at https://plato.stanford.edu/archives/spr2016/entries/race/. Accessed November 12, 2017.

Johnson, Odis, Jr. 2012. "Relocation Programs, Opportunities to Learn, and the Complications of Conversion." *Review of Educational Research* 82: 131–78.

Johnson, Alex M., Jr. 1993. "Bid Whist, Tonk, and *United States v. Fordice*: Why Integrationism Fails African Americans Again." *California Law Review* 81: 1401–71.

Johnson, Lyndon B. 1967. "Remarks of the President at Howard University, June 4, 1965." In Lee Rainwater and William L. Yancey, eds., *The Moynihan Report and the Politics of Controversy*. Cambridge: MIT Press, 126–32.

Johnson, Nuala. 1995. "Cast in Stone: Monuments, Geography, and Nationalism." *Environment and Planning D: Society and Space* 13: 51–65.

Jones, Jacqueline. 1998. *American Work: Four Centuries of Black and White Labor*. New York: Norton.

Joseph, Peniel E. 2006. *Waiting 'til the Midnight Hour: A Narrative History of Black Power in America*. New York: Henry Holt.

Joyce, Richard. 1999. "Apologizing." *Public Affairs Quarterly* 13: 159–73.

Kagee, Ashraf. 2006. "The Relationship between Statement Giving at the South African Truth and Reconciliation Commission and Psychological Distress among Former Political Detainees." *South African Journal of Psychology* 36: 10–24.

Kaplan, Jonathan and Andrew Valls. 2007. "Housing Discrimination as a Basis for Black Reparations." *Public Affairs Quarterly* 21: 255–73.

Kateb, George. 1997. "*Brown* and the Harm of Legal Segregation." In Austin Sarat, ed., *Race, Law, & Culture: Reflections on* Brown v. Board of Education. Oxford: Oxford University Press, 91–109.

Kateb, George. 2007. "Punishment and the Spirit of Democracy." *Social Research* 74: 269–306.

Katznelson, Ira. 2005. *When Affirmative Action Was White: An Untold History of Racial Inequality in Twentieth-Century America*. New York: Norton.

Keels, Micere. 2008a. "Neighborhood Effects Examined through the Lens of Residential Mobility Programs." *American Journal of Community Psychology* 42: 235–50.

Keels, Micere. 2008b. "Second-Generation Effects of Chicago's Gautreaux Residential Mobility Program on Children's Participation in Crime." *Journal of Research on Adolescence* 18: 305–52.

Keels, Micere. 2008c. "Residential Attainment of Now-Adult Gautreaux Children: Do they Gain, Hold or Lose Ground in Neighborhood Ethnic and Economic Segregation?" *Housing Studies* 23: 541–64.

Kelderman, Eric. 2013a. "10 States Are Shortchanging Historically-Black Land Grant Universities, Report Says." *Chronicle of Higher Education*, September 6.

Kelderman, Eric. 2013b. "4 Other States Could Be Affected by Desegregation Ruling in Maryland." *Chronicle of Higher Education*, October 18.

Kelly, Erin I. 2017. "The Historical Injustice Problem for Political Liberalism." *Ethics* 128: 75–94.

Kidder, William C. 2013. "Misshaping the River: Proposition 209 and Lessons for the *Fisher* Case." *Journal of College and University Law* 39: 53–126.

Kim, Claire Jean. 2000. "Clinton's Race Initiative: Recasting the American Dilemma." *Polity* 33: 175–97.

Kim, Claire Jean. 2002. "Managing the Racial Breach: Clinton, Black-White Polarization, and the Race Initiative." *Political Science Quarterly* 117: 55–79.

King, Desmond. 2007. *Separate and Unequal: African Americans and the US Federal Government*. Rev. ed. Oxford: Oxford University Press.

King, Martin Luther, Jr. 1963. *Why We Can't Wait*. New York: Signet.

King, Loren A. 2004a. "Democracy and City Life." *Politics, Philosophy, and Economics* 3: 97–124.

King, Loren A. 2004b. "Democratic Hopes in the Polycentric City." *Journal of Politics* 66: 203–23.

Kiss, Elizabeth. 2000. "Moral Ambition within and beyond Political Constraints: Reflections on Restorative Justice." In Robert I. Rotberg and Dennis Thompson, eds., *Truth v. Justice: The Morality of Truth Commissions*. Princeton: Princeton University Press, 68–98.

Kleinig, John and Kevin Murtagh. 2005. "Disenfranchising Felons." *Journal of Applied Philosophy* 22: 217–39.

Kort, Louis F. 1975. "What Is an Apology?" *Philosophy Research Archives* 1: 80–87.

Krauthammer, Charles. 1990. "Reparations for Black Americans." *Time*, December 31, 18.

Kritz, Neil J., ed. 1995. *Transitional Justice: How Emerging Democracies Reckon with Former Regimes*. 3 vols. Washington, DC: United States Institute of Peace Press.

Krivo, Lauren J. and Ruth D. Peterson. 1996. "Extremely Disadvantaged Neighborhoods and Urban Crime." *Social Forces* 75: 619–48.

Kukathas, Chandran. 2003. *The Liberal Archipelago: A Theory of Diversity and Freedom*. Oxford: Oxford University Press.

Kukathas, Chandran. 2006. "Who? Whom? Reparations and the Problem of Agency." *Journal of Social Philosophy* 37: 330–41.

Kurlaender, Michal and Eric Grodsky. 2013. "Mismatch and the Paternalistic Justification for Selective College Admissions." *Sociology of Education* 86: 294–310.

Kutz, Christopher. 2004. "Justice in Reparations: The Cost of Memory and the Value of Talk." *Philosophy and Public Affairs* 32: 277–312.

Kymlicka, Will. 1989. *Liberalism, Community, and Culture*. Oxford: Clarendon Press.

Kymlicka, Will. 1995. *Multicultural Citizenship: A Liberal Theory of Minority Rights*. Oxford: Oxford University Press.

Kymlicka, Will. 2001. *Politics in the Vernacular: Nationalism, Multiculturalism, and Citizenship*. Oxford: Oxford University Press.

Kymlicka, Will. 2002. *Contemporary Political Philosophy: An Introduction*. 2nd ed. Oxford: Oxford University Press.

Laden, Anthony Simon and David Owen, eds. 2007. *Multiculturalism and Political Theory*. Cambridge: Cambridge University Press.

LaFraniere, Sharon and Andrew W. Lehren. 2015. "The Disproportionate Risks of Driving While Black." *New York Times*, October 24. Available at http://nyti.ms/1jFXsFJ. Accessed November 11, 2017.

Leake, Donald and Brenda Leake. 1992. "African-American Immersion Schools in Milwaukee: A View from the Inside." *Phi Delta Kappan* 73: 783–85.

Lebron, Chris. 2013. *The Color of Our Shame: Race and Justice in Our Time*. Oxford: Oxford University Press.

Leebaw, Bronwyn. 2011. *Judging State-Sponsored Violence, Imagining Political Change.* Cambridge: Cambridge University Press.

Lefkowitz, Mary. 1997. *Not Out of Africa: How "Afrocentrism" Became an Excuse to Teach Myth as History.* New York: Basic Books.

Legal Action Center. 2009. "After Prison: Roadblocks to Reentry." 2009 update. Executive Summary. Available at http://lac.org/roadblocks-to-reentry/upload/lacreport/Roadblocks-to-Reentry--2009.pdf. Accessed August 11, 2016.

Leib, Jonathan. 2006. "The Witting Autobiography of Richmond, Virginia: Arthur Ashe, the Civil War, and Monument Avenue's Racialized Landscape." In Richard H. Schein, ed., *Landscape and Race in the United States.* New York: Routledge, 187–211.

Lenta, Patrick and Douglas Farland. 2008. "Desert, Justice and Capital Punishment." *Criminal Law and Philosophy* 2: 273–90.

Lerman, Amy E and Vesla M. Weaver. 2014. *Arresting Citizenship: The Democratic Consequences of American Crime Control.* Chicago: University of Chicago Press.

Levine, Michael P. and Tamas Pataki, eds. 2004. *Racism in Mind.* Ithaca: Cornell University Press.

Levinson, Meira. 1999. *The Demands of Liberal Education.* Oxford: Oxford University Press.

Levinson, Meira. 2012. *No Citizen Left Behind.* Cambridge: Harvard University Press.

Levinson, Meira. 2014. "It's (Still) All in Our Heads: Non-ideal Theory as Grounded Reflective Equilibrium." *Journal of Philosophy of Education.* Available at http://ojs.ed.uiuc.edu/index.php/pes/issue/current. Accessed November 11, 2017.

Levinson, Sanford. 1995. "They Whisper: Reflections on Flags, Monuments, and State Holidays, and the Construction of Social Meaning in a Multicultural Society." *Chicago-Kent Law Review* 70: 1079–1119.

Levinson, Sanford. 1998. *Written in Stone: Public Monuments in Changing Societies.* Durham: Duke University Press.

Levinson, Sanford. 2000. "Trials, Commissions, and Investigating Committees: The Elusive Search for Norms of Due Process." In Robert I. Rotberg and Dennis Thompson, eds., *Truth v. Justice: The Morality of Truth Commissions.* Princeton: Princeton University Press, 211–34.

Levy, Jacob T. 2000. *The Multiculturalism of Fear.* Oxford: Oxford University Press.

Levy, Jacob T. 2004. "National Minorities without Nationalism." In Alain Dieckhoff, ed., *The Politics of Belonging: Nationalism, Liberalism, and Pluralism.* Lanham: Lexington Books, 155–73.

Levy, Neil. 2002. "The Apology Paradox and the Non-identity Problem." *Philosophical Quarterly* 52: 358–68.

Lieberman, Robert C. 1998. *Shifting the Color Line: Race and the American Welfare State.* Cambridge: Harvard University Press.

Lilla, Mark. 2017. *The Once and Future Liberal: After Identity Politics.* New York: Harper.

Lippke, Richard L. 2001. "The Disenfranchisement of Felons." *Law and Philosophy* 20: 553–80.

Lipson, Daniel N. 2008. "Where's the Justice? Affirmative Action's Severed Civil Rights Roots in the Age of Diversity." *Perspectives on Politics* 6: 691–706.

Liptak, Adam. 2015. "A Test of Free Speech and Bias, Served on a Plate from Texas." *New York Times*, March 22. http://nyti.ms/1B63IOb. Accessed March 23, 2016.

Litan, Robert E. 1977. "On Rectification in Nozick's Minimal State." *Political Theory* 5: 233–46.

Londono, Oscar. 2013. "A Retributive Critique of Racial Bias and Arbitrariness in Capital Punishment." *Journal of Social Philosophy* 44: 95–105.

Los Angeles Times. 2017. "California Confederate Flag Ban Excludes Individuals, State Says." May 2. Available at http://www.latimes.com/local/lanow/la-me-ln-confederate-flag-ban-20170502-story.html. Accessed September 19, 2017.

Loury, Glenn C. 1997. "The Hard Questions: Double Talk." *New Republic*, August 25, 23.

Loury, Glenn C. 2002. *The Anatomy of Racial Inequality*. Cambridge: Harvard University Press.

Loury, Glenn C. 2007. "Transgenerational Justice—Compensatory Versus Interpretive Approaches." In Jon Miller and Rahul Kumar, eds., *Reparations: Interdisciplinary Inquiries*. Oxford: Oxford University Press, 87–113.

Lyons, David. 1981. "The New Indian Claims and Original Rights to Land." In Jeffery Paul, ed., *Reading Nozick: Essays on "Anarchy, State, and Utopia"*. Totowa: Rowman & Allanheld, 355–79.

Macedo, Stephen. 1995. "Liberal Civic Education and Religious Fundamentalism: The Case of God v. John Rawls?" *Ethics* 105: 468–96.

Macedo, Stephen. 2000. *Diversity and Distrust: Civic Education in a Multicultural Democracy*. Cambridge: Harvard University Press.

Madigan, Tim. 2001. *The Burning: Massacre, Destruction, and the Tulsa Race Riot of 1921*. New York: Thomas Dunne.

Magarrell, Lisa and Joya Wesley. 2008. *Learning from Greensboro: Truth and Reconciliation in the United States*. Philadelphia: University of Pennsylvania Press.

Main, Brian G. M. 1972. "Toward the Measurement of Historic Debts." *Review of Black Political Economy* 2: 22–42.

Manza, Jeff and Christopher Uggen. 2006. *Locked Out: Felon Disenfranchisement and American Democracy*. Oxford: Oxford University Press.

Margalit, Avishai. 2002. *The Ethics of Memory*. Cambridge: Harvard University Press.

Marketti, Jim. 1972. "Black Equity in the Slave Trade." *Review of Black Political Economy* 2: 43–66.

Martin, Jonathan and Jeremy W. Peters. 2017. "As G.O.P. Bends toward Trump, Critics Either Give In or Give Up." *New York Times*, October 25. Available at https://nyti.ms/2izLKBd. Accessed November 11, 2017.

Martinez, Michael J., William D. Richardson, and Ron McNinch-Su, eds. 2001. *Confederate Symbols in the Contemporary South*. Gainesville: University Press of Florida.

Massey, Douglas S. and Nancy A. Denton. 1993. *American Apartheid: Segregation and the Making of the Underclass*. Cambridge: Harvard University Press.

Matravers, Matt. 2013. "Political Neutrality and Punishment." *Criminal Law and Philosophy* 7: 217–30.

Matthew, D. C. 2017. "Rawls and Racial Justice." *Politics, Philosophy & Economics* 16: 235–58.

McAdams, A. James, ed. 1997. *Transitional Justice and the Rule of Law in New Democracies*. Notre Dame: University of Notre Dame Press.

McCarthy, Thomas. 2002. "Vergangenheitsbewältigung in the USA: On the Politics of the Memory of Slavery." *Political Theory* 30: 623–48.

McCarthy, Thomas. 2004. "Coming to Terms with Our Past, Part II: On the Morality and Politics of Reparations for Slavery." *Political Theory* 32: 1–23.

McCarthy, Thomas. 2009. *Race, Empire, and the Idea of Human Development.* Cambridge: Cambridge University Press.

McCartney, John T. 1992. *Black Power Ideologies.* Philadelphia: Temple University Press.

McDermott, Daniel. 2001. "A Retributivist Argument against Capital Punishment." *Journal of Social Philosophy* 32: 317–33.

McGary, Howard. 1999. *Race and Social Justice.* Oxford: Blackwell.

McIvor, David W. 2016. *Mourning in America: Race and the Politics of Loss.* Ithaca: Cornell University Press.

McPhate, Mike. 2016. "Record Number of False Convictions Overturned in 2015." *New York Times,* February 3. Available at http://nyti.ms/1mdrj8J. Accessed November 11, 2017.

Megret, Frederic. 2010. "Of Shrines, Memorials, and Museums: Using the International Criminal Court's Victim Reparation and Assistance Regime to Promote Transitional Justice." *Buffalo Human Rights Law Review* 16: 1–56.

Meister, Robert. 1999. "Forgiving and Forgetting: Lincoln and the Politics of National Recovery." In Carla Hesse and Robert Post, eds., *Human Rights in Political Transitions: Gettysburg to Bosnia.* New York: Zone Books, 135–76.

Meister, Robert. 2011. *After Evil: A Politics of Human Rights.* New York: Columbia University Press.

Mendenhall, Ruby, Stephanie DeLuca and Greg Duncan. 2006. "Neighborhood Resources, Racial Segregation, and Economic Mobility: Results from the Gautreaux Program." *Social Science Research* 35: 892–923.

Merry, Michael S. 2013. *Equality, Citizenship, and Segregation: A Defense of Separation.* New York: Palgrave Macmillan.

Michaels, Walter Benn. 2006. *The Trouble with Diversity: How We Learned to Love Identity and Ignore Inequality.* New York: Holt.

Mills, Charles W. 2005. "'Ideal Theory' as Ideology. *Hypatia* 20: 165–84.

Mills, Charles W. 2009. "Rawls on Race / Race in Rawls." *Southern Journal of Philosophy* 47 (Supplement): 161–84.

Mills, Charles W. 2013. "Retrieving Rawls for Racial Justice? A Critique of Tommie Shelby." *Critical Philosophy of Race* 1: 1–27.

Mills, Charles W. 2017. *Black Rights, White Wrongs: The Critique of Racial Liberalism.* Oxford: Oxford University Press.

Mills, Cynthia and Pamela H. Simpson, eds. 2003. *Monuments to the Lost Cause: Women, Art, and Landscapes of Southern Memory.* Knoxville: University of Tennessee Press.

Minow, Martha. 1998. *Between Vengeance and Forgiveness: Facing History after Genocide and Mass Violence.* Boston: Beacon Press.

Minow, Martha. 2000. "The Hope for Healing: What Can Truth Commissions Do?" In Robert I. Rotberg and Dennis Thompson, eds., *Truth v. Justice: The Morality of Truth Commissions.* Princeton: Princeton University Press, 235–60.

Minow, Martha. 2010. *In Brown's Wake: Legacies of America's Educational Landmark.* Oxford: Oxford University Press.

Moore, Margaret. 2003. "An Historical Argument of Indigenous Self-determination." In Stephen Macedo and Allen Buchanan, eds., *NOMOS XLV: Secession and Self-Determination*. New York: New York University Press, 89–118.

Moreno, Paul D. 2006. *Black Americans and Organized Labor: A New History*. Baton Rouge: Louisiana State University Press.

Movement for Black Lives. 2017. Available at https://policy.m4bl.org. Accessed November 10, 2017.

Morris, Christopher W. 1984. "Existential Limits to the Rectification of Past Wrongs." *American Philosophical Quarterly* 21: 175–82.

Mueller-Smith, Michael. 2015. "The Criminal and Labor Market Impacts of Incarceration." Working paper. Available at https://sites.lsa.umich.edu/mgms/wp-content/uploads/sites/283/2015/09/incar.pdf. Accessed November 14, 2017.

Muhammad, Khalil Gibran. 2011. *The Condemnation of Blackness: Race, Crime, and the Making of Modern Urban America*. Cambridge: Harvard University Press.

Munn, Nicholas. 2011. "The Limits of Criminal Disenfranchisement." *Criminal Justice Ethics* 30: 223–39.

Nagel, Thomas. 1973. "Equal Treatment and Compensatory Discrimination." *Philosophy and Public Affairs* 2: 348–63.

Narveson, Jan. 2009. "Present Payments, Past Wrongs: Correcting Loose Talk about Nozick and Rectification." *Libertarian Papers* 1: 1–17.

Nathanson, Stephen. 2014. "Why We Should Put the Death Penalty to Rest." In Andrew I. Cohen and Christopher Heath Wellman, eds., *Contemporary Debates in Applied Ethics*. Somerset: John Wiley and Sons, 175–88.

National Community Reinvestment Coalition. 2015. *Home Mortgage and Small Business Lending in Baltimore and Surrounding Areas*. Available at https://ncrc.org/home-mortgage-and-small-business-lending-in-baltimore-and-surrounding-areas/. Accessed November 14, 2017.

National Research Council. 2014. *The Growth of Incarceration in the United States: Exploring Causes and Consequences*. Washington, DC: National Academies Press.

Neubeck, Kenneth J. and Noel A. Cazenave. 2001. *Welfare Racism: Playing the Race Card against America's Poor*. New York: Routledge.

New York Times. 2017. "Confederate Monuments Are Coming Down across the United States. Here's a List." August 28. Available at https://www.nytimes.com/interactive/2017/08/16/us/confederate-monuments-removed.html?mcubz=1. Accessed September 19, 2017.

Nobles, Melissa. 2008. *The Politics of Official Apologies*. Cambridge: Cambridge University Press.

Nozick, Robert. 1974. *Anarchy, State, and Utopia*. New York: Basic Books.

Ogbar, Jeffrey O. G. 2004. *Black Power: Radical Politics and African American Identity*. Baltimore: Johns Hopkins University Press.

Ogletree, Charles J. and Austin Sarat, eds. 2012. *Life without Parole: America's New Death Penalty?* New York: New York University Press.

Oh, Sun Jung and John Yinger. 2015. "What Have We Learned from Paired Testing in Housing Markets?" *Cityscape* 17: 15–60.

Okin, Susan Moller. 1999. "Is Multiculturalism Bad for Women?" In Joshua Cohen, Matthew Howard, and Martha C. Nussbaum, eds., *Is Multiculturalism Bad for Women?* Princeton: Princeton University Press, 7–24.

Oliver, J. Eric. 2010. *The Paradoxes of Integration: Race, Neighborhood, and Civic Life in Multiethnic America*. Chicago: University of Chicago Press.

Oliver, Melvin L. and Thomas M. Shapiro. 2006. *Black Wealth / White Wealth: A New Perspective on Racial Inequality*. 10th-anniversary ed. New York: Routledge.

Omi, Michael and Howard Winant. 1994. *Racial Formation in the United States*. 2nd ed. New York: Routledge.

One America in the 21st Century: Forging a New Future. 1998. Washington, DC: Government Printing Office.

Orey, Byron D'Andra. 2004. "White Racial Attitudes and Support for the Mississippi State Flag." *American Politics Research* 32: 102–16.

Orfield, Gary. 2007. "Prologue: Lessons Forgotten." In Erica Frankenberg and Gary Orfield, eds., *Lessons in Integration: Realizing the Promise of Racial Diversity in American Schools*. Charlottesville: University of Virginia Press, 1–6.

Orfield, Gary and Erica Frankenberg. 2014. "*Brown* at 60: Great Progress, a Long Retreat, and an Uncertain Future." UCLA: The Civil Rights Project. Available at www.civilrightsproject.ucla.edu. Accessed 11 November 2017.

Pager, Devah. 2003. "The Mark of a Criminal Record." *American Journal of Sociology* 108: 937–75.

Pager, Devah. 2007. *Marked: Race, Crime, and Finding Work in an Era of Mass Incarceration*. Chicago: University of Chicago Press.

Pager, Devah and Hana Shepherd. 2008. "The Sociology of Discrimination: Racial Discrimination in Employment, Housing, Credit, and Consumer Markets." *Annual Review of Sociology* 34: 181–209.

Patten, Alan. 2014. *Equal Recognition: The Moral Foundations of Minority Rights*. Princeton: Princeton University Press.

Paul, Ellen Frankel. 1991. "Set-Asides, Reparations, and Compensatory Justice." In John W. Chapman, ed., *NOMOS XXXIII: Compensatory Justice*. New York: New York University Press, 97–139.

Peller, Gary. 1995. "Race-Consciousness." In Kimberlé Crenshaw, Neil Gotanda, Gary Peller, and Kendall Thomas, eds., *Critical Race Theory: The Key Writings That Formed the Movement*. New York: New Press, 127–58.

Peller, Gary. 2012. *Critical Race Consciousness: Reconsidering American Ideologies of Racial Justice*. New York: Routledge.

Peterson, Richard R. 2016. "Re-arrests of Homeless Defendants in New York City." New York City Criminal Justice Agency Research Brief No. 39. Available at http://www.nycja.org/library.php. Accessed August 11, 2016.

Pettit, Becky. 2012. *Invisible Men: Mass Incarceration and the Myth of Black Progress*. New York: Russell Sage Foundation.

Pfaff, John. 2017. *Locked In: The True Causes of Mass Incarceration and How to Achieve Real Reform*. New York: Basic Books.

Phillips, Anne. 2007. *Multiculturalism without Culture*. Princeton: Princeton University Press.

Phillips, Derek L. 1979. *Equality, Justice and Rectification: An Exploration in Normative Sociology*. New York: Academic Press.

Philpott, Daniel. 2006. "Beyond Politics as Usual: Is Reconciliation Compatible with Liberalism?" In Daniel Philpott, ed., *The Politics of Past Evil: Religion, Reconciliation, and the Dilemmas of Transitional Justice*. Notre Dame: University of Notre Dame Press, 11–44.

Piehler, G. Kurt. 1995. *Remembering War the American Way*. Washington, DC: Smithsonian.

Poe, Danielle. 2007. "On US Lynching: Remembrance, Apology, and Reconciliation." *Philosophy in the Contemporary World* 14: 88–98.

Pojman, Louis P. 2005. "A Defense of the Death Penalty." In Andrew I. Cohen and Christopher Heath Wellman, eds., *Contemporary Debates in Applied Ethics*. Somerset: John Wiley and Sons, 159–74.

Poole, Mary. 2006. *The Segregated Origins of Social Security: African Americans and the Welfare State*. Chapel Hill: University of North Carolina Press.

Poole, W. Scott. 2005. "Lincoln in Hell: Class and Confederate Symbols in the American South." In Michael E. Geisler, ed., *National Symbols, Fractured Identities: Contesting the National Narrative*. Hanover: University Press of New England, 121–48.

Portes, Alejandro and Rubén G. Rumbaut. 2006. *Immigrant America: A Portrait*. 3rd ed. Berkeley: University of California Press.

powell, john a. 1993. "Black Immersion Schools." *NYU Review of Law and Social Change* 21: 669–89.

Priced Out. 2017. Dir. Cornelius Swart. Syhonda Media. Film.

Prince, K. Michael. 2004. *Rally 'Round the Flag, Boys! South Carolina and the Confederate Flag*. Columbia: University of South Carolina Press.

"Protect Our Progress: State of Black America." 2017. National Urban League. Available at http://soba.iamempowered.com/2017-report. Accessed April 28, 2018.

Putnam, Robert D. 2007. "*E Pluribus Unum*: Diversity and Community in the Twenty-First Century. The 2006 Johan Skytte Prize Lecture." *Scandinavian Political Studies* 30: 137–74.

Raiford, Leigh and Renee C. Romano. 2006. "Introduction: The Struggle over Memory." In Renee C. Romano and Leigh Raiford, eds., *The Civil Rights Movement in American Memory*. Athens: University of Georgia Press, xi–xxiv.

Ramsay, Peter. 2013. "Voters Should Not Be in Prison! The Rights of Prisoners in a Democracy." *Critical Review of International Social and Political Philosophy* 16: 421–38.

Rawls, John. 1999. *A Theory of Justice*. Rev. ed. Cambridge: Harvard University Press.

Rawls, John. 2001. *Justice as Fairness: A Restatement*. Ed. Erin Kelly. Cambridge: Harvard University Press.

Rawls, John. 2005. *Political Liberalism*. Expanded ed. New York: Columbia University Press.

Reardon, Sean, Elena Tej Grewal, Demetra Kalogrides, and Erica Greenberg. 2012. "*Brown* Fades: The End of Court-Ordered School Desegregation and the Resegregation of American Public Schools." *Journal of Policy Analysis and Management* 31: 876–904.

Reed, Adolph L., Jr. 2002. "Black Particularity Reconsidered." In Eddie S. Glaude Jr., ed., *Is It Nation Time? Contemporary Essays on Black Power and Black Nationalism*. Chicago: University of Chicago Press, 39–66.

Reich, Rob. 2013. "Equality, Adequacy, and K-12 Education." In Danielle Allen and Rob Reich, eds., *Education, Justice, and Democracy*. Chicago: University of Chicago Press, 43–61.

Reiman, Jeffrey. 1996. *. . . and the Poor Get Prison: Economic Bias in American Criminal Justice*. Boston: Allyn and Bacon.

Reiman, Jeffrey. 2005. "Liberal and Republican Arguments against the Disenfranchisement of Felons." *Criminal Justice Ethics* 24: 3–18.

Reingold, Beth and Richard S. Wike, 1998. "Confederate Symbols, Southern Identity, and Racial Attitudes: The Case of the Georgia State Flag." *Social Science Quarterly* 79: 568–80.

Report of the National Advisory Commission on Civil Disorders. 1968. New York: Bantam.

Riley, Jason L. 2010. "Black Colleges Need a New Mission." *Wall Street Journal*, September 28, A21.

Risse, Mathias and Richard Zeckhauser. 2004. "Racial Profiling." *Philosophy and Public Affairs* 32: 131–70.

Robinson, Dean E. 2001. *Black Nationalism in American Politics and Thought*. Cambridge: Cambridge University Press.

Robinson, Randall. 2001. *The Debt: What America Owes to Blacks*. New York: Plume.

Rockquemore, Kerry. 1997. "Afrocentric Education: Understanding the Effects of Black Academies on Academic Achievement." In Cedric Herring, ed., *African Americans and the Public Agenda*. Thousand Oaks: Sage, 190–206.

Rockwell, Llewellyn H. 1994. "The Ghost of Gautreaux." *National Review*, March 7, 57–59.

Roeder, Oliver. 2015. "Releasing Drug Offenders Won't End Mass Incarceration." Available at http://fivethirtyeight.com/datalab/releasing-drug-offenders-wont-end-mass-incarceration/. Accessed August 11, 2016.

Rosewood Forum. 1994. *The Rosewood Massacre at a Glance*. Gainesville: Rosewood Forum.

Rotberg, Robert I. and Dennis Thompson, eds. 2000. *Truth v. Justice: The Morality of Truth Commissions*. Princeton: Princeton University Press.

Rothstein, Richard. 2013. "Racial Segregation and Black Student Achievement." In Danielle Allen and Rob Reich, eds., *Education, Justice, and Democracy*. Chicago: University of Chicago Press, 173–95.

Rothstein, Richard. 2017. *The Color of Law: A Forgotten History of How Our Government Segregated America*. New York: Liveright.

Ryan, Alan. 1997. "Justice and the City." In Robert Geddes, ed., *Cities in Our Future: Growth and Form, Environmental Health and Social Equity*. Washington, DC: Island Press, 13–31.

Sampson, Robert J. 2012. *Great American City: Chicago and the Enduring Neighborhood Effect*. Chicago: University of Chicago Press.

Sanbonmatsu, Lisa, Jeffrey R. Kling, Greg J. Duncan, and Jeanne Brooks-Gunn. 2006. "Neighborhoods and Academic Achievement: Results from the Moving to Opportunity Experiment." *Journal of Human Resources* 41: 649–91.

Sanbonmatsu, Lisa et al. 2011. Moving to Opportunity for Fair Housing Demonstration Program: Final Impacts Evaluation, Executive Summary. Available at http://www.huduser.org/portal/publications/pubasst/MTOFHD.html. Accessed November 11, 2017.

Sander, Richard H. 2004. "A Systematic Analysis of Affirmative Action in American Law Schools." *Stanford Law Review* 57: 367–483.

Sander, Richard H. 2005. "A Reply to Critics." *Stanford Law Review* 57: 1963–2016.

Sander, Richard H. and Stuart Taylor Jr. 2012. *Mismatch: How Affirmative Action Hurts Students It's Intended to Help, and Why Universities Won't Admit It.* New York: Basic Books.

Sanders, Eugene T. W. and Patricia L. Reed. 1995. "An Investigation of the Possible Effects of an Immersion as Compared to a Traditional Program for African American Males." *Urban Education* 30: 93–112.

Sanneh, Kelefa. 2015. "Body Count." *New Yorker*, September 14. Available at https://www.newyorker.com/magazine/2015/09/14/body-count-a-critic-at-large-kelefa-sanneh. Accessed November 20, 2017.

Satz, Debra. 2007. "Equality, Adequacy, and Education for Citizenship." *Ethics* 117: 623–48.

Satz, Debra. 2012. "Unequal Chances: Race, Class, and Schooling." *Theory and Research in Education* 10: 155–70.

Savage, Kirk. 1994. "The Politics of Memory: Black Emancipation and the Civil War Monument." In John R. Gillis, ed., *Commemorations: The Politics of National Identity.* Princeton: Princeton University Press, 127–49.

Savage, Kirk. 1997. *Standing Soldier, Kneeling Slaves: Race, War, and Monument in Nineteenth-Century America.* Princeton: Princeton University Press.

Schedler, George. 1998. *Racist Symbols and Reparations: Philosophical Reflections on Vestiges of the American Civil War.* Lanham: Rowman and Littlefield.

Schedler, George. 2000. "Minorities and Racist Symbols: A Response to Torin Alter." *Philosophy in the Contemporary World* 7: 5–10.

Schedler, George. 2001. "Are Confederate Monuments Racist?" *International Journal of Applied Philosophy* 15: 287–308.

Schelling, Thomas C. 1969. "Models of Segregation." *American Economic Review* 59: 488–93.

Schlesinger, Arthur M. 1992. *The Disuniting of America: Reflections on a Multicultural Society.* New York: Norton.

Schmidtz, David. 2006. *Elements of Justice.* Cambridge: Cambridge University Press.

Schuessler, Jennifer. 2017. "Princeton Digs Deep into Its Fraught Racial History." *New York Times*, November 6. Available at https://nyti.ms/2j75097. Accessed November 13, 2017.

The Sentencing Project. 2013. "Life Goes On: The Historic Rise of Life Sentences in America." Available at http://www.sentencingproject.org/wp-content/uploads/2015/12/Life-Goes-On.pdf. Accessed August 11, 2016.

The Sentencing Project. 2016a. "Felony Disenfranchisement: A Primer." Available at http://sentencingproject.org/wp-content/uploads/2015/08/Felony-Disenfranchisement-Primer.pdf. Accessed August 11, 2016.

The Sentencing Project. 2016b. "Felony Disenfranchisement." Available at http://www.sentencingproject.org/publications/felony-disenfranchisement-laws-in-the-united-states/. Accessed August 11, 2016.

Sewall, Gilbert T. 1996. "A Conflict of Visions: Multiculturalism and the Social Studies." In Robert K. Fullinwider, ed., *Public Education in a Multicultural Society: Policy, Theory, Critique*. Cambridge: Cambridge University Press, 49–61.

Sharkey, Patrick. 2013. *Stuck in Place: Urban Neighborhoods and the End of Progress toward Racial Equality*. Chicago: University of Chicago Press.

Shatz, Steven F. and Terry Dalton. 2013. "Challenging the Death Penalty with Statistics: Furman, McCleskey, and a Single County Case Study." *Cardozo Law Review* 34: 1227–82.

Shaw, Samuel C. 2009. "Resurrecting Martin Luther King." *Contexts* 8: 71–73.

Shelby, Tommie. 2004. "Race and Social Justice: Rawlsian Considerations." *Fordham Law Review* 72: 1697–714.

Shelby, Tommie. 2005. *We Who Are Dark: The Philosophical Foundations of Black Solidarity*. Cambridge: Harvard University Press.

Shelby, Tommie. 2007. "Justice, Deviance, and the Dark Ghetto." *Philosophy and Public Affairs* 35: 126–60.

Shelby, Tommie. 2013. "Racial Realities and Corrective Justice: A Reply to Charles Mills." *Critical Philosophy of Race* 1: 145–62.

Shelby, Tommie. 2014. "Integration, Inequality, and Imperatives of Justice: A Review Essay." *Philosophy and Public Affairs* 42: 253–85.

Shelby, Tommie. 2016. *Dark Ghettos: Injustice, Dissent, and Reform*. Cambridge: Harvard University Press.

Sher, George. 1979. "Compensation and Transworld Personal Identity." *Monist* 62: 378–91.

Sher, George. 1981. "Ancient Wrongs and Modern Rights." *Philosophy and Public Affairs* 10: 3–17.

Simmons, A. John. 2010. "Ideal and Non-ideal Theory." *Philosophy and Public Affairs* 38: 5–36.

Skocpol, Theda. 1995. "African Americans in U.S. Social Policy." In Paul E. Peterson, ed., *Classifying by Race*. Princeton: Princeton University Press, 129–55.

Skrentny, John David. 1996. *The Ironies of Affirmative Action: Politics, Culture, and Justice in America*. Chicago: University of Chicago Press.

Smith, Nick. 2008. *I Was Wrong: The Meanings of Apologies*. Cambridge: Cambridge University Press.

Smith, Rodgers M. 1997. *Civil Ideals: Conflicting Visions of Citizenship in U.S. History*. New Haven: Yale University Press.

Soja, Edward W. 2010. *Seeking Spatial Justice*. Minneapolis: University of Minnesota Press.

Song, Sarah. 2007. *Justice, Gender, and the Politics of Multiculturalism*. Cambridge: Cambridge University Press.

Southern Poverty Law Center. 2016. "Whose Heritage? Public Symbols of the Confederacy." Available at https://www.splcenter.org/20160421/whose-heritage-public-symbols-confederacy. Accessed November 18, 2017.

Southern Poverty Law Center. 2018. "Teaching Hard History: American Slavery." Available at https://www.splcenter.org/sites/default/files/tt_hard_history_american_slavery.pdf. Accessed May 1, 2018.

Spinner, Jeff. 1994. *The Boundaries of Citizenship: Race, Ethnicity, and Nationality in the Liberal State*. Baltimore: Johns Hopkins University Press.

Spinner-Halev, Jeff. 2005. "Autonomy, Association, and Pluralism." In Avigail Eisenberg and Jeff Spinner-Halev, eds., *Minorities within Minorities: Equality, Rights and Diversity*. Cambridge: Cambridge University Press, 157–71.

Spinner-Halev, Jeff. 2012. *Enduring Injustice*. Cambridge: Cambridge University Press.

Stanley, Sharon. 2014. "Toward a Reconciliation of Integration and Racial Solidarity." *Contemporary Political Theory* 13: 46–63.

Stanley, Sharon. 2017. *An Impossible Dream? Racial Integration in the United States*. Oxford: Oxford University Press.

Steele, Roberta. 1993. "All Things Not Being Equal: The Case for Race Separate Schools." *Case Western Reserve Law Review* 43: 591–624.

Steiker, Carol S. 2005. "No, Capital Punishment Is Not Morally Required: Deterrence, Deontology, and the Death Penalty." *Stanford Law Review* 58: 751–89.

Stein, Dan J., Soraya Seedat, Debra Kaminer, Hashim Moomal, Allen Herman, John Sonnega, and David R. Williams. 2008. "The Impact of the Truth and Reconciliation Commission on Psychological Distress and Forgiveness in South Africa." *Social Psychiatry and Psychiatric Epidemiology* 43: 462–68.

Steinberg, Stephen. 1995. *Turning Back: The Retreat from Racial Justice in American Thought and Policy*. Boston: Beacon Press.

Sterba, James P. 2009. *Affirmative Action for the Future*. Ithaca: Cornell University Press.

Stern, Sheldon M. and Jeremy A. Stern. 2011. *The State of the State U.S. History Standards 2011*. Washington, DC: Thomas Fordham Institute.

Stitcher, Matt. 2014. "The Structure of Death Penalty Arguments." *Res Publica* 20: 129–43.

Strauss, Valerie. 2010. "Teaching the Civil War: Debate Still Alive." *Washington Post*, April 8. Available at http://voices.washingtonpost.com/answer-sheet/history/the-debate-over-how-to-teach-t.html. Accessed November 10, 2017.

Student Nonviolent Coordinating Committee. 1997. "Position Paper on Black Power." In William L. Van Deburg, ed., *Modern Black Nationalism: From Marcus Garvey to Louis Farrakhan*. New York: New York University, 120–26.

Sum, Paul E., Steven Andrew Light, and Ronald F. King. 2004. "Race, Reform, and Desegregation in Mississippi Higher Education: Historically Black Institutions after *United States v. Fordice*." *Law and Social Inquiry* 29: 403–35.

Sunstein, Cass R. and Adrian Vermeule. 2005. "Is Capital Punishment Morally Required? Acts, Omissions, and Life-Life Tradeoffs." *Stanford Law Review* 58: 703–50.

Tamir, Yael. 1993. *Liberal Nationalism*. Princeton: Princeton University Press.

Taylor, Charles. 1994. *Multiculturalism: The Politics of Recognition*. Princeton: Princeton University Press.

Taylor, Robert S. 2009. "Rawlsian Affirmative Action." *Ethics* 119: 476–506.

Teitel, Ruti G. 2000. *Transitional Justice.* Oxford: Oxford University Press.

Thernstrom, Stephan and Abigail Thernstrom. 1997. *America in Black and White: One Nation, Indivisible.* New York: Simon and Schuster.

Thomas, Larry L. 1977–78. "Rawlsian Self-Respect and the Black Consciousness Movement." *Philosophical Forum* 9: 303–14.

Thompson, Janna. 2000. "The Apology Paradox." *Philosophical Quarterly* 50: 470–75.

Thompson, Janna. 2008. "Apology, Justice, and Respect: A Critical Defense of Political Apology." In Mark Gibney, Rhoda E. Howard-Hassmann, Jean-Marc Coicaud, and Nicklaus Steiner, eds., *The Age of Apology: Facing Up to the Past.* Philadelphia: University of Pennsylvania Press, 31–44.

Tonry, Michael. 2007. "Looking Back to See the Future of Punishment in America." *Social Research* 74: 353–78.

Tonry, Michael. 2011. *Punishing Race: A Continuing American Dilemma.* Oxford: Oxford University Press.

Tonry, Michael. 2016. *Sentencing Fragments: Penal Reform in America, 1975–2025.* Oxford: Oxford University Press.

Tucker, Sterling. 1971. *For Blacks Only: Black Strategies for Change in America.* Grand Rapids: William B. Eerdmans.

Ture, Kwame and Charles Hamilton. 1992. *Black Power: The Politics of Liberation.* New York: Vintage Books.

Turner, Nicholas. 2016. "A Home after Prison." *New York Times*, June 21. Available at http://nyti.ms/28JpmfQ. Accessed November 10, 2017.

United States Sentencing Commission. 2017. "Demographic Differences in Sentencing: An Update to the 2012 Book Report." Available at https://www.ussc.gov/research/research-reports/demographic-differences-sentencing.   Accessed November 21, 2017.

Upton, Dell. 1999. "Commemorating the Civil Rights Movement." *Design Book Review* 40: 22–33.

Vaca, Moisés. 2013. "Is Rawls's Theory of Justice Exclusively Forward-Looking?" *Revista de Filosofía* 45: 299–330.

Valls, Andrew. 1999. "The Libertarian Case for Affirmative Action." *Social Theory and Practice* 25: 299–323.

Valls, Andrew. 2002. "The Broken Promise of Racial Integration." In Stephen Macedo and Yael Tamir, eds., *NOMOS XLIII: Moral and Political Education.* New York: New York University Press, 456–74.

Valls, Andrew. 2003. "Racial Justice as Transitional Justice." *Polity* 36: 665–83.

Valls, Andrew. 2005. "Introduction." In Andrew Valls, ed., *Race and Racism in Modern Philosophy.* Ithaca: Cornell University Press, 1–15.

Valls, Andrew. 2009. "Racism: In Defense of Garcia." *Philosophy of the Social Sciences* 39: 475–80.

Van Deburg, William L. 1992. *New Day in Babylon: The Black Power Movement and American Culture, 1965–1975.* Chicago: University of Chicago Press.

Van Leeuwen, Bart. 2010. "Dealing with Urban Diversity: Promises and Challenges of City Life for Intercultural Citizenship." *Political Theory* 38: 631–57.

Vigdor, Jacob L. 2013. "Weighing and Measuring the Decline in Residential Segregation." *City and Community* 12: 169–77.

von Hirsh, Andrew and Andrew Ashworth. 2005. *Proportionate Sentencing: Exploring the Principles*. Oxford: Oxford University Press.

Wakefield, Sara and Christopher Wildeman. 2014. *Children of the Prison Boom: Mass Incarceration and the Future of American Inequality*. Oxford: Oxford University Press.

Waldron, Jeremy. 1992. "Superseding Historic Injustice." *Ethics* 103: 4–28.

Waligore, Timothy. 2016. "Rawls, Self-Respect, and Assurance: How Past Injustice Changes What Publicly Counts as Justice." *Politics, Philosophy, and Economics* 15: 42–66.

Walker, Margaret Urban. 2006a. *Moral Repair: Reconstructing Moral Relations after Wrongdoing*. Cambridge: Cambridge University Press.

Walker, Margaret Urban. 2006b. "Restorative Justice and Reparations." *Journal of Social Philosophy* 37: 377–95.

Warnke, Georgia. 1998. "Affirmative Action, Neutrality, and Integration." *Journal of Social Philosophy* 29: 87–103.

Warren, Samuel and Louis Brandeis. 1890. "The Right to Privacy." *Harvard Law Review* 4: 193–220.

Washington, Harriet A. 2008. "Apology Shines Light on Racial Schism in Medicine." *New York Times*, July 29. Available at http://www.nytimes.com/2008/07/29/health/views/29essa.html. Accessed November 11, 2017.

Webster, Gerald R. and Jonathan I. Leib. 2016. "Religion, Murder, and the Confederate Battle Flag in South Carolina." *Southeastern Geographer* 56: 29–37.

Weinstock, Daniel M. 2007. "Liberalism, Multiculturalism, and the Problem of Internal Minorities." In Anthony Simon Laden and David Owen, eds., *Multiculturalism and Political Theory*. Cambridge: Cambridge University Press, 244–64.

Weinstock, Daniel. 2014. "Cities and Federalism." In James E. Fleming and Jacob T. Levy, eds., *NOMOS LV: Federalism and Subsidiarity*. New York: New York University Press, 259–90.

Wellman, Christopher Heath. 2012. "The Rights Forfeiture Theory of Punishment." *Ethics* 122: 371–93.

Wellman, Christopher Heath. 2017. *Rights Forfeiture and Punishment*. Oxford: Oxford University Press.

Weschler, Lawrence. 1990. *A Miracle, a Universe: Settling Accounts with Torturers*. New York: Penguin.

Western, Bruce. 2006. *Punishment and Inequality in America*. New York: Russell Sage Foundation.

Western, Bruce. 2007. "Mass Imprisonment and Economic Inequality." *Social Research* 74: 509–32.

Weyeneth, Robert R. 2001. "The Power of Apology and the Process of Historical Reconciliation." *Public Historian* 23: 9–38.

Wicker, Tom. 1966. "Time to Pay the Piper." *New York Times*, August 4, 32.

Widener, Ralph W., Jr. 1982. *Confederate Monuments: Enduring Symbols of the South and the War Between the States*. Washington, DC: Andromeda Associates.

Wilkins, David B. 2005. "A Systematic Response to a Systematic Disadvantage: A Response to Sander." *Stanford Law Review* 57: 1915–61.

Williams, Justin. 2018. *Spatial Justice as Analytic Framework*. Ph.D. dissertation, University of Michigan. Forthcoming.

Williams, Melissa S. 1998. *Voice, Trust, and Memory: Marginalized Groups and the Failings of Liberal Representation*. Princeton: Princeton University Press.

Williams, Melissa S., Rosemary Nagy, and Jon Elster, eds. 2012. *NOMOS LI: Transitional Justice*. New York: New York University Press.

Williams, Timothy. 2016. "Official Apologizes for Police Role in Mistrust by Minorities." *New York Times*, October 17. Available at https://nyti.ms/2edSHlB. Accessed November 18, 2017.

Williamson, Thad. 2010. *Sprawl, Justice, and Citizenship: The Civic Costs of the American Way of Life*. Oxford: Oxford University Press.

Wilson, Bradley. 2012. "Justice with Mercy: An Argument against Capital Punishment." *International Journal of Applied Philosophy* 26: 119–35.

Wilson, Mabel O. 2001. "Between Rooms 307: Spaces of Memory at the National Civil Rights Museum." In Craig Evan Barton, ed., *Sites of Memory: Perspectives on Architecture and Race*. Princeton: Princeton Architectural Press, 13–26.

Wilson, William Julius. 1980. *The Declining Significance of Race: Blacks and Changing American Institutions*. 2nd ed. Chicago: University of Chicago Press.

Wilson, William Julius. 1987. *The Truly Disadvantaged: The Inner City, the Underclass, and Public Policy*. Chicago: University of Chicago Press.

Wilson, William Julius. 1996. *When Work Disappears: The World of the New Urban Poor*. New York: Vintage.

Wilson, William Julius. 2009. *More Than Just Race: Being Black and Poor in the Inner City*. New York: Norton.

Winter, Stephen. 2015. "Theorizing the Political Apology." *Journal of Political Philosophy* 23: 261–81.

Woliver, Laura R., Angela D. Ledford, and Chris Dolan. 2001. "The South Carolina Confederate Flag: The Politics of Race and Citizenship." *Politics & Policy* 29: 708–30.

Woodward, C. Vann. 2001. *The Strange Career of Jim Crow*. Oxford: Oxford University Press.

Wright, Joshua D. and Victoria M. Esses. 2017. "Support for the Confederate Battle Flag in the Southern States: Racism or Southern Pride?" *Journal of Social and Political Psychology* 5: 224–43.

Young, Iris Marion. 1990. *Justice and the Politics of Difference*. Princeton: Princeton University Press.

Young, Iris Marion. 1997. "A Multicultural Continuum: A Critique of Will Kymlicka's Ethnic-Nation Dichotomy." *Constellations* 4: 48–53.

Young, Iris Marion. 2000. *Inclusion and Democracy*. Oxford: Oxford University Press.

Young, Iris Marion. 2011. *Responsibility for Justice*. Oxford: Oxford University Press.

Young, Whitney M., Jr. 1963. "Domestic Marshall Plan." *New York Times Magazine*, October 6, 240, 283–84.

Young, Whitney M. Jr. 1965. "For a Federal 'War on Poverty.'" In Francis L. Broderick and August Meier, eds., *Negro Protest Thought in the Twentieth Century*. Indianapolis: Bobbs-Merrill, 383–90.

Zutlevics, T. L. 2002. "Reconciliation, Responsibility, and Apology." *Public Affairs Quarterly* 16: 63–75.

COURT CASES

Brown v. Board of Education of Topeka, 347 U.S. 483 (1954).

Brown v. Board of Education of Topeka, 349 U.S. 294 (1955).

Fisher v. University of Texas, 570 U.S. ___ (2013).

Fisher v. University of Texas, 579 U.S. ____ (2016).

Floyd, et al. v. City of New York, et al., 959 F. Supp. 2d 540 (2013).

Fullilove v. Klutznick, 448 U.S. 448 (1980).

Glossip v. Gross, No. 14-7955, 576 U.S. ___ (2015).

Graham v. Florida, 560 U.S. 48 (2010).

Grutter v. Bollinger, 539 U.S. 306 (2003).

McCleskey v. Kemp, 481 U.S. 279 (1987).

Miller v. Alabama, 567 U.S. 460 (2012).

Parents Involved in Community Schools v. Seattle School District No. 1, 551 U.S. 701 (2007).

Plessy v. Ferguson, 163 US 537 (1896).

Regents of the University of California v. Bakke, 438 U.S. 265 (1978).

San Antonio Independent School District v. Rodriguez, 411 U.S. 1 (1973).

United States v. Fordice, 505 U.S. 717 (1992).

United Steelworkers of America v. Weber, 443 U.S. 193 (1979).

Utah v. Strieff, 579 U.S. ___, 136 S. Ct. 2056 (2016).

Vinter and Others v. The United Kingdom, ECHR 66069/09 (2013).

Walker v. Tex. Div., Sons of Confederate Veterans, Inc., 576 U.S. ___ (2015).

Wisconsin v. Yoder, 406 U.S. 205 (1972).